ROBERT LOUIS STEVENSON

James Pope Hennessy was born in 1916 and educated at Downside and Balliol. He won the Hawthornden Prize at the age of 21 for his *London Fabric* and followed this with a successful career as a journalist, travel writer and biographer. In 1959 he published his much acclaimed biography of Queen Mary.

Robert Louis Stevenson was published by Jonathan Cape in 1974 soon after the author was violently murdered.

CASSELL BIOGRAPHIES

ROBERT LOUIS STEVENSON

James Pope Hennessy

With an Introduction by
Nigel Nicolson

CASSELL

Jan 21, 2007

Cassell Publishers Ltd
Artillery House, Artillery Row
London SW1P 1RT

Originally published by Jonathan Cape Ltd 1974
Published in Cassell Biographies 1989

ISBN 0-304-31703-9

British Library Cataloguing in Publication Data

Pope-Hennessy, James, *1916-1974*
    Robert Louis Stevenson. — (Cassell biographies)
    1. English literature. Stevenson, Robert
    Louis, 1850-1894 — Biographies
    I. Title
    828′.809

Cover: 'The Road of the Loving
Heart' by G. Pieri Nerli, reproduced
by permission of the Lady Stair's
House, Edinburgh City Museum

Printed and bound in Great Britain by Biddles Ltd, Guildford and King's Lynn

Contents

For my brother
John Pope Hennessy

Illustrations

Introduction by Nigel Nicolson

I am writing about a friend, a friend who led a coruscating life and died a violent death, and I write it with gratitude and sadness, gratitude for all he gave to me and many others, and sadness for his loss at a moment when he had so much more to give. I would like to write more fully about him, but that would require many pages, a whole book perhaps, and a deep delving into his personality and life such as he devoted to the subjects of his many biographies.

He would not have minded this. He was not a secret person, except about his writing, which he never would discuss, changing the subject when I asked him about it, being most reticent about what he intended to be most public. For him a book in gestation was an intimate affair, and a book published was a book soon forgotten: he was thinking of the next. But about his adventures, his friendships, he was joyfully communicative, mischievously indiscreet.

For forty years I touched James's life tangentially. We might not see each other for many months, and when we met again he was always in a flurry of excitement about some new acquaintance, some new experience. Then he would turn on me, demanding equivalent revelations which could never match his own, provoking, teasingly inquisitive, solicitous if there was a hint of trouble, drawing back his long dark hair as a new fantasy occurred to him about what *ought* to have happened to me, his voice rising to a new note of amusement; or he would throw himself into the depth of an armchair, still boyishly sprawling when he reached middle age, and then suddenly lean forward gesticulating, fashioning phrases out of images, always eager, as anxious to catch as to throw.

In between our infrequent meetings we corresponded. At the time his letters seemed expendable, lightly tossed in my direction like paper darts, and to my present infinite regret, I threw most away, knowing that our next reunion would bring James alive again, for he, and our friendship, were eternally renewable. His personality emerged much more clearly from his letters than from his books, because, like Virginia Woolf, like Robert Louis Stevenson, he took less trouble with them. Typewriting carelessly and at top speed, correcting himself as he went along ('No I don't mean that. Forget it. What I really mean is this ...'), he splashed his letters with dashes, question-marks, dots, and then, in manuscript, with additions, underlinings, postscripts scribbled above, below, sideways on the typed page, a medley of affection, reproach, comment, inquiry, his typewriter a substitute for his tongue. Then he would telephone, plunging straight into chatter after months of silence, knowing that his voice was so unlike any other man's that any self-identification was needless, assuming a delighted response however busy I happened to be. Sometimes his news was scandalous, for he could be feline; more often it was self-mocking, if he had involved himself in some new muddle, whether financial (he was carelessly generous of the considerable sums he earned), or amatory, or simply a confession that he missed the train to Staplehurst or the plane to Hong Kong.

Occasionally one was in temporary disgrace. He could be unexpectedly offended by a chance remark. As undergraduates we went on a walking-tour to Normandy, and found ourselves in Bayeux cathedral. I observed to him, 'How odd it is that the descendants of the people who built this marvellous church could now fill it with such hideous effigies of painted wax.' James turned on his heel without a word, his Catholic susceptibilities outraged, strode to the hotel, packed in a temper, and took the next train to Paris, alone. A week later I caught sight of him in Notre Dame. I crept up behind him. 'How odd it is ...', I began. He turned, laughing, and we resumed our journey together without referring to the incident again. This was the James I knew, quick to anger, quicker to forgiveness, never sullen, expecting welcome because he was always welcoming, assuming the best in people until confronted with the worst.

Other friends may have seen him differently, because although he always remained the same himself, the variety of his acquaintance was one of his greatest charms. At his memorial service I was surprised that I knew so few people in the congregation. Who was that elderly woman weeping openly as she walked down the aisle? Who that coloured youth? Who that grey-haired man who might have been a librarian, or James's bank-manager? We might have been a magnification of one of his parties at Ladbroke Grove. His flat was a clutch of small rooms filled by low sofas, low lights, the glowing bindings of old books, a drawing of Angelica Kauffman, a mottled stone picked up on a South Sea beach, a fringe of tassels, warm carpets. There would be a well-known actress, an Indonesian friend, Cecil Beaton, an American publisher, a man whom he had met the night before. James did not compose his parties. He threw them together, and because he liked his guests, he assumed that they would like each other, and they did, because of him.

The memory of James Pope Hennessy may fade, as we, his friends, fade, for he wrote no autobiography, though he once told me, with a slight smirk of anticipation, that he was planning one. What will live in his books is a slightly different James. He gave to them the serious side of his mind. His frivolity is faintly detectable in everything he wrote, but he had a profoundly professional approach. He was a scholar, treating facts with a respect that he seldom accorded to his friends, and he could appreciate in his biographies qualities which were quite alien to his own. 'One of the few benefits of growing older,' he once said to me, 'is that envy is replaced by admiration.' When he disliked the subject of his book, he made a generous effort to understand him. On finishing *Lord Crewe*, the book which gave him least pleasure, he wrote to my father: 'You don't know the inward history of the writing of this book, far the worst two years in my life. I hated writing it. I read over 60,000 pieces of paper, all of uniform boredom, and my only aim was that the reader should be less bored than I was. I am thinking of patenting it as an insomnia cure.'

Reading the book, one detects no sign of the effort it cost him. Like all his others, it runs on rubber tyres, powered by a smooth engine. In *Queen Mary*, his longest and best-known biography, and *Verandah*, which gave him the greatest enjoyment since *London Fabric*, his first, his personality shines through another's stronger than his own. Describing the life of the central European courts, or a Colonial Governorship with which he had little sympathy, he touched both with a faint irony that never descended to ridicule, and his amusement at Queen Mary's foibles never became disrespectful. He dipped his fingers deep into the treasury of the language, fishing out strange words like rubies and his sentences, paragraphs, chapters, finish when another writer's might simply end. With a lick of the lips he sets himself to the task of depicting a place, mixing his colours as if on a palette. Landscape, houses, the shape and arrangement of rooms and furniture, play a great part in all his books. He believed that environment was as important as friendship and culture in moulding a man's mind. His biographies are three-dimensional. Instead of observing objects, he handles them. 'On the evening of 15th September 1883, a little group of exiles stood, surrounded by their trunks and shrouded in their travelling capes and ulsters, on the gas-lit departure platform of Victoria Station.' Thus he wrote typically in *Queen Mary*, his sense of period as accurate as his date.

Robert Louis Stevenson was his last book, though at the moment of his death he was deep in the research for another, the life of Noël Coward. He may have intended a final revision of his *Stevenson*, since it is on record that he agreed with his American publisher that the book needed a new opening, a summing-up of Stevenson's literary achievement and its influence. He attempted this rather coolly in the concluding pages, and it is unlikely that he would have left the passage as it stands, for it suggests to the reader what he certainly did not feel, that Stevenson's reputation lacks lustre. 'His personages seem to return to the puppet-box whenever you put a book of his down,' wrote James. He explains that this was partly because Stevenson died at 44, before he had had time to give the world his best. But he never denies Stevenson's genius. a word he uses more than once. He saw him as a romantic, and not only because of the remarkable circumstances of his life and death, and as a writer who struggled with and perfected his art, a great story-teller who was unrivalled in his evocation of a scene or an atmosphere, unsolemn, eternally youthful, the sort of man whom James would have liked immensely, indeed the sort of man who James, in many unexpected ways, actually was. 'His mind was alerted by a plangent voice or a passionate gesture, or an ambiguous smile.' So was James's. Henley described Stevenson as 'A deal of Ariel, just a streak of Puck'. He might have been describing James. If he was unaware of the parallel between himself and Stevenson which strikes me so forcibly, it must at least have created strong bonds of sympathy with him. Both wrote highly egotistical letters; both enjoyed travel, being vagabonds at heart; both were devoted practitioners of their art; both could switch suddenly from carousel into profound study and reflection, and take scrupulous care with their writing; both were rather vain, enjoying a sudden glimpse of themselves in a mirror (it is typical of James that he should begin with a minute description of Stevenson's appearance). And both were spared the degradation of old age.

It would be too much to claim that James Pope Hennessy has restored Stevenson to us, for Stevenson has never faded. What he has done is to re-present him to us as a 'major romantic', whose books spun silk out of cotton, and whose charm and 'disarming candour' as a man and writer were so close to James's own. *Si Monumentum Requiris*, read on.

Preface

MORE than two thousand five hundred letters of Robert Louis Stevenson's have survived, and many of these are of great length. The chief collections of these letters are in the National Library of Scotland in Edinburgh; in the Beinecke Library at Yale University; in the Houghton Library at Harvard; and in the Silverado Museum at St Helena, California. For the purposes of this book I have examined the letters in these collections, and I wish to thank the authorities in charge of them for their help in my researches. I am also grateful to Chatto & Windus Ltd for permission to reproduce the letter from Stevenson to Andrew Chatto on p. 173.

I wish further to thank Mr and Mrs John Macfie, the present owners of the Stevenson house in Heriot Row, Edinburgh, for their unvarying kindness and hospitality to me while I was staying as their guest in that city. I wish also to thank Miss Ellen Shaffer, curatrix of the Silverado Museum, St Helena, California, for all her assistance and for showing me the site of the Silverado mine head at which Robert Louis Stevenson spent his honeymoon.

The preparation for this book has taken me to such faraway places as Monterey and Apia, Samoa. My work on it has been greatly facilitated by my research assistant, Anne Mockett. I must also record my thanks, as usual, to Len Adams, who came with me to Grez-sur-Loing and other places relevant to Stevenson.

Since this book is intended for the general reader I have not thought it necessary to print reference notes for the extracts from manuscript letters and diaries which it contains.

For Stevenson's own published works I have throughout relied on the *Tusitala Edition* and on the *Collected Poems* edited in 1950 by Miss Adam Smith, and reissued in 1971 by Rupert Hart-Davis. Some of the other books consulted will be found in the selective bibliography at the end of this volume.

London   J.P.H.
November 1973

1

The Night-Hag's Victim

IN January 1880, penniless and emaciated, Robert Louis Stevenson sat shivering over the fire of his shabby room in a San Francisco lodging-house and began to write a paper entitled *Memoirs of Himself*. As, towards evening, the clammy fog he hated rolled uphill from the Bay, this scarecrow of a man swivelled his mind back to a childhood likewise dominated by sea-fog in a dimmer, colder city, Edinburgh, where he had been born twenty-nine years before. 'On the whole,' he wrote in the *Memoirs*, 'I have not much joy in remembering these early years. I was as much an egotist as I have ever been; I had a feverish desire for consideration ... I was sentimental, snivelling, goody, and morbidly religious. I hope and do believe I am a better man than I was a child.'

Stevenson felt it suitable to begin writing his recollections in isolation in San Francisco because, after two years made hideous by mental and emotional anxieties, and now suffering from what was loosely diagnosed as malaria, he had convinced himself that he had 'altogether changed into another character'. Although he had been in the new Pacific capital for several weeks he had so far explored only a few blocks in the neighbourhood of Mrs Carson's Irish lodgings on Bush Street. He seemed to himself spiritually diminished and to have lost not merely his 'adventurous whims', but his 'human curiosity' as well. These dark conclusions were, of course, due to the fact that Louis Stevenson was still suffering from the effects of his cruel westward journey on the cars from New York, described in one of the most evocative of all his several travelogues, *The Amateur Emigrant*. This spare, short work, which irritated his insular British friends, is written in a less contrived manner than most of those previous essays which had already brought him, in eclectic circles of

London and Edinburgh, a reputation for literary promise and, indeed, an extremely local fame. Undertaken on a characteristic impulse and for the most sympathetic of all reasons — romantic love — his headlong journey had smashed the delicate balance of his health. It was thus, in part, responsible for the next fourteen years of semi-invalidism which were to culminate in his sudden death on Samoa at the age of forty-four.

Broken off in San Francisco, to be resumed many years later in Samoa, the *Memoirs of Himself* were never finished, and have come down to posterity as a fragment. In Louis Stevenson's case this loss seems of no great consequence. In the works of hardly any other British writer do we find so much that is so consistently autobiographical and, indeed, egotistical as in those of Stevenson. His earlier critics complained of his egotism, but he was perfectly aware of this aspect of his own character.

'I am a rogue at egotism myself,' he wrote when he was twenty-seven to an Australian admirer, 'and, to be plain, I have rarely or never liked a man who was not.' The waspish sister of one of his most intimate Edinburgh friends, Sir Walter Simpson, recalled how frequently Louis in his youth would report on the state of his own often precarious health: 'Stevenson, with that captivating egotism of his which took you into his confidence, would often start an evening of brilliant talk with a health bulletin as to a vanished cold, delivered smilingly, and amusingly, if he was better.' Everything that happened to Louis Stevenson seemed to him worthy of public record, whether it was a ten days' tramp with a small French donkey in the Cevennes, or his own squatters' honeymoon at the mouth of a deserted silver-mine on the slopes of Mount St Helena in the idyllic scenery of the Napa Valley. It was noticed that whenever he happened to be in a room with a wall-mirror Louis Stevenson was unable to refrain from glancing at his own reflection in it as he glided swiftly to and fro with rapid, nervous movements — perfectly caught by John Singer Sargent in the more famous of the two portraits of Louis which he painted at Bournemouth in 1885. In his embittered posthumous attack on his old friend and benefactor this harmless weakness was held up to ridicule by the poet W. E. Henley. Such a practice admittedly would never have done for Henley himself, one of the ugliest and most hirsute of Victorian literary figures; but the image which the glass revealed to Stevenson was that of a slight man of rare physical distinction and of an almost elfin beauty. In his dark eyes 'with the gypsy light behind' (as he himself expressed it) a smile was always lurking: 'A child-like mirth leaped and danced within him,' Edmund Gosse wrote of Louis as a youth, 'he seemed to skip upon the hills of life.'

In his twenties Robert Louis Stevenson's face had been likened to that of the young Raphael in the self-portrait in the Louvre. All contemporary accounts of his appearance concur in dwelling upon the visionary quality of Stevenson's eyes; they have been described as 'luminous', as 'gleaming' as 'wonderful, dark, far-apart', as 'very bright and penetrating', 'large', 'lucid', 'quick-glancing and observant' and, on occasions, 'brimful of banter'. In repose his eyes looked dark and melancholy, but illuminated by his eager smile they seemed to lighten to a violet-blue. In retrospect, after her husband's early death, his wife defined the colour of these eyes 'the sort of brown that is called black—with very little yellow or red; a cool brown, with ... lights and great changes of expression.' She explained that Louis's eyes were 'unusually far apart with level eyebrows, one of which he sometimes lifted in an odd Japanese sort of way. They were large, with black eyelashes, and exactly like—in shape—the patterns given in drawing-books.' Fanny Stevenson remembered that her husband could 'languish' his eyes 'like any South Sea native'. When angry (and he was a high-tempered man) his eyes would sparkle 'and seemed to emit electric lights'. The only other man she ever saw whose eyes would, on occasion, flash in the same way was Louis Stevenson's first cousin, Both Stevenson, the Edinburgh painter and most intimate friend of Louis's youth. From this fact she conjectured that this sudden sparkle was 'a Stevenson characteristic'.

These magnificent eyes were set in a long oval face, which seemed even thinner than it was for being framed in the glossy light-brown locks which flowed carelessly to his shoulders, a Bohemian fashion at which Edinburgh people looked askance. It was this hair-style, together with his sparse figure, gesturing, nervous, tapered fingers and classically beautiful profile that sometimes gave people a totally false impression of effeminacy. 'More like a lass than a lad,' Andrew Lang had opined on first meeting him at Menton in 1874, while an Edinburgh lady, Mrs Miller, remembered having, in girlhood, watched young Stevenson being taunted on George Street by urchins chanting, 'Hauf a laddie, hauf a lassie, hauf a yellow yite!'

Louis Stevenson was as agile as he was slender, and carried with him a general indefinable air of having emerged from some earlier, more aristocratic epoch and background than his own. His extreme refinement of body and feature owed nothing to his father's family, the stalwart engineering Stevensons whose lighthouse experiments and successes had won them international acclaim and gratitude throughout the seafaring world. It was, rather, to be traced to his mother's family, the Balfours of Pilrig, and those conversant with the Balfour portraits in the old house at Pilrig on the Water of Leith would declare that the long oval faces and sensitive hands of his seventeenth- and eighteenth-century ancestors seemed clearly to foreshadow the somewhat overbred appearance of Robert Louis Stevenson himself. His American wife, who had at once recognized Louis's likeness to the Louvre Raphael, was always impressed by her husband's grace of movement — 'an alert grace of movement,' she wrote, 'that is seldom seen except in half-civilized countries.' Fanny Stevenson took a pride in the superiority of Louis's looks over those of more humdrum human beings — 'Something royal, ain't it?' she had overheard a Negro waiter on the Newport boat declare. A traveller who came across Stevenson on Waterloo Station about the year 1885, and who did not then know his identity, thought that he looked like a man 'who had just been rescued from the sea or a river' — a notion confirmed by a Waterloo cabbie who remarked, 'Looks like a sooercide, don't 'e, sir? One of 'em chaps as take their down-on-their-luck 'eaders inter the Thimes.' But in a few moments the cabbie's client was astounded to observe 'the supreme change' which came over Stevenson's melancholy face on meeting an expected friend on the platform; the sad dark eyes lightened and 'were filled with sunshine and laughter. An extraordinarily winsome smile invaded the face ... pervaded the whole man, I was about to say.' Other strangers who did actually make Louis Stevenson's acquaintance quickly forgot the surprise which their first sight of him had caused them. The excessive thinness, the narrow, stooping shoulders, the long silken hair, the 'weird' Bohemian garb, all seemed irrelevant once he spoke to them or smiled. Exposed to the full radiation of Louis Stevenson's character and manner they remained captive for ever after — slaves to a rare, authentic and irresistible charm. It was Robert Louis Stevenson's destiny to be loved wherever he went. This should have compensated him, and to some extent did, for a life which was short and was only intermittently happy, and which there is good reason to think that he relinquished without regret.

This process of being loved began on November 13th, 1850, in a small two-storied house in a modest terrace in Edinburgh New Town. All his life he needed, and customarily inspired, extreme devotion, but at no time was his need greater than in his earliest years when (as he reminds us in his *Memoirs*) he was 'an only child and, it may be in consequence, both intelligent and sickly'. From this childhood he retained three 'powerful impressions': ' ... my sufferings when I was sick, my delights in convalescence at my grandfather's manse of Colinton, near Edinburgh, and the unnatural activity of my mind after I was in bed at night.' This 'unnatural activity' in dreaming stayed with him until his death. Its influence upon his creative writing as well as upon his whole taut nervous system was important and profound.

[II]

In his own words Louis Stevenson was 'from a child an ardent and uncomfortable dreamer'. Briefly in the *Memoirs of Himself*, and more fully in the significant *A Chapter on Dreams* (written at Saranac in the Upper Adirondacks during the winter of 1887–8 as one of a series of essays commissioned by Scribner's), he has described areas of his childish world of nightmare. Born with a weakness of chest inherited from his mother, he would often as a small boy spend long nights awake, wracked by painful bouts of coughing. Bad as these nights were, the alternative of drifting off to sleep offered terrors far more formidable. His fevered eyes would watch his bedroom walls as they seemed to swell and then to shrink, while his clothes on their hanger would take on 'the bigness of a church' only to dwindle into 'a horror of infinite distance and infinite littleness'. By this time he was well aware that the menace of sleep was imminent, and he would struggle valiantly to fight it off: 'But his struggles were in vain; sooner or later the night-hag would have him by the throat, and pluck him, struggling and screaming, from his sleep.' His father alone could pacify the child after these ghastly awakenings, telling him stories and inventing conversations to divert his mind.

Like Hawthorne before him, and Rudyard Kipling later, Stevenson took an extremely enlightened interest in the world of dreams and of what came subsequently to be called the subconscious, although there is no evidence that he ever read the first works of Freud, who was his junior by six years. Louis's dreams were complex and vivid, and in their earliest manifestations seemed to him as meaningless as they were fearful. He dreamed for example that he had to 'swallow the world' and the terror of this conception arose from his childish knowledge of the 'hugeness and populousness of our sphere'.

This and other dreams were suffused by 'a peculiar shade of

brown, something like that of a sealskin'—a colour which, entirely harmless in his waking hours, became ineffably threatening when he was asleep. As he grew a little older, and could observe more of the world, scenery—that is to say landscapes and buildings—came to play a prominent part in his dreams, which now also seemed to be more sequential and took on the succinct shape and style of short stories. When he was a youth with the ambition to write, and later still when he was an established author, he came to rely on such dream-sequences to supply him with some of his plots. In *A Chapter on Dreams* he has described how essential ideas for both *Olalla* and *The Strange Case of Dr Jekyll and Mr Hyde* came to him as terrifying dreams—although, naturally, it was up to his waking mind to fill them out by drawing on his daytime imagination and using his literary skill. By this period he would positively look forward to dreaming, in the hope that something 'mercantile' and saleable to a magazine would emerge. He began to think of these dramatic dreams as being arranged for him by a race of clever 'little people' who would adroitly unfold to him a plot complete with characters, while he sat watching their efforts as though from a stage-box. Often the 'little people' would tire, and bungle their job, but on the whole he felt that they served him well. By this period of his life he no longer screamed so much at night and his 'physical contortions passed away, seemingly forever'. His visions were 'still for the most part miserable but they were more constantly supported.' For those puzzled by the fact that Robert Louis Stevenson preferred to write historical rather than contemporary romances it is interesting to note that 'an odd taste' he had for the Georgian costume and for stories laid in that period of English literature began to rule the features of his dreams. In these dream-sequences he would find himself masquerading in a three-cornered hat and 'much engaged with Jacobite conspiracy between the hour for bed and that for breakfast'.

In the larger part of this essay on dreams, Stevenson wrote in the third person, only revealing himself near the end of it: ' ... who is the dreamer? Well, as regards the dreamer, I can answer that, for he is no less a person than myself—as I might have told you from the beginning, only that the critics murmur over my consistent egotism.' Now it may be argued that the corollary of egotism is romanticism—and, both in his lifetime and for a good many years after his death, Robert Louis Stevenson was widely recognized as a major romantic. His amazing marriage, his South Sea voyages, his persistent fight against what always seemed to be imminent death, his Samoan adventure and his burial on the top of Mount Vaea, all appealed to the public imagination to a degree which slowly tended to obscure his true worth as a writer. The final gesture of choosing a grave on the almost inaccessible summit of a tropical mountain confirmed his renown as a mythical figure. The publication, in 1901, of his official biography by his mother's connection Graham Balfour unwittingly emphasized the interest of Robert Louis Stevenson's bizarre life at the expense of that of his work. Writing to congratulate Balfour on the book, Henry James, a devoted friend of both the Stevensons, formulated this unforeseen result with a comparative clarity:

> ... The question really is, however, for the critical spirit, whether Louis's work itself doesn't pay somewhat for the so complete exhibition of the man & the life ... the books are jealous and a certain supremacy and mystery (above all) has, as it were, gone from them. The achieved legend and history that has *him* for subject, has made, so to speak, light of *their* subjects, and their claim to represent him ... He had of course only to be then himself less picturesque and none of us who knew him would have had him so by an inch. But the fact remains that the *exhibition* that has overtaken him has helped and that he is thus as an artist and creator in some degree the victim of himself ...

Stevenson's reputation was assiduously kept alive by his widow and his stepchildren (who continued to benefit from his rich literary royalties) as well as by his devoted friend Sidney Colvin, who produced edition after edition of his letters. In these years the relict and her family, and to a lesser degree Sidney Colvin, were intent on presenting Robert Louis Stevenson as a species of latter-day saint. Their attitude, and that of the reading public who took from them their cue, later produced a natural reaction amongst the younger critics, and Stevenson's memory became a prey to intellectual iconoclasts in the sceptical period that followed on the First World War. Nowadays we may fancy that we can assess him more justly than could either his contemporary devotees or his subsequent detractors.

Childhood is seldom a fascinating subject, but in the case of Robert Louis Stevenson it is vital to consider the moulding effect on his career and on his writings of his earliest upbringing in the ancient and mysterious city of Edinburgh, where the history of the past still lingers more potently than in any other place within the confines of the United Kingdom.

[III]

I saw rain falling and the rainbow drawn
On Lammermuir. Hearkening I heard again
In my precipitous city beaten bells
Winnow the keen sea wind.

These lines from the dedication of his fragmentary masterpiece, *Weir of Hermiston*, were written very shortly before Stevenson died. They form testimony to his yearning loyalty to the image rather than to the spirit of Edinburgh. As a youth he had passionately loved the Old Town, with its steep narrow wynds falling away from the High Street and St Giles, with the tall top-heavy 'lands' or tenement buildings which reach sternly towards the sky. He would slither down the darkened alleys at night-time, his hands touching the walls on either side, and try to sense the teeming life within the high rickety-looking buildings, the blunt summits of which glimmered above him by the light of a winter moon. The majestic outlines of the Castle brooding on its crag haunted him all his life long. Neither the seductive scented air of Samoa nor the bewitching enchantments of Polynesian living could allay the nostalgia that he felt for the grey historic city from which he had, all the same and quite deliberately, fled. Always he remained faithful to the city of his birth.

Louis believed that the Old Town of Edinburgh, high against the background of hills and sky, was ideally complemented and balanced by the New Town, that superb pattern of noble streets and squares, terraces and rows and circles and crescents which forms the great legacy left to Edinburgh by its citizens of the reign of George III. No. 8 Howard Place, where he was born in 1850 in a comfortable ground-floor bedroom overlooking the back garden, was, however, neither in the Old Town nor the New. Howard Place consists of a set of terraced houses on low-lying ground; the opposite side of its street is called Inverleith Terrace, and both are separated from the New Town proper by the Water of Leith, which here flows sluggishly beneath a road-bridge and marks the northern boundary of the fashionable and affluent Georgian development. Then, Howard Place was within easy access of the surrounding countryside, and was anyway near the new, extensive Botanic Gardens. Seen from the pavement of Inverleith Terrace the string of houses in Howard Place look modest, squat and almost mean. They consist of only two stories and a sunken basement with an iron area railing. They are set back behind other iron railings protecting scrubby, nine-foot-deep front gardens from pedestrians on the road. The roofs are of grey slate, the house-fronts of grey stone: the general sense evoked is that of a blurred greyness and of undistinguished iron-work; you would not be surprised to be told that the basements were dank. To the right of the front door of No. 8, which, like all the Howard Place front doors, is reached by a flight of stone steps, are the two windows of the dining-room, while on the upper floor there are three windows of the same size, regularly placed. In the young Thomas Stevenson's day each of these sash-windows boasted astragals holding twelve small panes to each window, but a later, more progressive generation has replaced these with commonplace sheets of plate glass. Yet once the front door of No. 8 is opened and you find yourself within the outer hall, an impression of order and even of spaciousness takes over. Above the doorway to the inner hall is set a plaster bas-relief of the Massacre of the Innocents. Through this doorway may be seen a good, wide staircase, winding up to a large double drawing-room above. The rooms in this house in Howard Place are lofty and dignified. They have about them an air of classical restraint.

Although the Stevenson couple moved across the road to Inverleith Terrace two years after Robert Louis was born, the house in Howard Place was the setting for the start of their great adventure—that of a marriage squarely based on love. One of Mrs Stevenson's bridesmaids came on a visit to the couple in Howard Place. During her stay she said that she had opportunity to watch the friend of her girlhood turning into 'a wife and mother, and to study the character of her grave and scientific husband'. It must have been borne in on her how very much her host and hostess were in love; a surviving letter from Margaret Isabella Stevenson, written from Howard Place in January 1852 to her husband when he was away on one of his frequent engineering journeys, brims with solicitude and affection: 'Good night sweet life,' it ends, 'think often of your own dear wee wife.' Like her famous son, Mrs Stevenson spoke English with a pronounced Edinburgh accent to her dying day.

Margaret Isabella Stevenson was the twelfth child and fourth daughter in the large family of the Reverend Lewis Balfour and his Ayrshire wife. Thirteen altogether, the Balfour progeny were all reared in their father's manse at Colinton, a village four miles south-west of Edinburgh. The old clergyman, who had been one of the sons of a Balfour laird of Pilrig, was born in the old house there in 1777. At twenty, symptoms of a chest weakness had despatched him to the Isle of Wight. He returned to take a cure in Ayrshire, married a local girl up there, and came finally to rest in the manse at Colinton in

1823 when he was in his middle forties. He remained there until his death thirty-seven years later. When Robert Louis Stevenson first knew this grandfather, Mr Balfour still had a noble face and a head of thick, silvery hair, a look of absolute integrity and a strict, remote manner which disturbed his grandchildren and kept them in awe. His fourth daughter, Margaret Isabella, began her life under the awkward pet-name Maggabella, but this was soon changed to 'Maggie', the name by which her husband and all their relatives knew her. Maggabella was a slender, elegant, lithe girl with very blonde hair and a fresh complexion, a slightly Roman nose and a distinct gift for seeing only the best side of any problem. She was soon known as 'the Angel of the Family', and could be relied upon to pour oil on to the most troubled of waters. She was a fresh-faced girl with courage and a buoyancy of spirit which, in the words of her brother George Balfour, a much-respected physician, enabled her much later in her marriage 'to make a perfect heaven upon earth of a household which contained within itself the elements of discord'. In this oblique reference the discreet old doctor was hinting at tempera-mental difficulties which, in after years, seemed liable to set Maggie Stevenson's husband and their growing son at permanent logger-heads.

Her intimates considered that as an old lady Maggie Stevenson was more beautiful even than in her youth, when the Colinton villagers had known her as 'the Minister's white-headed lassie' who was 'daft about weans'. Her thirst to reach babies to fondle would lead this lissome girl to 'kilt her coats' and wade through parish burns; sometimes even through the Water of Leith, that ubiquitous Edinburgh stream which tumbled down a mill-race at the bottom of Colinton Manse garden after gliding past the Balfours' ancestral home at Pilrig, and creeping along the northern boundary of the New Town to sever Howard Place from the world of uphill fashion. When her own son was born in the year after her marriage she idolized him. A wife and mother at barely twenty, Maggie was delightfully spoiled by her devoted thirty-year-old husband, and together they worshipped at the cradle of their only son. The young mother began to keep a series of small almanack books, one for every year, in which she recorded the winning, the prodigious remarks of her baby as soon as he could speak. These records she kept, in the form of a diary, all through Louis's life. She continued to make entries of her own bereft state during the three years that she survived the swingeing blow of his death.

Selfless and light-hearted, only existing 'to shed happiness around her', Mrs Thomas Stevenson was entirely devoid of the black streak of stark Calvinism which made her husband at times so moody, and melancholy to the point of despair. Such defects as she had were due to her professional optimism, her robust determination to look only at the pleasant sides of life and to ignore anything ugly, forbidding or sad. Such natures may float through life unscathed, but this can often be at the expense of members of their family who wish to come to terms with some obtrusive but unpleasant reality. It is no solution to pretend, as Mrs Thomas Stevenson pretended, that a scorching problem simply does not exist. No doubt it was this quality for sailing the summer seas of life, refusing to recognize a squall when one blew up, that led the sagacious Henry James to select the adjective 'complacent' when describing Louis's mother: 'A fresh, youthful, complacent Scotch mother' he once called her when she was already well on in middle age. Maggie Stevenson specialized in a form of sweet evasion and indirect speech: 'She says nothing, but as her habit is, she implies much,' Louis Stevenson confided to a woman friend when he was a restive and angry twenty-three. During her son's very first years, however, his mother was a perfect companion, romping with him all over the house, looking perennially young, the source of pride to her son at Edinburgh children's parties when her bright quality contrasted with the dinginess of the other 'quite old and sedate' parents of his playmates. Yet, despite her humour and her sheen, Mrs Thomas Stevenson did manage to project across her son's earliest years a sombre and impenetrable shadow — that of her own increasing ill-health.

The lung weakness which had sent her father to recuperate in his youth upon the Isle of Wight soon declared itself in her. A union for which the husband's brilliant triumphs and researches in the light-house engineering field should have set the tone was soon bedevilled by quite another consideration — that of keeping the young wife alive. Winters were spent in the South of France or in Italy. The choice of healthy summer residences became a prime consideration. Mrs Stevenson was told not to rise until lunchtime, and for little Louis the gay companion was too often a smiling personage in a lace night-cap recumbent upstairs on a bed. Health and illness became daily topics in the house in Howard Place, and then in that across the road in Inverleith Terrace to which the Stevenson family migrated in the year 1853. It would be unfair to call their domestic atmosphere hypochondriacal; but when their only child, who was waiflike and puny from birth, showed the same symptoms as his mother and proved highly strung, feverish and subject to nightmare, a sick-room atmosphere prevailed. Thomas Stevenson was a solid man, of remarkable physique, yet he was doomed to watch over the two beings he most loved in the world—his wife and his child—with a gnawing anxiety about their sheer day-to-day survival.

We might say that Louis Stevenson thus acquired a thorough grounding in all the hazards of ill-health, and a profound preoccupation with it. Given his own obscure medical history, this knowledge may be regarded either in the light of a handicap or of a help. Granted the fact that the mid-Victorians were as self-consciously aware of illness as they were of death, we may still conclude that Louis's childhood scene was an unusually unhealthy one. This was further complicated by his precocious religiosity and his morbid interest in, say, the Colinton churchyard or his contentment in trotting, hand-in-hand with his nurse, down the paths between the worn, mossy gravestones in Warrington Cemetery. The little creature suffered, amongst other ills, from acute earaches, and, when not totally house-bound in winter, would be taken forth on to the streets of Edinburgh with his head muffled up in protective flannel. A fractious baby and an under-sized, ill-developed child, Louis was called 'Smout' by his doting parents, from the Scots colloquial noun denoting 'small fry' in fish. Thomas Stevenson's profound consciousness of the overpowering presence of a just God and of the certainty of his own salvation, together with his truly warm and chivalrous nature, precluded his resenting a fate which had allotted him the care of two remarkably frail dependants. This life governed by medicine bottles and embrocations was in no way what he had bargained for when that 'trig' girl, Maggabella Balfour, had agreed to become his wife.

[IV]

For a man known to be thoughtful and deliberate, Thomas Stevenson's proposal to Miss Balfour was strangely sudden. It stemmed from an emotion inspired by brief acquaintance. The pair had first set eyes on each other in September 1847 on the train to Glasgow, to which city Margaret Isabella Balfour, aged just eighteen, was travelling in the charge of an uncle and aunt. The encounter left the girl with a conviction that she would surely meet the young lighthouse engineer again, and so she did, at a dance given by his brother, Alan Stevenson. Then at the beginning of May 1848, as Maggie and her sister Jane were striding into Edinburgh from Colinton Manse, Thomas Stevenson chanced to emerge from the grounds of Merchiston Castle as they were passing the lodge-gates. He joined the two girls on their walk. Some weeks later Tom Stevenson took part in one of the Balfours' communal country rambles, their goal being Mount Parnassus, 'a beautiful little valley at the bottom of the Pentlands'. Here Maggie Balfour and Tom Stevenson somehow got separated from the rest of the walkers. He proposed to her, she replied that she did not know him, he suggested that this could be 'mended', and later spoke to her clergyman father at Colinton. Maggie's sister Jane, to whom this account of the courtship is due, declared that there had never been a happier marriage — 'she was always so bright'.

As time went on Maggie Stevenson needed to summon up all her brightness to counteract the fits of grim Calvinistic pessimism and deep melancholia to which her husband, ordinarily the most humorous and indeed whimsical of men, fell a victim from time to time. She had not been reared as he had in the fiercest form of Presbyterian bigotry, and, though deeply religious, she respected God as an all-powerful beneficent being, not as a merciless, exacting judge of men. There were other marked differences between herself and her husband, but these contrasts merely served a complementary purpose. As the granddaughter of the landowner at Pilrig, and able to claim kinship with several ancient branches of the Balfour family, Margaret Isabella was more than marginally better-born than Thomas Stevenson, whose own paternal grandfather, a West Indian merchant with a background of malting, had married into the family of a Glasgow builder. His son Robert Stevenson, young Thomas's father, served as engineer to the Scottish lighthouse board for almost half a century, and had made his name by achieving the allegedly impossible feat of building the hundred-foot-high tower lighthouse on the ominous Bell Rock. Robert Stevenson's three sons, Alan, David and Thomas, all joined him in his business. Thomas, who had an aptitude for mathematics, combined this with a liking for the Latin and English classics, an absorbing love for stray dogs, a tendency towards collecting books and old furniture, and made a personal speciality of experimental lighthouse illumination. By his efforts 'the great sea-lights in every quarter of the world' shone more brightly. He steadfastly refused to take out patents for any of his inventions, preferring to give the world the free benefit of his pioneering work rather than selfishly to accumulate fame and fortune. He was a high-minded man who revelled in his work and eagerly looked forward to the time when his own son, little Smout, should follow in his footsteps and himself enter the family firm. So far as his cherished plans for Louis went, Thomas Stevenson was in for ashen disappointment.

Because of their religious controversies and Louis's tormented complaints, it has been customary among the writer's biographers and memorialists to tend to underrate Thomas Stevenson's very human characteristics, and to present him as a species of dour, covenanting ogre, malignly blocking his son's upward path to literary success. In fact those who knew Thomas Stevenson well took a far more tolerant and appreciative view of him. His crony the Lyon King-at-Arms wrote after Tom Stevenson's death that he had been:

> ... one of the most delightfully quaint and interesting of men. It is from him I am sure that his son got most of his character-istic humour. His mother of course was charming, but that has been universally acknowledged, and I don't think his father has been sufficiently appreciated ...

When his daughter-in-law from California, Fanny Stevenson, first met Louis's father in 1880 she called him 'a most lovely old person', far better-looking than Louis, with eyes that sparkled and twinkled, full of jokes and spouting comic verses thought up by himself; 'a most delightful person' who would come into their hotel sitting-room at Strathpeffer of a morning 'with a sprig of heather in his hat, looking so pert and wholesome that it does one good to see him'. Many years later, when Louis and both his parents were long dead, Fanny Stevenson published her final verdict upon her father-in-law:

> I shall always believe that something unusual and great was lost to the world in Thomas Stevenson. One could almost see the struggle between the creature of cramped hereditary con-ventions and environment, and the man nature had intended him to be. Fortunately for my husband he inherited from this tragic father his genius and wide humanity alone.

In Fanny's view it was the natural gaiety he had inherited from his mother — 'who lives as a bird sings, for the very joy of it' — that carried Louis 'safely through the monotony of suffering that he endured for so many years ... ' Fanny perceived that her father-in-law 'adored' his wife and spoilt her 'like a baby'. It was this intimate, devoted relationship between his father and mother that, in Louis Stevenson's youth, gave him, within the family, a sense of isolation: 'For my mother is my father's wife,' he wrote in his twenty-fifth year to the lady with whom he was currently in love, ' ... the children of lovers are orphans.' To the same correspondent, Mrs Frances Sitwell (whom we shall shortly meet again), he had also described a form of claustrophobia which had overcome him in Edinburgh the previous year. Here he uses the imagery of being shut in by heavy doors:

> ... I know what you mean about doors shutting—brazen doors. They are now noiselessly closing about me, through my parents' kindness. I may say that each parent is one wing of the imperial portals and that, with smiling faces, they are closing fatally about my future happiness. That's a lie, of course, only I don't like Edinburgh, and there are people with whom I can be so much happier than I can be with my parents ...

But all these worries, some concrete, some purely subjective, lie in the future. We must first further consider Louis Stevenson's happy though invalidish childhood. We now come upon the third great influence in his youngest years—his nurse, Miss Alison Cunningham, known to himself and his parents, and afterwards to the widening international circle of his works' admirers, by the affectionate diminutive, 'Cummy'.

[V]

His mother's tricky health and late mornings meant that the role of nurse to Smout was a responsible and demanding one. It was some months before the parents were satisfied that they had found the ideal female. Meanwhile it seems that two or three nurses had been tried and found wanting. One of these, tradition says, was sacked for taking the precious baby to a local pub and depositing him as a bundle on the bar whilst she flirted and drank gin. In 1851, however, the Stevensons decided to take on a young nurse who had been with the little son of Professor Garden and Mrs Blaikie of Pilrig Manse, near the Balfours' Pilrig House on the Water of Leith. Alison Cunningham was a handsome, stalwart woman with piercing blue eyes, who had been born in the remote Fifeshire village of Torryburn. She was well educated and prepared to devote hserelf with ferocious loyalty to her new charge and his delicate mother. She was an admirable human being, a fine example of the old Scots family servant, independent and self-respecting. To Louis in his sickly childhood 'Cummy' seemed to be an angel, for she would sit up with him at night when he was feverish and could not sleep, would read to him or tell him stories at any hour of the day and gave him at times the cosy security which he craved. It was to Cummy that he wrote the once-famous dedication to *A Child's Garden of Verses*, published in 1885:

> For the long nights you lay awake
> And watched for my unworthy sake:
> For your most comfortable hand
> That led me through the uneven land: ...
>
> My second Mother, my first Wife,
> The angel of my infant life—
> From the sick child, now well and old,
> Take, nurse, the little book you hold!

In the tale of Robert Louis Stevenson's childhood Cummy can never be underrated, nor should she be debunked. At the same time there is no question that with her murky Calvinist and Covenanting convictions, her vivid awareness of the flicker of Hell-fire and of eternal damnation as well as in her choice of morbidly religious literature for reading aloud, she did implant in the little boy's mind many of the terrors that haunted him in the watches of the night. As a grown man he looked back on these 'ecstasies and terrors', and in the unfinished *Memoir of Himself* he faces up to the fact that it was to Cummy's conversation that they primarily were due:

> It is to my nurse that I owe these last [ecstasies and terrors]: my mother was shocked when, in days long after, she heard what I had suffered. I would not only lie awake to weep for Jesus, which I have done many a time, but I would fear to trust myself to slumber lest I was not accepted and should slip, ere I awoke, into eternal ruin. I remember repeatedly ... waking from a dream of Hell, clinging to the horizontal bar of the bed, with my knees and chin together, my soul shaken, my body convulsed with agony.

It was thus that Cummy, with the best intentions in the world, managed to inflame the child's mind and diligently to facilitate the awful entrance of the night-hag into the shadowy bedroom which his nurse shared with little Lou. Psychologically it is also interesting to reflect upon the fact that Cummy was inducing a state of mental tumult which only she could calm. As we have noticed, Louis's father was able to coax him back to sleep after a nightmare, but Thomas Stevenson was often away from home and it fell mainly to Cummy's part to allay the fears that her own religious tenets had spawned. Mrs Stevenson seems to have had no very clear idea of what was going on in the nursery when she was absent, although she did once veto the reading of the life of a Scots fanatic named Brainerd. Judging by her pocket diaries she regarded Louis's precocious interest in religion with a distinct pride. The boy's favourite game in his earliest years was 'playing at church', making a pulpit from a chair, and alternately standing up as preacher and sitting down as precentor. 'I piped and snivelled over the Bible,' Louis recalled, 'with an earnestness that had been talked into me. I would say nothing without adding "If I am spared", as though to disarm fate by a show of submission; and some of this feeling still remains upon me in my thirtieth year.' During this phase of precocious religious mania, Smout would fret about his parents' spiritual welfare, since in his view the Thomas Stevensons were imperilling their immortal souls by giving worldly dinner-parties and by playing cards. So was the spring-board inescapably prepared for Louis's gay and headlong plunge into agnosticism once he had reached the age of reason. This agnosticism, which his shocked parents misinterpreted as atheism, had a sarcastic ring to it. 'It was really pathetic to hear my father praying pointedly for me today at family worship,' Louis wrote of the daily dining-room prayers when he was twenty-two, 'and to think that the poor man's supplications were addressed to nothing better able to hear and answer than the chandelier. I could have bit my tongue out ... '

Loyal and religious, Cummy was not by any means a sentimentalist. Less than three years after the death of 'her laddie' in Samoa, and while she was basking to the full in his posthumous glory, the old lady, deaf and permanently wearing crêpe, was busily selling to a London agent the autographed copies of *Kidnapped*, *Memories and Portraits*, *Travels with a Donkey* and other of Louis's books which he had given to his 'second mother'. 'But I can't sell them unless I get something handsome for them,' this auxiliary parent wrote frankly. 'Mrs Riggs offered me £5 for one,' Miss Cunningham explained in another letter. 'She has not got it, but she got a lock of dear L's hair.'

[VI]

The Stevensons' move across the road from Howard Place to Inverleith Terrace did not turn out to have been a wise one. Number 1 Inverleith Terrace was an exposed corner-house, facing north. It was larger than Howard Place, but, it, too, was sited on the wrong bank of the Water of Leith. The previous tenants, Professor William

Aytoun, author of *Lays of the Cavaliers*, and his young wife had left the house after only four years in it, and bought another in Great Stuart Street in the New Town. The Professor frankly told a friend that they had left Inverleith Terrace because of the damp; a former wedding-dress of white silk 'hanging peacefully on a peg' had been attacked by blight and mildew and 'was spotted like a Leopard's skin'. This unhealthy residence immediately gave Smout the croup, followed afterwards by bronchitis; and though he still beguiled his parents and his nurse with quaint and artless religious questions his health was worsening. 'You can never be good unless you pray,' he remarked one day when he was four years old. How did he know this? he was asked. 'Because I've tried it,' the pious child replied. Summoned because Louis was 'feverish', the doctor brought common sense to bear. 'Christison ... says it is nothing but bronchitis,' Mrs Stevenson noted in her diary, 'but this house is bad for him, from being an end house.' Number 1 Inverleith Terrace was not merely an end house, it had no fewer than three exposed walls.

Like their predecessors the Aytouns, the Thomas Stevensons stuck it out there for four years. They then made a rather spectacular and, as it proved, a final move to one of the finest of the New Town terraces, Heriot Row. This was in all senses a step up, for Heriot Row, facing south and overlooking a very large private garden to which the tenants alone had the key, was considered one of the most delectable residential streets in Edinburgh. It was far away from the Water of Leith and built upon a hill.

Thomas Stevenson bought No. 17 Heriot Row in the spring of 1857. He died there thirty years later, having never moved house again. The Stevensons had, in fact, no incentive whatsoever to move further, for this tall, imposing terrace-house suited them perfectly, and gave each member of the family of three plenty of space. Heriot Row had been built towards the close of the Napoleonic wars. Like the rest of the New Town it is faced with stone of a colour which almost eludes description—it is neither a bleak grey nor a glowing honey-colour, but has an element of both of these, a light warm stone seen, as it were, through a blackish veil.

Louis Stevenson was six years old when the move took place. As he grew to manhood, 17 Heriot Row, for all its sunny rooms and cheerful aspect, began to seem to him a gaol. The dignified house became a setting for family scenes not unworthy of Strindberg. All that cumulative misery and all those bitter rows and misunderstandings have, on the other hand, left no trace behind them. The atmosphere of No. 17 today is as halcyon and welcoming as it must

No. 17, Heriot Row, Edinburgh, from a drawing by John Knight

have seemed to the Stevensons when they first went to inspect their prospective purchase on a clear March day in 1857.

A paramount feature of the Heriot Row houses, as of the rest of those in the New Town, is the well-designed ironwork which shuts in the area from the street, runs up on each side of the steps to the front doors, and, in the case of No. 17, forms three separate ornamental balconies outside the drawing-room windows, which look down over the street and the gardens from the first floor. Number 17, like the rest of Heriot Row, has an outer and an inner hall, a broad handsome flight of stairs to the first and second floors and, on the dining-room and drawing-room floors, tall elegantly proportioned windows with astragals, facing due south. The spacious, high-ceilinged dining-room, with an alcove in it, is lit by the two windows on the right of the solemn front door. At the back of the dining-room is a smaller, more intimate study, with a view of a narrow strip of walled garden, at the end of which, in the Stevensons' day, stood a privy. This study would have been Thomas Stevenson's own 'den'.

Upstairs was his wife's domain—the big L-shaped drawing-room, lit by three tall windows; in the western and central windows Mrs Stevenson placed 'kangaroo vines', which she tended with solicitude. 'I envy you your vines,' a visitor one day remarked. 'I envy you your daughters,' Mrs Stevenson answered. 'Will you exchange?' It must have been Maggie Stevenson's precarious state of health which persuaded herself and her husband to have no more children. Smout was left to reign supreme and imperial in Heriot Row, as he had got used to doing in Inverleith Terrace and Howard Place.

The large bedroom with a dressing-room attached which lay behind the drawing-room would have been that of Louis's parents. The boy's own quarters were on the floor above, where a fine oval dome made of glass-panes and ornamented with lions' heads lets the light into the staircase well. Louis's day-nursery, in later years his workroom, has two large windows whence, held up in Cummy's arms, he could peer at the gardens on the other side of the Row and, in winter through bare trees, at Queen Street far over the way. When he could not sleep and had the night horrors, his faithful nurse would hold him up to the window, suggesting that the few lights glimmering in the blackness of Queen Street proved that there were other children, too, who kept awake. Louis's night-nursery, in which Cummy had her bed until he was nearly ten years old, was a small room to the east of the day-nursery, and likewise commanding garden and street. The two back rooms on the top floor may have been guest rooms—as Louis grew up Mrs Stevenson would hopefully ask his girl-cousins to stay—or may have been used by the maids. At the bottom of the house is a huge kitchen and other offices. In the Stevensons' day there were no bathrooms but merely hip-baths in the bedrooms. Commodes in bedrooms or closets served the purpose of the modern W.C., and 'night-soil' was collected by carts each morning to be sold to the market-gardeners on the outskirts of Edinburgh for their plots of vegetables.

Altogether Heriot Row bespoke an unmistakable prosperity, and was an outward symbol of Thomas Stevenson's success. It was, anyway, a positive advance on the two previous Stevenson homes. The new house was furnished in a plain, conservative fashion, typical of which was the long mahogany dining-room table into which several extra leaves could be inserted for dinner-parties. This table later found its way to Samoa, and was used to support Louis's coffin during the brief lying-in-state that preceded his hasty burial on Mount Vaea. With the rest of the Heriot Row furniture (including Mrs Stevenson's little Regency desk, a wedding-present) this dining-room table may now be seen at the old adobe Robert Louis Stevenson House in Monterey.

In the drawing-room at Heriot Row Maggie Stevenson had her desk placed in the easternmost of the three windows, facing outwards so that she could watch the privileged children of the local residents at play round the pond in the gardens below and could benefit by every gleam of the fitful Edinburgh sun. We may safely assume that Mrs Stevenson's drawing-room was, like her own character, feminine and gay, whereas her husband's ground-floor den would have been book-lined, serious and of a sober colour.

Up on the third floor Smout's kingdom was doubtless an organized confusion of lead soldiers, picture-books (he did not begin to read until he was seven), paint-boxes, coloured chalks, and the intricate cut-out sheets for *Aladdin, The Old Oak Chest, Jack Sheppard, Der Freischütz* and the other pieces to be mounted for those toy theatres that were then called *Skelt's Juvenile Dramas* and which a later, London, generation knew as Pollock's of Hoxton. 'Penny Plain and Twopence Coloured', these sheets of characters, with other sheets of backdrops and wings, were sold at Mr Smith's shop in a neighbouring side-street, a shop which 'was dark and smelt of bibles'.

Louis tells us, in his essay *Penny Plain and Twopence Coloured*, that the whole excitement of the Skelt projects lay in choosing and actually buying the sheets at Mr Smith's: 'The purchase and the first half-hour at home, that was the summit. Thenceforth the interest declined little by little.' This declension of interest in his enthusiasms was a problem with which Robert Louis Stevenson lived all his adult life. He had inherited his mother's tenacious optimism, but, unlike her, he gave it full rein and was an optimist without restraint. Over and over again the events of his life proved a disappointment of his greatest expectations. The famous canoe trip through Belgium and Northern France, subject of his first published book, *An Inland Voyage*, turned out to be infinitely more soggy and rain-bound and dull than he had anticipated. From being a paradise, a rented house outside Marseilles named Campagne Delfi became a germ-pit from which he and his wife found that they had to flee. A châlet at Hyères, which he declared had provided the only unalloyed happiness of his life, had to be abandoned because it also proved unhealthy. From seeming a revelation of shimmering snow-mountains, the Swiss resort of Davos fast gave him claustrophobia. The American West, of which he had expected so much, was harsh and unromantic. A cottage at Saranac Lake in the Adirondack Mountains, that had seemed deliciously strange and rural at first, was soon judged untenable from cold. Even the islands and the atolls of the South Seas were in some ways other than he had expected to find them. Samoa itself, and the spacious halls at Vailima, were infected by the intrigues of the third-rate Europeans of 'the Beach' with whom Louis found it politic to keep on good terms. It was, of course, in part his ill-health which caused zest to fade and wither on the stem. But it was the same story with many of his writing plans—an idea for a book would arise in his brain, obsessive and alluring, but enthusiasm would falter and, tired of it all, he would either leave the work uncompleted or botch the end of it impatiently, as he did with that otherwise strong and splendid novel, *The Master of Ballantrae*.

The optimism he shared with his mother made it hard for him to believe in evil and loth to portray it. In his brilliant study, *Robert Louis Stevenson and the Fiction of Adventure* (1965), Professor Robert Kiely of Harvard University has drawn attention to the pains which Louis took to give even his villains—Long John Silver, for instance—a lovable side to their character and so to minimize their capacity for doing real harm. In *Ballantrae* and in *Weir of Hermiston* he finally abandoned his seat on the fence, and overcame his reluctance to probe evil to its depths. Hitherto he had flinched before it, like a timorous child clutching a lighted candle in a pitch-dark room.

As a child in Heriot Row Louis's terror of the darkness, with its promise of visitations from the night-hag, was increased by the winter sea-wind which would bluster along the New Town terraces

The drawing-room of No. 17, Heriot Row, from a drawing by John Knight

like a galloping horseman. This fear of night made the child always conscious of anything that glistered through it—the stars overhead, the moonlight, the stray lit-up window in Queen Street. One of the best-known jingles in his *A Child's Garden of Verses* concerns Leerie, a New Town lamp-lighter who was responsible for the lighting of the gas-lamps in Heriot Row, those gas-lamps which Stevenson in an essay once termed 'biddable domestic stars'. Leerie on his round was a signal that the day was closing, and the fell hours of night were about to begin. But to the little boy peering down from his nursery windows in Heriot Row there was a magic touch about the way in which Leerie on his ladder could conjure up light so dexterously:

My tea is nearly ready and the sun has left the sky;
It's time to take the window to see Leerie going by;
For every night at teatime and before you take your seat
With lantern and with ladder he comes posting up the street ...

For we are very lucky, with a lamp before the door,
And Leerie stops to light it as he lights so many more;
And O! before you hurry by with ladder and with light,
O Leerie, see a little child and nod to him to-night!

Leerie and his activities were, like shopping for Skelt's theatrical scenes, among little Louis Stevenson's urban pleasures. As many of the verses in *A Child's Garden* reflect, country pastimes were also available to him, at Colinton Manse.

[VII]

We have earlier noticed that, in his uncompleted *Memoir of Himself*, Louis Stevenson listed three 'powerful impressions' which he had retained from childhood—his sufferings when ill, his 'delights' in convalescing at his maternal grandfather's house, Colinton Manse, and the 'unnatural activity' of his brain when in bed at night. It is the second of these items, his sojourns at the manse, that we may now reasonably consider.

Colinton Manse, which as we may remember was, at four miles out, within easy walking distance of Edinburgh, is a building of uncertain date. That it was designed to be a manse and nothing else is known, and it was long supposed to have been built in 1784 by a Colinton minister who was a botanist and became Professor of Natural History in Edinburgh University; the subsequent discovery, during repairs, of a stone with the date 1636 upon it indicates, however, that the original manse may have dated from the seventeenth century. It is a square house, homely and straight-forward, built on a flat rock in the centre of a garden of three-quarters of a Scots acre. In Louis's childhood this garden was ringed by a beech hedge lined with holly, and the side walls of the house were swathed in climbing roses; an espalier plum covered the front of the house up to the top of the first-floor windows. The slate roof boasted many chimney-pots. In a corner of the garden there was, and still is, a giant yew-tree with a child's swing hanging from an inner branch. Maggie Stevenson's father, Mr Balfour, had trenched and replanted the garden, which he had found full of weeds and red earth, with the yew, two hollies, a small apple-tree and some marigolds as its only embellishments. By Louis's day the garden was a mass of roses and other flowers.

What makes the old manse at Colinton unique, and so memorable to children? The answer is its curious, somehow secret situation. You turn right off the road just before the bridge over the Water of Leith — 'that dirty Water of Leith' as Louis, who loved the clouded stream, would call it — and plunge down a very steep track, passing the church upon your left, and you arrive at the manse, which crouches between the Water of Leith and the ten-foot containing wall of the churchyard. You cannot but be conscious of this crowded churchyard, which lies so far above your head, yet fails to give the house and garden a wholly morbid tone. As a child Louis Stevenson would fancy that he could see the souls of the dead 'peeping through the chinks of the churchyard wall', and he christened the path in that region of the garden 'the Witch's Walk'. The Water of Leith, which curls round the manse so that the house seems to stand on a small promontory, is no longer harnessed at Colinton to drive a mill-wheel. Apart from bird-song in early summertime, the house and its garden used to echo and re-echo to the 'sound of rushing waters that pervaded the old manse, and that has never left the ears of those who were brought up there'. Streams babbled down the hillsides and through Colinton woods, but it was the roar of the Water of Leith, sweeping round the manse and over Hole Mill dam, which seemed the dominant noise to those living in the rectory. Colinton Manse was a very private place, ideal for imaginative children, combining verdant lawns and flowerbeds with churchyard shivers and the fascination of the mill at work:

> Over the borders, a sin without pardon,
>   Breaking the branches and crawling below,

Out through the breach in the wall of the garden,
  Down by the banks of the river we go.

Here is the mill with the humming of thunder,
  Here is the weir with the wonder of foam.
Here is the sluice with the race running under—
  Marvellous places, though handy to home! ...

Years may go by, and the wheel in the river
  Wheel as it wheels for us, children, today,
Wheel and keep roaring and foaming for ever
  Long after all of the boys are away.

Colinton Manse was usually full of some of the old minister's grand-children, for his family of thirteen had proved fertile. Many of these boys and girls came from as far away as India, and Indian pictures and curios were scattered through the manse. Louis's mother shared her father's view that the manse was fundamentally bracing and healthy, and she would for weeks at a time settle there with Louis, convinced that this low-lying, water-bound house and garden were as curative to invalids as any spa. Thomas Stevenson also liked Colinton. When staying there with his wife and son he would conduct experiments in the garden with a holophote, an apparatus for throwing a lighthouse beam in one single direction. His only complaint was his being awoken in what he called 'the middle of the night' by the bell for family prayers which was rung punctually at eight o'clock each morning, summer and winter. At one period the manse clocks were kept half an hour fast to trick sluggards out of bed.

At Colinton Manse Louis did not lead the life of an only child, for he had many small cousins to romp with; but when he was ten years old these delightful times at Colinton ended, for his grandfather died and a new minister with his own family was installed. One Colinton figure remained steadily in his mind and heart—his aunt Jane, a sister of his mother's, who had kept house for the old minister and was beloved by all the children. Aunt Jane, or more simply 'Auntie', was deaf and almost blind from a riding accident in her youth. She wore a deep eye-shade and used a large ear-trumpet, but her kindly, generous personality was undimmed by either disability or age:

> *Chief of our aunts*—not only I,
> But all your dozen of nurslings cry—
> *What did the other children do?*
> *And what were childhood, wanting you?*

Outliving both Louis and his mother, Miss Jane Balfour became, in the early years of this century, a major source of authentic information not only for Louis's official biographer Graham Balfour, but for many Stevenson pilgrims who would make their way to Edinburgh to ask her questions and to prod her memory. A contributor to the legend of Robert Louis Stevenson, Aunt Jane did not take every aspect of her gifted nephew too seriously. In 1901 she wrote to a young friend about a long-ago evening in Heriot Row when Louis had been reading aloud: 'I never heard anything more beautiful or more pathetic.' Late in the evening, as Louis was walking Auntie home through the New Town he confided that 'the only thing he was proud of was his feet & then he took me to a lamp & held up one in a big boot and overshoe! I said I could not judge of it in that dress.' With this vision of Louis Stevenson standing on one leg beneath a greenish gas-lamp we may now move on from his childhood to his infrequent school-days and mutinous youth.

2

Pressures and their Releases

Louis Stevenson's spontaneous tribute to the neatness of his feet was but one symptom of an interest in his own appearance which had started very soon indeed, and already at two years old embraced a grave approval of photographs of himself. Writing her a reminiscent letter about Louis's death, a woman friend of Maggie Stevenson recollected how she once had called at Howard Place and, finding Louis's mother out, had joined Cummy and her little charge as they set off to walk to town over Cannonmills Bridge and past St Mary's Church. Louis looked a 'darling' in a navy-blue pelisse, beaded hat, swansdown ruff and white woollen gloves. To entertain his chance companion the child 'repeated hymn after hymn ... emphasizing so prettily with the dear little baby hands'. Near St Mary's Church he stood stock-still, gazing up into her face. 'But by the bye,' he remarked, 'did I not give you my likeness?' The strange lady replied that he had not done so and that she had not even known that he had got his own photograph. 'Oh yes,' Louis replied, 'I *have* got it and I *will* give it to you. I'll send it *tomorrow* by the *Real Post*.' It seemed to Miss Rymer that he 'had been considering what other kind thing he could do to me besides repeating the hymns'. The likeness, brought by Louis's mother, duly arrived next day.

Photography was at that moment in its infancy, but later, when it had ceased to be a magical novelty and when the exchange of *carte-de-visite* photographs became a norm of Victorian friendship, Louis Stevenson was as a young man as pleased with pictures of himself as he had been when a child. 'You do not know the pleasance I have had out of my two photographs,' he wrote to Mrs Sitwell when he was twenty-three, '... it is very egotistical, is it? or no? but, egotistical or no, so it is — I am as pleased, as proud of my two

42

photographs as I can be.' In later years, and especially when he and his wife lived at Bournemouth in the mid-1880s, Louis was being constantly photographed by enthusiastic amateurs, but, according to the reliable testimony of his close friend Edmund Gosse, hardly any representations of Louis at all resemble him. The painted portraits seemed to Gosse 'positively appalling', because the artists had been defeated by the fugitive quality of Stevenson's expression and the extreme mobility of his features. Gosse considered that the famous Sargent portrait of 1885, and the bas-relief by another great American artist, the sculptor Augustus Saint-Gaudens, alone recaptured the actual appearance of their original. It seems likely that Louis Stevenson's very human partiality to pictures of himself arose from the same need for reassurance that led him to gaze into wall-mirrors to watch his own reflection as he passed.

Although during his youth certain Edinburgh personages judged him, and his clothes, as affected and deliberately eccentric, Louis Stevenson was in fact natural and merely self-conscious. Once the rule of Cummy was over, and the days of beaded caps and swansdown long gone by, young Robert Louis Stevenson, with his flowing hair, dark blue flannel shirts and old velvet jacket, often looked unkempt and also unwashed. Writing from Edinburgh to a Californian friend in the summer of 1880, Louis's newly wed American wife described her mother-in-law as 'so like Louis' and only differing from him 'in one thing; she is generally well dressed and always clean. Louis, as you doubtless remember, is seldom either.' Paradoxically, Louis Stevenson's disregard of fashion and of sartorial convention did not imply that he cared little or nothing for the impression he made on strangers. On the contrary, he cared very much and he was forever wondering what other people thought when they saw him. 'My hair, as I think I have said, is long,' he wrote in 1874 to his friend Sidney Colvin from a Welsh seaside hotel where he was spending the autumn with his parents. ' ... I eat, I am seen about the garden with large and aged quartos, making cigarettes and inhaling the seductive pipe ... I go down to the drawing-room in the evening, where I listen to the music and say nothing. I wonder what the *devil* they think of me. I shd rather contemn one in my own style, I think. You will observe that I do think of what they think of me ... ' Louis was not deliberately setting out to be an enigma. He simply realized that the way he dressed and behaved was, like his ideals and his ambitions, out of the ordinary run of the Edinburgh mill. On occasions he would take as many mischievous pains as Lord Byron himself to startle the bourgeoisie, but by and

43

large his clothes and his manner of living were a sincere form of self-expression. In any case, the derisory monthly sum—seven pounds—his father allowed him in those days precluded his dressing himself at anything but the cheapest shops, and drinking anything but cheap spirits in dirty grog-shops.

That recital of hymns which had formed a prelude to Smout's benevolent gift of his photo to Miss Rymer was but a portion of the repertory with which his Fifeshire nurse endowed him. He could repeat psalms or the story of the Shunammite's son 'with appropriate inflections'. He would weep over Christ's agony on the cross. He early developed what he has termed 'a great fund of simplicity', he 'believed all things and the good rather than the evil, was very prone to love and inaccessible to hatred.' As a child the sight of hunchbacks and other deformed persons made him panic, but he was always trying to conceal this revulsion from the beings who had inspired it. He had an inborn respect for age, and struggled against his natural reaction to the old and the ugly. Looking back when he was thirty at his boyhood, Louis detected in all this 'something that was saintly'. Nevertheless Cummy's teaching and what he defined as her 'over-haste to make me a religious pattern' had at times the opposite effect to that intended. He afterwards judged his nurse's system as not only severe but unwise: 'The idea of sin attached to particular actions absolutely, far from repelling, soon exerts an attraction on young minds … I can never again take so much interest in anything as I took, in childhood, in doing for its own sake what I believed to be sinful. And generally, the principal effect of this false, common doctrine of sin, is to put a point on lust.' But the child kept his mute rebellion secret. He later remarked that had he died in childhood he might perhaps have figured in a tract. Long before he had learned to read—which he did quite suddenly, at seven, from scanning pictures in the illustrated papers whilst recovering from gastric fever—Smout would chant to himself impromptu verses of a religious tinge, some of which his parents copied down and preserved. He referred to this corpus ejaculations as his 'Songstries'.

When he was five years old he entered into a lasting friendship with his cousin Bob Stevenson, who was eight. Possibly to offset their son's loneliness as an only child, or for some domestic reason connected with the household of Thomas Stevenson's eldest brother, Alan, Louis's parents had asked their young nephew Bob to come to stay in the Edinburgh house. Bob, whose full name was Robert Alan Mowbray Stevenson, was also an only son and is described by Louis as an 'imaginative child who had lived in a dream with his sisters, his parents, and the *Arabian Nights*, and more unfitted for the world, as was shown in the event, than an angel fresh from heaven.' The friendship of these two gifted boys was immediate and became intense. 'We lived together in a purely visionary state,' Louis has written. They invented two countries, one of which was ruled by each. Concerning these two countries they drew maps 'and made wars and inventions'. They were forever dressing up, colouring their own drawings, and, of course, snipping out the sheets of Skelt's Juvenile Drama. When Bob's sojourn was over, the boys remained devoted friends, and in their first youth they were far closer than any brothers. As we shall see when we come to Louis Stevenson's prolonged and turbulent adolescence, his parents thought they had reason bitterly to regret the cousins' intimacy, and at one moment young Bob Stevenson was actually banned from Heriot Row. Remembered by those who knew him as a conversationalist even more brilliant than his cousin Louis, Bob became a professional painter and, when inspiration failed him, an art historian, whose study of Velasquez is still well regarded today. As Louis's swing away from church-going Christianity came to the notice of his appalled parents, it began to suit old Thomas Stevenson to blame his nephew Bob for this and other disquieting features of his own son's thinking and behaviour. In retrospect, Louis's wife declared that 'Uncle Tom' (as she called her father-in-law) always held Bob to account for Louis's deficiencies: 'Uncle Tom's idea was that anything he objected to in Louis was due to Bob's influence, but it was the other way round.'

'Bob was fascinating, but he gave like putty,' Fanny Stevenson has recorded. 'It is a hard thing to say, but Bob was a physical, moral and mental coward. Louis was just the opposite. That was why Bob never came off.' When in July 1875 Fanny Osbourne first met the two Stevenson cousins, then wild and coruscant youths in the painters' summer colony at Grez on the skirts of the forest of Fontainebleau, she was far more attracted by Bob than she was by Louis. This original mistake may have biased her subsequent harsh judgment on the young painter. All that we need note about Bob Stevenson at the moment is that the childhood friendship blossomed ultimately into an unholy alliance. They pursued girls together and smoked hashish (when they could get it). They professed agnosticism and derided every tenet that their parents held sacrosanct. Seen together they were always laughing, and when Louis was at Edinburgh University Bob would collect him for luncheon almost daily in term-time and seemed to Louis's fellow-students ever to have come prepared to share some outrageous new joke with his cousin. A letter which Bob wrote to Louis from Antwerp in 1873 shows, however, that it was Bob who was the dependent party in the friendship. As an extreme expression of the electrical effect of Louis Stevenson's company even on a man who had grown up with him in circumstances of unique *camaraderie*, Bob's Antwerp letter deserves to be quoted:

> ... I have been so accustomed to living entirely with you and see and do everything with, or with reference, to you that the being unable to tell you everything day by day, to hear what you say and to have you for public audience, world and everything that I am now quite stumped. Talking I find was talking with you, talking with other people I must always have thought this I will tell Louis that I won't so that it was merely collecting material for my next talk with you ... [Everything] I do mean you, success means you, everything means you. I was not aware of this, I have never felt alone before. At Edinburgh I never knew that I had got into this state mais que faire ...

The rare, almost moonstruck, quality with which Louis Stevenson invested friendship, and which such dissimilar people as Edmund Gosse and Henry James frankly acknowledged, survived distance and even death. ' ... the world seems changed and darkened,' Bob Stevenson wrote to his Aunt Maggie in December 1894 when he had heard the sombre news from Samoa. ' ... I know that, far away as he was and long as it is since I saw him—I did everything thinking of him who was my first and best friend. It does not seem as if there could be much pleasure or interest in what happens now ... There was no one else like him to me ... '

Bob's passionate friendship was reciprocated by Louis, though in more clear-sighted terms. 'I am tired of people misjudging him,' Louis wrote to Sidney Colvin in Paris in January 1874. 'You know *me* now. Well, Bob is just such another mutton, only somewhat further wandered and with perhaps a little more mire on his wool. He has all the same elements of character that I have; no two people were ever more alike only that the world has gone more unfortunately for him, although more evenly.' When he wrote this note to Colvin, Louis was staying at Menton for his health, and it was at the hotel there that Bob's Antwerp declaration of dependence had reached him. To another friend Louis wrote that Bob's letter had 'both pained and pleased' him. 'Should I—I really don't know quite what to feel; I am so much astonished, and almost more astonished that he should have expressed it than that he should feel it; he never would have *said* it, I know. I feel a strange sense of weight and responsibility.' Until he had met his future wife, Louis's sense of responsibility for other people's happiness was a slow and stunted growth. He would agonize over what he was making his parents suffer during his voluble and liberated youth; but he would re-assure himself that it was their rigid minds and their bourgeois attitudes that were causative and fundamentally to blame.

[II]

It was not until Louis Stevenson was nine that his mother ceased to refer to him as 'Smout' in her pocket diaries. She then began to write of him as 'Lew'. The child had been christened Robert Lewis Balfour Stevenson. The spelling 'Lewis', which his maternal grand-father had used for his own name, was changed to 'Louis' when the boy was about eighteen. The replacement of the Scots by the French spelling was said to be due to his father's prejudice against a prominent Edinburgh citizen of radical tendencies whose surname was Lewis. Although spelt 'Louis', it was always pronounced 'Lewis'. His American wife unintentionally pronounced the name 'Loo-us'. The pet-name 'Smout' nevertheless remained current for a few years longer, until in fact Louis put an end to this himself, by exacting a penny fine from any grown-up who made use of it. In his seventh year, that is to say in 1857, the boy's parents decided that he was old enough to go to day-school. Mr Henderson's small school in India Street, a short walk from Heriot Row, was selected; but Louis's prevailing ill-health made his attendance at Mr Henderson's sketchy, and he did not clock in at the school systematically until 1859 and 1860. He was next moved on to the Edinburgh Academy, where he remained for eighteen months. After this, whilst his mother went abroad for her own health, Louis was despatched to a school in Middlesex where some of his Balfour cousins were already boarding; disliking this English school he was withdrawn after one term and went as a day pupil to Mr Thomson's establishment in Frederick Street which he 'attended with more or less regularity' until the year 1867, when he entered Edinburgh University. There he worked for three and a half years in a tepid manner, his aim being a degree in science which would equip him to follow the Stevenson family pattern of lighthouse engineering; his summers were expended in gaining practical knowledge in this latter field. Although his grand-father, his father and the two uncles, Alan and David Stevenson, were highly accomplished lighthouse engineers, the qualifications for their job were in a way nebulous and psychological, or, as Louis's official biographer Graham Balfour puts it, 'elusive': 'The family capacity for the work, though undeniable, was very elusive,' he writes, 'consisting chiefly of a sort of instinct for dealing with the forces of nature and seldom manifesting itself clearly till called forth in actual practice.'

During his schooldays, partly because of his delicacy, and partly because it was an old Edinburgh tradition, Louis was often coached at home by tutors. One of these, a master at his first school, Henderson's in India Street, always looked forward to his evenings with Louis in the library at Heriot Row. For the Reverend Mr Peter Rutherford, who once went on a seaside holiday with the Stevenson family, the boy's overwhelming charm already worked at the age of eight: 'He was without exception the most delightful boy I ever knew. Every recollection of him is delightful. Full of fun, full of tender feeling. Ready for his lessons, ready for fun.' Mr Rutherford's appreciation of his small pupil was written in the year after Louis's death, when any connection with his past gave surviving friends and acquaintances a special public aura. Yet there is no reason to suppose that Louis was not an attractive little boy, as eager for knowledge as he was for relaxation.

Thomas Stevenson's library at 17 Heriot Row gave his son the impression of 'a spot of some austerity'. The bookshelves were disappointingly crowded with the proceedings of learned societies, with books of Latin divinity, physical science and optics — 'it was only in holes and corners that anything really legible existed as by accident'. There were a few Walter Scotts, the third and moralistic section of *Robinson Crusoe*, one novel by Harrison Ainsworth, an unexpected tale by Georges Sand in French, and four old bound volumes of *Punch*. It was on this slender and patchy diet that the boy Louis was forced for some years to subsist at home. At his third school, Mr Thomson's in Frederick Street, which catered for a dozen boys aged from nine to fifteen, literary interests were encouraged and so were literary projects in the way of handwritten, hand-illustrated school magazines. In fact Louis Stevenson's first effort at serious composition dates from 1856 when, as a child of five and a half, he had dictated to his mother a *History of Moses*, that theme having been chosen by his uncle David Stevenson as subject for a prize competition amongst the related children. At Colinton Manse the boy would dictate little stories to some patient amaneunsis, while at thirteen he wrote a satire on 'the inhabitants of Peebles' in the style of the *Book of Snobs*. At four-teen he composed an opera libretto in rhyme, *The Baneful Potato*, which has since, perhaps happily, disappeared. Were it not for his later fame, and his mother's assiduity in piously recording his sayings and doings as a child, it is likely that Louis Stevenson's juvenilia would seem to differ little from the normal exercises in self-expression of any other mid-Victorian child reared in a cultivated atmosphere.

For a long time in his early childhood Louis's knowledge of story-books was limited by what Cummy liked and deemed suitable to his age. Yet at times his mother would herself read aloud to him, and on at least one occasion Mrs Thomas Stevenson took a bold literary line; she read to him from the tragedy of *Macbeth*. By chance this reading was begun on 'a disastrous day of storm, the heaven full of turbulent vapours, the street full of the squalling of the gale, the windows resounding under bucketfuls of rain.' Louis has written that wherever he re-read *Macbeth* in later life the play would conjure up for him 'the gale howling up the valley of the Leith.' He did not find this introduction to Shakespeare 'agreeable'. It was 'something new and shocking to be thus ravished by a giant, and I shrank under the brutal grasp', he wrote in an article for *Scribner's Magazine* in 1888. He felt that, as audience, a child 'is conscious of interest, not in literature, but in life', and he describes himself as listening 'for news of the great vacant world upon whose edge I stood'. Louis likened learning to read to a second weaning: 'In the past all was at the choice of others ... In the future we are to approach the silent, in-expressive type alone, like pioneers.' In another essay he confesses that he is puzzled to find that as a grown man he had retained the literary prejudices—the preference for *Rob Roy*, the passion for one chapter in *The Book of Snobs*—which he had formed in his father's library in childhood. Did this mean that he was right in his judg-ments when he was a child? Or did it mean that he had never grown up; 'that the child is not the man's father but the man? and that I came into the world with all my faculties complete, and have only learned sinsyne to be more tolerant of boredom?' The pioneer-ing aspect of choosing his own books was quickly superseded by a sheer gusto for the act of reading. Louis gives no precise date for the revelation, indeed he probably no longer knew how old he was when it had dawned. He chiefly remembered that he and his parents were staying in some country place, that he was sent down into the village on an errand, and, taking a book of fairy-tales with him, he walked through a fir-wood reading as he went. He said that he had never forgotten and never could forget 'the shock of that pleasure ... for it was then that I knew I loved reading.'

[III]

The winter's gale howling up the valley of the Leith was only one aspect of Edinburgh weather which affected Louis. An Edinburgh childhood and youth is enervating, and even today Edinburgh demands a certain physical resilience of its citizens. In the years before central heating, when a big house like that of the Stevensons in Heriot Row was entirely dependent upon open coal fires for warmth, those who were not tough either succumbed to the chilling draughts of passages and stairways or, if they were able to do so, went south for the winter. 'The delicate die early,' Louis Stevenson wrote in his *Picturesque Notes on Edinburgh*, a fine book which gave offence to some Edinburgh readers when it was first published in folio format in 1879: 'The delicate die early and I, as a survivor among bleak winds and plumping rain, have been sometimes tempted to envy them their fate.' He was very conscious of the commanding position which 'the ancient and famous metropolis of the North' occupies, overlooking 'a windy estuary from the slope and summit of three hills', but he asserted that Edinburgh 'paid cruelly for her high seat in one of the vilest climates under heaven'. He wrote of the winds which blew from all directions, of the icy rain, of the cold sea fogs from out of the east and of the snow which came fluttering down from the Highland hills. He categorized the city's winter weather as raw and boisterous, the summer weather as shifty and ungenial and the spring as 'a downright meteorological purgatory'. As he grew up the Edinburgh winters seemed to age him: 'I am always an old man in winter as you know,' Louis wrote to a correspondent when he himself was only twenty-five. It is probable that the inhabitants of 17 Heriot Row were more alert to Edinburgh weather and its harshness than many of their friends or neighbours. There was an emphasis on illness in that house, bred both by the long-established chest ailments of the mother and by the anxious fear that these had been passed on to the undersized, narrow-chested little boy who was her only child. For weeks together, in the long, cruel winter-time, he did not cross the doorstep of his parents' house out into the bleak street. As an adolescent, and even later, Louis would stand on the bridge that links Princes Street to the old Town and watch the trains heading south with envy for their passengers in his heart.

Louis's image of the South had nothing to do with his unsatisfying

single term at a Surrey boarding-school. When he thought of the
South he pictured the Mediterranean, as he had first seen it in his
parents' company at the age of twelve. On January 3rd, 1863, Mr
and Mrs Thomas Stevenson, their son, his nurse Cummy and his
girl-cousin Bessie Stevenson left Edinburgh for York on the first stage
of a happy exile which lasted for the best part of five months. They
went via Marseilles, Toulon and Nice to Menton, where they took a
furnished flat from the first week in February until the last day of
March. From Menton they went in a private carriage to Genoa,
where they took ship for Naples. Sometimes by train, but more often
by road, they wound their way to Rome, and thence to Florence,
Ferrara and Bologna. Their last Italian stop was Venice, where they
spent four nights in an hotel near the Rialto, afterwards crossing the
Brenner Pass and visiting Munich. By this time they wearied for
home; on entering yet another strange town after a long day's
journey Louis would exclaim petulantly: 'O I wish this was Auld
Reekie!'

Louis's cousin Bessie recalled in later life that Lew at this time was
'in some ways … more like a boy of sixteen'. His father firmly
believed in the educational value of foreign travel and made Louis
sight-see wherever they went. In the hotel at Nice Mr Stevenson
began taking his son into the smoking-room, where Louis watched
his father become the witty centre of an animated group of other
men. It is a curious fact that, although he was known to be enjoying
Pompeii and the Roman catacombs and the gondola rides in Venice,
his rich experiences seem to have left no palpable imprint upon
Louis Stevenson's mind. Many years later, at Davos Platz, he made
friends with the historian of Venice, Horatio Brown, but never once,
during their conversations, did Louis hint that he knew Venice or
indeed had ever travelled in Italy at all. His nurse Cummy, who
kept a careful diary of this, her first and last visit to the Continent,
seems to have benefited more by the journey than her charge, who
had fits of the sulks, or as she called them in Scots idiom 'the touts'—
which he only lost when safely settled at Menton. Mrs Stevenson
remained in a semi-invalid state for much of the journey, and her
hacking cough was to Cummy a cause of much concern.

Alison Cunningham was four years younger than Mr Thomas
Stevenson, and seven years older than his wife. Her devotion to the
latter, and to her 'dear bit Lewis', was complete; Mr Stevenson was
not included in this close affection, though she expresses sorrow that,
at Genoa, his piles were giving him unusual pain. Cummy's diary is
written in a notebook bought for her by her friend 'Cashie', nurse to

the family of Louis's uncle David Stevenson. Several of the journal's comments take the form of ejaculations addressed to this absent friend. 'Oh, Cashie, woman, I think I love her more than ever now I am with her in a foreign land,' she writes of her employer's wife. ' ... What a different house it is now since she has been able to sit up all day!' Cummy notes at Menton: 'She really has the knack of making others happy; I am sure she cheers her husband when he is cast down.' At Menton Cummy had ceased to be a traveller upset by the promiscuity of *table d'hôte* meals and distressed by the weakness of French tea; in their apartment she took control, aided by a little local girl called Marie, whom she harangued about Presbyterianism in broad Scots. Although always treated as a friend, and sometimes as a butt for Mrs Stevenson's well-intentioned jokes, Cummy shows that she knew her place, travelling outside in the *berline* and appraising the other members of the little party from a reliable domestic's angle: 'Lew is a good bit boy, no trouble indeed. None of them are much,' she noted—the word 'much' being doubtless the key to this remark. From her diary Cummy emerges as intelligent and individual, very much alive to natural beauty, inquisitive about foreign habits, distressed by Lenten carnivals and grubby friars, intrigued by confessionals ('I saw a great many small places with a door, large enough to hold one person ... Mrs S. whispered in my ear—"Now is your chance, Cummy, if you wish to confess!"') and very conscious of what she terms her own cold heart in relation to God.

Typically, Edinburgh is the yardstick by which foreign cities and towns are judged: 'Rome is about the size of Edinburgh, though not nearly as bonny as Auld Reekie.' The place of Cummy's preference was Venice, and like her mistress she became 'quite *daft* about boating'; on her last night she went out with three new friends (probably ladies' maids) in a gondola, and, reclining on the carpeted deck, she gazed up at the star-strewn sky. Cummy's diary for these months of 1863 reveal a less pessimistic side to her nature than Louis's accounts of his nurse's ominous bedtime stories suggest.

Why his visions of Italy left no mammoth or even lasting impression on Louis's mind is hard to understand. A second visit to Menton, where he joined his mother in the winter of 1863 to 1864, doubtless confirmed his longing for sunshine and olive trees, for orange groves and the seemingly carefree atmosphere of the South. One asset which Louis brought back with him from his two visits to the Mediterranean would seem to have been a working knowledge of how to talk French easily, although he never attained grammatical accuracy in writing the language. At Menton, in the spring of 1863, we know that he had lessons from a tutor; his mother, whose French was fluent from her youth, would surely have helped him as well. At one time, in Menton, Mrs Thomas Stevenson was trying to learn Italian, but she had found that this effort did 'permanent harm' to her brain, and she afterwards confessed that she could remember only one phrase of all she had learnt. Her subsequent search for winter health led her to Torquay, where Louis once again accompanied her.

I do not wish to imply that the Mediterranean sojourns, the sight of Venice and the Brenner Pass left Louis's mind a *tabula rasa*; it is only that what caught his attention abroad were tiny details, sometimes of a literary nature. His cousin Bessie may have thought that he had on the Italian journey acted like a boy of sixteen, not twelve, but in fact his reactions were still very much those a child—the child whom he recalled in the *Garden of Verses*, that fetching record of the workings of the child-mind. Thus, his most durable memory of Nice was centred on a set of dessert plates ornamented with pictures of incidents from the novels of the younger Dumas. These plates first brought to the boy's attention the character and the adventures of the Vicomte de Bragelonne. The novel of this name then became and remained one of his favourite works of fiction. In the essay *A Gossip on a Novel of Dumas*, which was published in *Memories and Portraits* in 1887, when Louis Stevenson was thirty-six, he is still revelling in *The Vicomte de Bragelonne*, which he compares favourably with Shakespeare's *Richard III*, a play there denounced as 'a big, black, sprawling melodrama, written with infinite spirit but no refinement by a man who had the world, himself, mankind and his trade still to learn.' He thinks *Bragelonne* 'better done of its kind' than *Richard III*, although he does admit that the Dumas tale could not be mentioned 'in the same part of the building' as *Hamlet*, *Lear* or *Othello*. Louis's thirst for adventure stories, which gave us, for example, *Treasure Island*, could, like his preference for the eighteenth century as the site for his own novels, seem to be allied to the braggadocio poses and heroic stances of his old nursery playmates, the coloured cut-out figures of Skelt's toy theatres. Similarly, at the end of his short life, we find him interpreting the age-long rivalries and helter-skelter squabbles of Samoan chieflets in clannish, romantic and vaguely Jacobite terms.

Whilst his glimpses of Mediterranean sunshine did clearly leave him with a yen to escape from Edinburgh and head South, there was another variety of Edinburgh climate against which, in his adolescent years, he reacted as peremptorily as he did against the dark weather.

This was the heavy cloak, almost the pall, of Presbyterian conformity which still, fold upon fold, Sunday after Sunday, smothered the whole city in a deathly hush, a palpable silence splintered only by the echoing of church bells that summoned, by the patter of belated loiterers' feet, and by the consequent harmony of hymn-singing which, at set hours, was wafted out upon the empty streets from each Covenanting places of worship that you passed. 'Everything here is utterly silent,' Louis Stevenson wrote to a London friend on an autumn Sunday morning at Heriot Row; 'I can hear men's footfalls streets away; the whole life of Edinburgh has been sucked into sundry pious edifices ... I wish I could make you feel the hush that is over everything, only made the more perfect by rare interruptions ... '

In a lively and sinister Christmas story, *The Misadventures of John Nicholson*, published in *Yule Tide* for 1887, Louis describes his young hero imagining his father, brother and sister in church on a Sabbath morning which he himself is personally celebrating by rifling his father's money-drawer: 'An hour and a half, perhaps an hour and three-quarters, if the doctor was long-winded,' John Nicholson calculates for this the first church-going of the day. ' ... He saw, in a vision, the family pew, the somnolent cushions, the Bibles, the Psalm-books, Maria with her smelling-salts, his father sitting spectacled and critical; and at once he was struck with indignation, not unjustly. It was inhuman to go off to church, and leave a sinner in suspense, unpunished, unforgiven ... ' John's father—'that iron gentleman'—is a pillar of the Church of Scotland, but perfectly aware that the English and men of other nationalities who do not take that institution as seriously as he himself does form part of an evil, rebellious world, 'lying sunk in dozedness, for nothing short of a Scots word will paint this Scotsman's feelings'. But once back at home, in his house on the most sunless segment of Randolph Crescent, Mr Nicholson feels secure—'Here was a family where prayers came at the same hour, where the Sabbath literature was unimpeachably selected ... and over which there reigned all week, and grew denser on Sundays, a silence that was agreeable to his ear, and a gloom that he found comfortable.'

Even on the Sabbath, 17 Heriot Row was never as gloomy as Louis represents the Nicholsons' household to have been. It did, after all, contain Mrs Thomas Stevenson in all her brightness, the unpredictable if pious Smout, and Coolin the Skye terrier, who had come to the household in 1857 and was a spoiled favourite of Thomas Stevenson, drinking water from a huge *bénitier* (actually a tropical stone clamshell) in the hall. Nevertheless, Sunday was set apart from the weekdays in that house. The reading of novels or children's story books was strictly forbidden; the *Shorter Catechism* and such edifying if lurid works as *Foxe's Book of Martyrs* were substituted. Although Louis's wife, Fanny, had been brought up as a member of the Second Presbyterian Church in Indianapolis, she was surprised to find how portentously her parents-in-law took the matter of 'Sabba'-day reading'. When the whole family were staying in a rainswept cottage at Pitlochry, in the summer of 1881, the elder Stevenson confiscated a two-volume life of Voltaire which Louis, then thirty, and his wife, aged forty-one, were found reading on a Sunday. Fanny was also shocked to discover that a sick little girl could not have fairy-stories read to her on the Sabbath. She may have been unaware that when Louis was a child his mother conformed to Sunday rules for children, though in her own somewhat charming and disingenuous way: little Smout could only play with his toy soldiers on the Sabbath after his mother had sewn a tiny sack on the shoulders of one of them and Louis had promised that his only game should be Christian's adventures from *Pilgrim's Progress*.

Even the dust-cart men and the collectors of night-soil did not sully the Sabbath silence by work or the cobblestone rumble of wheels. Saturday nights were, however, saddened for Thomas Stevenson, who knew that householders put out no refuse-boxes or 'backets' that the dustmen might collect next morning; for one of the old man's endearing qualities was an affection for the stray dogs, forlorn and friendly creatures who 'raked the backets' for food at night-time. A particular stray, a liver-and-white spaniel which he had christened Bob, and which haunted the west end of busy Princes Street, was a great friend of Mr Stevenson, who would stop to talk to it, scratch its chin or pull its ears, ending by buying the dog a lunch at a confectioner's.

Seated at his own comfortable board on wintry Saturday nights, Louis's father would express anxiety about Bob; had he taken refuge in the Caledonian Station, had he had the foresight to bury a bone in the West Kirkyard against his Sunday dinner? It is such traits as these that make one realize why Thomas Stevenson was fundamentally loved by his son.

In one of his early letters Louis tried to define the effect of his father's overweening concern with Death and the Hereafter. He wrote that Thomas Stevenson had declared that he regarded life itself as 'a shambling [and presumably unsatisfactory] sort of omnibus' taking him to his hotel. It is interesting to note that although the old man's whole existence was often darkened by what his son called a 'morbid sense of his own unworthiness' and an apprehension 'of the fleetingness of life and his concern with aching death' he would never consent to be an elder of their local church, St Stephen's, just round the corner from Heriot Row in St Vincent Street. Like many of his Presbyterian contemporaries, Mr Thomas Stevenson could preach well, but he instinctively shrank from imposing himself on a congregation. It would seem that his didactic gift, like his obsession with ethics, was inherited and developed by his only son. Essays such as those contained in the volume *Virginibus Puerisque* (collected and published in 1881) have charmed two or three successive generations, and yet are neither very original nor, to our modern eyes, very gripping. They are, basically, obvious truths presented in a manner at once insidious, intimate and engaging. A violent youthful reaction against a harsh doctrinal upbringing does not mean that the deep effect of such doctrines is either slight or ephemeral. For all his humanity and gentleness, Robert Louis Stevenson can, at times, be something of a prig.

[IV]

In November 1867 Robert Louis Stevenson entered Edinburgh University. He has described himself in his student days as 'lean, idle, ugly, unpopular'. He was certainly lean and, by deliberation, idle, but he was never ugly and probably not unpopular. Young Stevenson pursued a course of planned truancy. For instance, he scarcely attended the Greek classes so that he never knew Greek. The result of his valiant efforts not to learn resulted, in his own perhaps exaggerated words, in his being 'sent ... forth into the world and the profession of letters with the merest shadow of an education'. Later in life, when he made friends with such an erudite scholar as John Addington Symonds, he felt conscious of this lack, and would joke about reading his Greek classics in Boehm translations. Yet he was secretly and manfully working at a private life-project of his own — to learn how to become a writer. He always kept two books in his pocket, one to read, the other to record what he observed. This aim and intention of becoming a writer was what he himself called his 'own private end'. Whenever he came across a new book which excited or impressed him he would try to imitate its author's style, thus, in a famous phrase of his, 'playing the sedulous ape' to such diverse predecessors as Hazlitt, Lamb, Wordsworth, Sir Thomas Browne, Defoe and Montaigne, whilst also studying contemporary writers—Baudelaire, for example, or Nathaniel Hawthorne. This frank recognition of the art of writing as something that could and should be learned has at times been derided by critics of Stevenson, and may seem self-conscious or laborious to modern eyes. But it was held by other writers of Stevenson's day, including his friend the poet and critic Edmund Gosse. 'Perhaps', wrote Gosse to a young author in 1895, ' ... you will not think me disagreeable if I ask you whether you are not a little rash in supposing that you can, without training, at once write in such a way as to be successful. No one expects to be a painter or a lawyer or an engineer in a couple of months. Those professions require long training ... : why should not literature?' It was on such a theory that young Stevenson was working at what he termed his 'monkey tricke', and though he did not aspire to publish his juvenilia he did contribute articles to a short-lived college magazine founded by himself and three other friends, all members of the respected Speculative Society, which had, and still has, its rooms inside the building of Edinburgh University. Although he never made any notable or impressive speeches in 'the Spec' debates, he liked the company and also the atmosphere of the turkey-carpeted hall, where on winter evenings the firelight flicked on the portraits of earlier illustrious members along the walls. It formed, too, an escape from Heriot Row and when in 1873 he fell in love he would use the Spec. as a *poste restante*.

The real and immediate reason for Robert Louis Stevenson's college career was, however, understood in the family to be that he should learn engineering so as to enter the Stevenson lighthouse firm. He had first come into contact with the uncanny, isolated life of lighthouse-keepers when his father took him as a boy on a tour of harbour lights round the shores of Fife. This was in 1863, when Louis was thirteen. The idea of taking him along on the tour arose from a strange scene in which the boy, about to be sent away to boarding-school in England, had burst into tears sitting on a doorstep in the London Road, and had been comforted by a cat which 'fawned upon the weeper, and gambolled for his entertainment, watching the effect, it seemed, with motherly eyes'. Back in Heriot Row Louis could not resist speaking of the cat's kindness (and, of course, of his own outburst of tears) and it was decided that he needed a change. In consequence he was taken to the old kingdom of Fife. He could see the distant prospect of Fife from the back-windows at Heriot Row; now the historical seaboard places at which they put in by boat stirred him with their names: Donbristle, Burntisland, King-horn, Kirkcaldy, Wemyss 'with its bat-haunted Caves' and the two

Anstruthers. He was struck by the relationship between the visiting engineer, his own father, and the keepers of the lighthouses, who might prove slovenly and need upbraiding, or might, on the other hand, have the brasses shining and all the storm-panes in place. 'As soon as the boat grates on the shore,' Louis wrote reminiscently in *Random Memories*, 'and the keepers step forward in their uniformed coats, the very slouch of the fellows' shoulders tells their story, and the engineer may begin at once to assume his "angry countenance".' While these inspections were in progress the boy would hang about with 'the east wind humming in [his] teeth', hands deep in his pockets.

In 1868, when he was seventeen, Louis Stevenson was sent to acquire practical knowledge of engineering by watching the new harbour works at Anstruther in Fife, and at Wick in Caithness; this last he considered 'one of the meanest of men's towns, and situate certainly upon the baldest of God's bays'. The one interesting aspect of the Wick harbour-works he found to be the diving, and he became determined to put on the padded suits, helmet and heavy weights then necessary for the diver. This idea obsessed him, and 'with the countenance of a certain handsome scamp of a diver, Bob Bain by name' he succeeded in going down into the green depths and learned that by jumping upwards only slightly he 'blew out sideways like an autumn leaf'.

Although he was bored by Wick, and repelled by the ugliness of Caithness, Louis Stevenson did not at heart despise the profession of harbour and lighthouse engineer. It could involve visits to strange rocks and wild islands reached through dangerous seas, and it also often involved 'hanging-about at harbour sides, which is the richest form of idling'. At Wick he kept himself going by his own writing in the evenings, and by reading *The Moonstone* and other modern novels. What he most objected to in his imposed career was the idea of the periods when he would not be at harbour-mouths, or diving—long stuffy, claustrophobic periods when he would be shut up in the Edinburgh office as his father so frequently was. There is no reason to assume that Louis Stevenson could not have made a fairly competent engineer. In March 1871 he read his first and last professional paper, *A New Form of Intermittent Light*, before the Royal Scottish Society of Arts, by which it was judged 'highly creditable to so young an author'. But on April 8th, scarcely a week after this minor triumph, he went for a walk with his father and told him that he did not want an engineering career at all but wished to become a writer. Old Mr Stevenson was shocked and shaken, but, according to his wife, was 'wonderfully resigned'. He merely stipulated that from engineering his son should now at the university embark on law, so as to find himself with a steady income and occupation should writing fail.

At this particular phase of his dealings with Louis, Thomas Stevenson showed wisdom and restraint. There was, however, one vital direction in which the father showed restraint without wisdom. This was in the matter of pocket-money: until the age of twenty-three the young man was restricted to a weekly sum of half a crown or sometimes of five shillings. As Louis's first biographer explained, the Stevensons were perfectly ready to give dinner-parties and dances for Louis and his friends in their Heriot Row house. By some quaint thought-process they must have believed that by keeping him on so taut a financial tether, they would be keeping him out of mischief; instead they were ensuring that he haunted the lowest and cheapest taverns and howffs, and mixed happily with prostitutes and other denizens of the Lothian Road, Calton Hill and the port of Leith. Since his monthly pound was usually spent the first night of the day he got it, Louis tells us in his *Memoirs* that he often did not have five shillings in his pocket. 'I was the companion of seamen, chimney-sweeps and thieves; my circle was being continually changed by the action of the police magistrate.' He would sit in a little sanded kitchen, 'generally in silence and making sonnets in a penny version-book'. Everyone petted him — 'the women were most gentle and kind to me; I might have left all my money for a month, and they would have returned every farthing of it'. From the black velvet jacket he habitually wore he was nicknamed 'Velvet Coat' by these new friends. It is an irony that this distinctive garment had been bought for Louis by his father himself. For a future novelist this experience of a life antithetic to that of 17 Heriot Row was surely admirable. To cut free from the parental atmosphere Louis Stevenson once set up his headquarters in a tobacconist's shop.

In a paper which Graham Balfour did not publish, but which he appreciated, Stevenson has left us a portrait of Mary H—, 'a robust, great-haunched, blue-eyed young woman, of admirable temper, and, if you will let me say so of a prostitute, extraordinary modesty'. Every now and then she would go to work for months in a factory, and during these stretches of respectability she refused to be recognized when Louis Stevenson passed her on Leith Walk. She had sometimes tried to arouse his jealousy, but it had never occurred to him 'that she thought of me otherwise than in the way of business', until he met her by chance again years later, when she was about to emigrate to the United States: 'I can still·hear her recalling the past in her sober, Scotch voice, and I can still feel her good honest loving hand as we said goodbye.' Chance encounters were a part of Stevenson's philosophy of life. His strange compelling charm worked vertically, and reached into the most disparate circles.

In the 1920s, when as we have seen a reaction against the plaster-saint version of Robert Louis Stevenson propagated by his widow and her family had violently set in, a great deal of idle gossip about his allegedly excessive virility and his liking for low-life was rife in Edinburgh. The facts seem no more intensely exciting than that, in the stringent society of Victorian Edinburgh, he was driven to go to brothels by poverty, curiosity and desire. There was in Victorian Edinburgh an underworld which was officially ignored by the bourgeoisie but which fulfilled a definite purpose as an outlet for young men. In the 1920s, also, a youth who declared himself to be Robert Louis Stevenson's bye-blow came to Edinburgh. He created a nine days' wonder from his resemblance to his putative father, but was generally judged to be a fraud.

[V]

To much of the polite Edinburgh society which his parents frequented Louis Stevenson seemed erratic and bohemian. They were inclined to ridicule this strangely clad youth, and foresaw for him neither fame nor future. In university circles he would come and go as he wished, vanishing for weeks together and giving to one of his contemporaries the hint of being 'a comet with no calculable orbit or recognizable period'. This was after he had graduated from the university and had begun to flee abroad. But there were some discerning people in Edinburgh who understood and loved him, and suspected him of great capacities so far untapped. Chief amongst these were Mr and Mrs Fleeming Jenkin, he the famous Professor of Engineering in the University of London, she an erudite and charming Englishwoman with a passion for private theatricals. Amongst her friends, Mrs Jenkin was always lovingly referred to as 'Madam'.

After her husband's appointment to the new chair of Engineering at Edinburgh University in 1868, Madam busied herself paying or returning calls. One winter's evening in that year, she went for the first time to tea with Mrs Thomas Stevenson in Heriot Row. They were seated by the tea-table probably placed before the cheerful fire in the grate at the east end of the big drawing-room, which seems to have been at that moment very dimly lit. Mrs Stevenson was no doubt engaging her new acquaintance in that form of stately but endearing conversation for which she was known. Suddenly, from out of a dark corner beyond the fireplace there came 'a voice, peculiar, vibrating; a boy's voice I thought at first'.

Mrs Stevenson exclaimed that she had altogether forgotten her son was in the room. She introduced him. 'The voice', writes Mrs Jenkin, 'went on: I listened in perplexity and amazement. Who was this son who talked as Charles Lamb wrote? this young Heine with the Scottish accent?' She writes that she stayed long and that when she left 'the unseen converser' came down with her to the front door. As he opened it the light of Leerie's gas-lamp fell full on his face and she saw 'a slender, brown, long-haired lad, with great dark eyes, a brilliant smile, and a gentle, deprecating bend of the head'. She thought him a boy of sixteen but he was in fact, as she found out later, already eighteen. She asked him to call on her and he at once agreed to do so the next day. Mrs Jenkin says that she 'ran home. As soon as I sat down to dinner I announced, "I have made the acquaintance of a poet." He came on the morrow and from that day forward we saw him constantly. From that day forward, too, our affection and our admiration for him, and our delight in his company, grew.'

Louis Stevenson's friendship with the Jenkins was the first of the many that he afterwards formed with intellectual Londoners who were prepared to take him at his face value. He began to act in the Jenkins' annual amateur theatrical productions, which were always very professionally organized and rehearsed. He was never, apparently, a brilliant stage actor, but he enjoyed the dressing-up and the lobster-and-champagne suppers which rounded off each evening's performance. During the bitterly cold winters of the 'seventies, when 'all Edinburgh was skating on Duddingston Loch', that idyllic sheet of water near Duddingston village, and almost under the shadow of the parish church, Louis would walk out there through the crisp air, and skate with, or rather round, the Jenkin couple. The Jenkins had somehow appropriated to themselves at Duddingston an oval of well-swept ice on which they would skate together. When Mrs Jenkin, who was delicate, got tired she would kneel down on the ice looking like a church effigy, her profile outlined against the white ice and the banks of reeds. Professor Jenkin would pirouette round her while she rested, and Louis Stevenson would dart about them skating alone 'like a melancholy minnow', with a muffler round his neck. After Professor Jenkin's premature death at the age of fifty-two, Louis Stevenson was asked to write his biography, which forms a lengthy preface to Jenkin's collected papers. In a passage from this, recording the professor's first arrival in Edinburgh, he presents a mature view of his native city. 'Edinburgh, which was henceforth to be his home, is a small metropolitan town; where college professors and the lawyers give the tone ... Not, therefore, an unlettered place, yet not pedantic, Edinburgh will compare favourably with much larger cities.' Pointing out that Jenkin never took up golf, Louis remarks that 'golf is a cardinal virtue in the city of the winds'.

The *Memoir of Fleeming Jenkin* is Robert Louis Stevenson's only biography, and, unlike many similar volumes undertaken from piety or from a sense of duty, it is candid and entertaining. He was writing it at Bournemouth in 1886 when he wrote to Edmund Gosse:

> I am very full of Jenkin's life, it is painful, yet very pleasant to dig into the past of a dead friend, and find him, at every spadeful, shine brighter. I own, as I read, I wonder more and more why he should have taken me for a friend. He had many and obvious faults upon the face of him; the heart was pure gold. I feel it little pain to have lost him, for it is a loss in which I cannot believe; I take it, against reason, for an absence ... Yes, if I could believe in the immortality business, the world would indeed be too good to be true; but we were put here to do what service we can, for honour and not for hire; the sods cover us, and the worm that never dies, the conscience sleeps well at last.

Stevenson was at this time thirty-five, and, in fact, still an agnostic.

[VI]

It was on the last day of January 1873, when he was twenty-two years old, that Louis Stevenson shattered his father's peace of mind for ever by first declaring that he was an agnostic. Hitherto he had been the subject of many suspicions and manifold anxieties. He now came out into the open and announced that he belonged to the one category of human beings which to both his parents was purest anathema. To Thomas Stevenson doubts about the truth of Christianity were quite simply not credible. 'If a man does not hold Christianity,' Louis wrote of him at this time, 'he must be to him ever a knave, a madman, or an inconsiderate and culpable fool.'

How much or how little Louis's parents knew of his escapades in the lower haunts of Edinburgh and in the port of Leith we can no longer judge. Edinburgh, however, was a small and gossipy city, and the Thomas Stevensons must at least have been aware of their son's irregular hours, for when Louis let himself into Heriot Row with his latchkey long after midnight, he had not only to pass through the hall, where a low gas-jet was left burning, but to creep to the very top of the house to reach his own bedroom. Some of the Stevensons' friends thought that Louis's attitude to his father at the dinner-table was impertinent, for he would contradict him outright. Other guests found the Stevenson boy quaint and puzzling, ill-dressed and excitable. There is a story that driving one day down the High Street with her sister Miss Jane Balfour, Louis's mother saw 'a queer-looking ragamuffin walking along the pavement with a bag of bones over his shoulder'. A third lady in the carriage exclaimed 'Do look at that queer old-bones-man.' Aunt Jane Balfour looked, only to recognize that it was her nephew. 'Oh, Louis, Louis!' she cried out. 'What will you do next?' Argument and eccentricity were bad enough. A declaration of religious doubt was an outrage and thoroughly unspeakable. 'You have rendered my whole life a failure,' was Thomas Stevenson's first bitter comment, while his wife simply said that her son's scepticism was the 'heaviest affliction' that had ever befallen her.

In the winter of 1872–3 Louis had been very ill; he had thought that he might die. His mother took him to recuperate in Great Malvern, where his only pastime was playing billiards with one of the hotel waiters. He returned home with what he called 'a new-found honesty' which he personally attributed to the dangers of his recent illness. One evening soon after this return to Edinburgh he came back to the house in Heriot Row, having spent some hours with his closest boon crony, a young Writer to the Signet* named Charles Baxter. Louis's father waylaid him, and in the course of conversation questioned him about his religious beliefs. Inspired by the new-found honesty Louis ceased to prevaricate—'I really hate all lying so much now,' he wrote later to Baxter—but the effect of his confession of disbelief was so catastrophic that he said he wished that he had continued to lie. His parents treated him as 'a horrible Atheist' and 'a careless infidel'. Owing to his candour, the atmosphere at 17 Heriot Row became that 'of a house in which somebody is still waiting burial'. He described his parents' faces as grim and wretched, their voices hushed, their step quiet; everything in the

* A member of a society of legal practitioners in Edinburgh, so named because they were originally clerks to the office of the King's secretary, their duties being to prepare all warrants or charters for sealing with the King's signet.

Heriot Row household had suddenly become 'real Hell'. Thomas Stevenson had solemn recourse to Butler's *Analogy of Religion*, a famous work by an eighteenth-century Bishop of Durham which was thought by many Protestants to be second only to the Bible in value. While the old man raked through Bishop Butler's book for arguments to convince his infidel son, Mrs Stevenson begged Louis to join a class for young men currently organized by a clergyman named Nicholson, the minister of St Stephen's church. 'I don't know whether I feel more inclined to laugh or cry over these naivetés', Louis wrote in despair to Charles Baxter, 'but I know how sick at heart they make me ... What a pleasant thing it is to have just *damned* the happiness of (probably) the only two people who care a damn about you in the world.' Henceforth he began referring to Heriot Row as 'our ruined, miserable house', and to his own behaviour under the strain as 'rough and sour'. Regarding life as a 'pilgrimage from nothing to nowhere' he began to feel an 'utter polar loneliness' of spirit.

From that disastrous January evening onwards, Louis was subjected to a seemingly endless series of discussions on religion. At most of these Mrs Stevenson was present, but, as she declared many years later, neither she nor her husband 'had the least idea that they were so painful to Louis—I never knew till I was living with him at Vailima, his father never knew at all.' Out of these discussions there sprang up and burgeoned a whole crop of virulent scenes, scenes in which the father would tell his son that he even regretted his own marriage. 'A poor end for all my tenderness,' Thomas Stevenson remarked on one occasion, 'I have worked for you and gone out of my way for you and the end of it is that I find you in opposition to the Lord Jesus Christ—I find everything gone.' He fancied that Louis was proselytizing for atheism amongst his young contemporaries : 'I would ten times sooner have seen you lying in your grave,' remarked this highly Christian parent, 'than that you should be shaking the faith of other young men and bringing such ruin on other houses, as you have brought already upon this. I had thought', he added, 'to have had someone to help me when I was old.' 'These scenes,' Louis wrote to a friend, 'seem to tell more and more on me at each repetition. I don't get acclimatized.' He thought that if only he could 'cease to like' his father he would mind it all less; as it was he loved him and found it 'insupportable' to see the old man's emotion —'an impotent emotion to make things worse, his sort of half-threats of turning me out.' 'If I were not an exceptionally light-hearted man, I do not think that I could survive all that has been concentrated in my head,' he wrote on another occasion. He no longer really trusted those periods when his parents were amiable to him, likening such interludes to 'a pic-nic on a volcano'. He also felt that he had killed his father's gaiety. Lying in bed in the morning he would hear Thomas Stevenson going out to get the newspapers and hoped that his father would whistle to himself as he used to do on his return: 'But of course he did not. I have stopped that pipe.'

[VII]

Charles Baxter, with whom Louis had been dining on that fatal last Friday of January 1873, was one of the four close friends who did a great deal in these early days to alleviate his sporadic sense of polar loneliness. The others included, as we have seen, his devoted cousin Bob, who was not too much in Edinburgh, frankly preferring the Latin Quarter of Paris to his native city. Then there was Sir Walter Simpson, a youthful baronet, whose father had owed his fame and title to the discovery of chloroform for use as an anaesthetic. Lastly, and perhaps the best beloved of all, was James Walter Ferrier, beautiful, genial and witty, who died in the prime of his youth of tuberculosis and advanced alcoholism. It was on these four that Louis Stevenson relied at this storm-struck period of the early 1870s.

Charlie Baxter was, like Louis himself, a law-student. He became a Writer to the Signet and in later years proved himself dedicated and invaluable in managing Louis's financial affairs, for he possessed what another friend termed 'an extraordinary automatical faculty of picking up and assorting facts and figures'. Louis Stevenson's letters to this *fidus Achates* constitute a substantial volume, recently issued by the Yale University Press. Many of these letters are jocular, and in some of them the humour is boisterous and distinctly porky. They would, for instance, randomly address each other as Johnston and Thomson, never quite clear which was which; and in these particular missives they would write in broad Scots. Louis's widow described Charlie Baxter as her husband's 'friend of the heart'. 'Louis's affection for Charles never wavered,' she wrote. 'For that reason I can forgive Charles much; and, besides, Charles drunk is not the real Charles.' Under the strain of the situation in Heriot Row, Louis was himself at this time drinking fairly heavily. In this pursuit he was bravely aided and abetted by Charlie Baxter. They treated their law studies with apparent frivolity, entering a lecture-room late, interrupting the speaker on the rostrum, and suddenly leaving again after a few moments. Baxter was a burly individual.

An acquaintance afterwards recalled that the pair of them resembled 'a slim and graceful spaniel with a big bull-dog, jowled and "pop-eyed" following in its wake'. When they had stumbled out of the classroom, Louis and Charlie 'left behind a spirit of unrest that made concentration on legal quiddities impossible'. Yet both passed their law examinations with distinction.

Stevenson and Baxter would spend their evenings in public-houses, and, some ten years later, Louis composed a series of sonnets, *Brasheanna*, in honour of a dead and detested publican, Peter Brash. The first of these sonnets seems worth quoting, for it gives the atmosphere of night-time Edinburgh during these gin-sodden jaunts:

> We found him first as in the dells of May
>> The dreaming damsel finds the earliest flower;
>> Thoughtless we wandered in the evening hour;
> Aimless and pleased we went our random way:
> In the foot-haunted city in the night,
>> Among the alternate lamps, we went and came,
>> Till, like a humorous thunderbolt, that name,
> The hated name of BRASH assailed our sight.
> We saw, we paused, we entered, seeking gin.
>> His wrath, like a huge breaker on the beach,
>> Broke instant forth. He on the counter beat
>> In his infantile fury; and his feet
> Danced impotent wrath upon the floor within.
>> Still as we fled, we heard his idiot screech.

Writing to Louis's biographer in 1901, Fanny Stevenson declared that she did not 'care for the vulgarity' of *Brasheanna* and did not think the sonnets need be referred to in the forthcoming book. She may indeed have thought Charlie Baxter vulgar himself. Neither she nor anyone else could have applied that adjective to Sir Walter Simpson.

Walter Simpson, known to his family and to his intimates as 'Wattie', was seven years older than Louis Stevenson, who would speak of him affectionately as 'the Bart'. Although, like Louis, he had been educated at the Edinburgh Academy, he was so much his senior that they had never met there. Simpson was later sent to Cambridge University, and after that spent a while in a merchant's office in Cairo. He was a deliberate, thoughtful man of the world, with twinkling blue eyes, a pleasant squatly-designed person who smoked a meerschaum pipe and did not shine in conversation;

Louis called him 'the stalwart woodman of thought ... never hurry-
ing, never flagging'. He, his brother Magnus and his sister Eve
Blantyre Simpson had been reared in a house in Queen Street, across
the gardens from Heriot Row, but as children they had played in
another part of the gardens to that frequented by little Louis. The
house in Queen Street is famous today as the place in which the first
operation under chloroform was performed. The Simpsons' father,
Sir James, who had accepted 'the first baronetcy offered to a
physician north of the Tweed', had been an expert on the mysteries
of the uterus and had written a treatise on hermaphrodites.

On his death in 1870 Walter (who inherited the baronetcy),
Magnus and Eve Blantyre moved to a smaller house in the New
Town, and here they would entertain their young friends with taste
and enthusiasm. Particular friends, of whom Louis Stevenson was
one, would be welcomed at any hour of the evening, but a house-
rule was laid down that the front-door bell should never be rung after
ten o'clock; callers were admitted by rattling on the letter-box. The
establishment was colloquially known as 'the Republic' and thither
Louis would often repair, bubbling with excited ideas which the
Simpson family accepted with discretion and, at times, with ridicule.
The Simpsons acted as lightning-conductors to Louis Stevenson.
Like the Fleeming Jenkins, they believed in him, but in a sober and
ruminative manner. Louis had first made the acquaintance of
Wattie Simpson at the Speculative Society. In the summer of 1872
he was allowed to go to Frankfurt with Simpson for some weeks, for
the Bart was the sort of responsible, respectable friend of whom
Louis's parents highly approved. Such approval was soon withheld
from James Walter Ferrier, for in those days alcoholism was not
recognized as a medical disease and was attributed to weakness and
to moral squalor.

Ferrier was a very gifted man who laughed internally, and wore
coral waistcoat studs in the evening. Louis wrote that Ferrier
believed in himself profoundly — 'but he never disbelieved in others'. He
also wrote that he himself had learned 'more, in some ways, from
Ferrier than from any other soul I ever met; and he, strange to
think, was the best gentleman, in all kinder senses, that I ever knew.'
He had 'fine, kind, open dignity of manner', yet ended up as 'such
a temporal wreck'. Walter Ferrier died in 1883. Not long before his
death his mother wrote Louis Stevenson a letter, which goes far to
suggest the stringent tone of polite Edinburgh in those days:

As the mother of your friend Walter Ferrier, I am about to

inform you of what you will feel grief and surprise at. This miserable victim has just escaped Delirium Tremens and has been indulging in a very terrible way in the Isle of Wight, quite apart from his Relatives and as usual deceiving those he has been with ... May a Mother's affection send me to my God in prayer but my Heart seems drying up within me when I think of all that has been done for this Son.

Walter Ferrier lies buried in the family tomb in the wall of the West Kirk. After this death, which distressed him terribly, Louis would remember Ferrier's many charming oddities—his 'romantic affection' for pharmacies, for instance, where the coloured bottles in the windows 'were for him a poem. He said once that he knew no pleasure like driving through a lamplit city, waiting for the chemists to go by.' His death seemed to Louis to undermine the earth: 'All my friends have lost one thickness of reality since that one passed.'

How much he told his cousin Bob and his other friends of the storms raging inside 17 Heriot Row is hard to assess; to Baxter he wrote about it all freely, but the Simpson menage may have been too conventional for such recitals of disbelief and consequent parental woe. The confession of agnosticism had been made in January 1873. That summer the elder Stevensons devised a plan which was probably inspired by a desire to place Louis for some weeks in a safely religious household. Maggie Stevenson had a Balfour niece, Maud, who had married a wealthy English clergyman, the Reverend Churchill Babington. The Babingtons lived in a roomy Georgian rectory in the village of Cockfield, near Bury St Edmunds in Suffolk. Louis had already stayed with the Babingtons on several occasions and seemed to like his cousin Maud. What could be more spiritually therapeutic than for him to go to the Babingtons again that summer? Accordingly, July 26th, 1873, found him walking up the drive of Cockfield Rectory, wearing a straw hat and with a knapsack at his back. It was in every sense a momentous walk for Louis Stevenson; for watching him from the rectory window was a young and almost notoriously beautiful woman, who had a head like a cameo and was Maud Babington's particular friend and guest. This lady, who was separated from her husband—another clergyman—was called Mrs Albert Sitwell. With her Robert Louis Stevenson, who was twenty-two years old, fell headlong and desperately in love. This intense emotion changed the whole tenor of his youth and life.

3

The Cockfield Madonna

THE Old Rectory, Cockfield, stands back from a typically winding Suffolk road and hidden behind a belt of elms. It is a distinguished, mainly eighteenth-century house with airy, elegant rooms. From the high downstairs windows you can step out on to a wide green lawn. Beyond the lawn is a moat, and beyond the moat a meadow. Until the Churchill Babingtons' day this moat had been filled up as a sort of marsh at the behest of a previous vicar's maiden sister, who thought water near the house unhealthy. Louis found Suffolk cold even in summer, and, according to his cousin Maud, 'was afraid of the clay soil'. On this particular visit he was once again amazed at 'the hopeless gulf' between England and Scotland; he felt as 'outlandish' as if he were in France or Germany, and though he admired Long Melford and Lavenham he felt that he was walking 'amongst surprises, for just where you think you have them, something wrong turns up'. In the person of Mrs Sitwell, however, something exceptionally right had turned up for him. Through her he met her official admirer Sidney Colvin, who became an intimate friend and launched Louis upon the literary and intellectual world of London. For the next two years Fanny Sitwell was the dominant factor in this Scots lad's existence.

Frances Sitwell had been born a Featherstonehaugh, of an impoverished Irish landed family. She had lived in Ireland, Germany and, for a short time, with her father in Australia, whence she returned in her 'teens to marry the Reverend Albert Sitwell, who took her out to Calcutta. Two sons had been born, but one had died in April of the year in which Louis met her; the other boy, Bertie, was staying at Cockfield and was much attracted by Stevenson. After leaving India Mr Sitwell had been given a parish in Bethnal Green, and after that in the Isle of Thanet. By this time the marriage had broken down, since the husband had proved 'a man of unfortunate temperament and uncongenial habits'. Whether these habits involved drink or choir boys is no longer known; but after the death of her son Mrs Sitwell left her husband — a bold step for a Victorian clergyman's wife — and kept herself in London by reviewing and writing articles. Her greatest friend in the world was Sidney Colvin, who in 1873 had become Slade Professor at Cambridge and was later keeper of the Department of Prints and Drawings at the British Museum. This precise, earnest man she was unable to marry until after her husband's death; the marriage took place finally in 1903. In London they lived separately, but Mrs Sitwell was the recognized hostess in Colvin's chambers at the British Museum, and the liaison was approved by all their many friends.

When Louis met her at Cockfield, Mrs Sitwell was thirty-four, twelve years older than himself. She was dark, with almost orientally senuous eyes, and was said by Tennyson's biographer to have had more men in love with her than any other woman he knew. 'In the fearlessness of her purity,' wrote Colvin, 'she can afford the frankness of her affections, and show how every fascination of her sex may in the most open freedom be honourably secure. Yet in a world of men and women such a one cannot walk without kindling once and again a dangerous flame before she is aware.'

Another admirer wrote of Frances Sitwell: 'Beauty like hers was genius ... Divine intuition like hers was genius. Vitality like hers was genius.' Such was the woman with whom Louis Stevenson fell in love, calling her 'Madonna', 'Consuelo' and, finally, 'mother of my soul'. At Cockfield they read Browning aloud to one another, wandered through the summer fields, in the old walled kitchen garden, or along the margin of the moat on which water-lilies were floating, while he poured out his soul to her.

Maud Babington had hoped that Louis and Mrs Sitwell would hit it off, though whether she quite realized the atomic effect on her romantic cousin one can but wonder. She had already talked of Louis to her beautiful friend, and shown her an essay or two of his from the short-lived Edinburgh University magazine. When Mrs Sitwell actually met and talked with Louis she became so enthusiastic about him that she sent post-haste for Sidney Colvin to come over from Cambridge to meet the marvellous boy. Colvin came, and was equally impressed by Louis's conversation. It was dazzlingly clear to him that young Stevenson had a literary future. From then onwards Louis had in Colvin and in Frances Sitwell two quintessential, lifelong friends. His days of misery at Heriot Row were by no means over, but Mrs Sitwell gave him a sense of release from tensions, and when he got home he began to send her a cataract of daily letters which, if at times adolescent and at others self-pitying and egocentric, form, as a corpus, some of the most moving love-letters in the English language. He wrote of his troubles with his parents, of his dislike of Edinburgh society, of his constant anxiety about his own efforts at composition, and, indeed, of every detail of his daily life, including his efforts to 'be good' and not dissipate his energies by weakness. She sent her replies to him at the Speculative Society; once, when a careless porter forgot to give him her letters, Louis became hysterical with doubts. Mrs Sitwell's own letters do not exist, as Louis burned them at her request. His to her have survived and are now lodged in a cedar-wood box in the National Library of Scotland in Edinburgh. Garbled and excised extracts from them were published by Sidney Colvin after his wife's death.

During the period after the First World War when certain writers (mainly American) were busy debunking Stevenson it was, not surprisingly, suggested that he had a real affair with Mrs Sitwell. The love-letters, which were not then available for perusal, leave no doubt that this was not so; in addition, Mrs Sitwell's very delicate marital position and her affection for Colvin make the supposition most unlikely. It seems probable that he did try to make a pass at her one evening in London, but this was followed by protestations·that it would never happen again, by his attitude of reverence and, finally, by his asking her to be his mother. Sometimes in London he would stay in the same house as she did, 15 Chepstow Place, behind Notting Hill Gate, but little importance attaches to this merely geographical proximity. How Mrs Sitwell, with her beauty, her vitality and 'divine intuition', managed so adroitly to fend off an ardent and slightly frustrated Edinburgh youth remains puzzling; yet do it she did. On his side he regarded her as a deity before settling down to regard her as a surrogate for Mrs Thomas Stevenson. We do know that in 1921, many years after Louis's death, Mrs Sitwell, by then Lady Colvin, wrote to a friend to whom she was sending a holograph of Robert Louis Stevenson's that he had been used 'to write kind of diary letters to me with no formal beginning. This one was written in April 1875 from Edinburgh ... he was 25 then or nearly 25 — and very young in all his ways.' This comment suggests a feeling that had been maternal rather than amorous. Health, we need hardly add, forms one of Louis's chief topics in a good many of the love-letters — his own health and hers, for as chance would have it Mrs Sitwell, apart from being unhappy over her marriage and her lack of money, seems also to have cherished a respiratory complaint not dissimilar to Louis's own. This was yet another bond between them. He always shows a most touching concern for her health and her happiness. At Christmas 1874 he wrote:

> ... But you will see, dear madonna, that I am very happy as I write; and that will make you happy, as you read, will it not? You must be happy: I will not have a sad deity in my chapel, she must be all smiles and peace must look eloquently out of her eyes ... I do feel all that she could wish, happy and good and industrious ... And now let us put out the tapers for a while ... only the little red heart-shaped lamp, let us leave burning, just before the shrine: it has not been extinguished since it was first lighted, eighteen months ago among the summer trees ... so madonna, I give you a son's kiss this Christmas morning, and my heart is in my mouth, dear, as I write the words, ever your faithful friend and son and priest, R.L.S.

In another letter he writes of using her as a confessional: 'If I had not known you, where should I have been?' Again: 'Let me think of you, as you said yourself, still ready to grasp at every cause of happiness, still your own beautiful self. And do not be sad about me: it is enough to know that you still live and have not forgotten me.' 'The thought of you, Madonna, upholds and cherishes me like strong wine,' he wrote at another time, '—I do not fear anything in life so long as you are left to me, and this cursed God does not torment you too much.' 'I believe in you as others believe in the Bible,' was another earnest assertation. Louis was intermittently afraid of 'wearying' his correspondent, but these moods were transitory. 'I wish to God I did not love you so much,' he wrote in the autumn of 1874. 'But I do, and it's as well for my best interests as I know well enough. And it ought to be nice for you; for you need not fear any bother from this child except petulant moments. I am good now; I am; am I not?'

Whilst this torrid correspondence was in progress, religious arguments were still rocking the foundations of 17 Heriot Row. On his return from Cockfield he discovered that Thomas Stevenson now attributed Louis's state of spiritual danger to his cousin Bob, had had a scene with Bob in the public street and 'prayed ... that he should never see him between the eyes again'. In the November after the Cockfield visit, Thomas Stevenson and Louis were persuaded by the Lord Advocate during a railway journey, that Louis had better take his exams at the English Bar. This relief from Edinburgh, and the fact that through the good offices of Sidney Colvin an essay by Louis on Suffolk roads was to be published in the December *Portfolio*, was cheering; but when Louis got to London he was looking so thin and ill that Colvin and Mrs Sitwell urged him to consult the distinguished London physician, Andrew Clark, who looked after Mr Gladstone's health and practised from a large house in Cavendish Square. The Stevenson parents came down from Edinburgh in an agitated way when they heard that Clark had forbidden Louis to sit for the law examinations or to spend the winter in a cold climate. He had diagnosed potential tuberculosis, and when Mrs Stevenson suggested taking Louis to Torquay, wisely answered that he should go away to the Riviera and quite alone. Louis's mother suspected that Clark's verdict was a put-up job between Louis and his two new friends Colvin and Mrs Sitwell. She half-believed that he never intended to come back home; and when Louis, on his last Sunday in London, went to church with Mrs Sitwell instead of with herself she was mortified and jealous. 'My parents utterly puzzle me,' Louis wrote to Baxter from London that November, 1873. 'I have sometimes a notion that the atheist son is almost in the way. My head is about done for, so goodby, old man. Poste Restante, Mentone, is my next address.'

[II]

Soon after his arrival at Menton, which he reached by easy stages through Paris, Sens and Avignon, Louis Stevenson went to consult an English doctor in Nice, who confirmed that he was not consumptive. He continued however in a listless state, feeling wretchedly ill, afraid of noises, shy of strangers, forgetting how to speak French and subject to a nervous facial tic. He found that he could not at first react naturally to the beauty of the Mediterranean nor do any work. His condition at this time is well described in an essay, *Ordered South*, which he wrote later on at Menton and which *Macmillan's Magazine* published in the spring of 1874. In London, before his departure, his parents had developed an astonishing new theory of the source of his winter breakdown. They had met Mrs Sitwell and Colvin, and, though Thomas Stevenson took a pronounced fancy to Mrs Sitwell, both parents told Louis that he had been 'in the very worst possible hands' and that his illness was entirely due to his new friends' society. 'Are they not perplexing people to deal with?' Louis wrote to Mrs Sitwell while waiting to board the channel packet at Dover.

He settled on the top floor of the Hôtel du Pavillon, which was full of dreary and not conversible English people. He spent his first few days revisiting parts of Menton that he remembered from his childhood, noting many changes in the townscape. Then he would lie languidly on a bench, watching falling plane leaves as they swirled beneath the clear blue sky, looking like 'little pieces of gold leaf'. In December, Sidney Colvin came out for the Christmas holidays. They stayed some days in Monaco and then moved back to Menton, but to a different hotel with a cosmopolitan clientèle. The presence of Colvin strengthened and diverted Louis, but it was company at the Hotel Mirabeau that really brought him back to life. Chief amongst this company were two youngish Russian sisters from Georgia, Princess Zassetsky and Madame Garschine, who had taken a private villa but ate at the hotel. There were two children belonging to them —Louis was never quite certain which was the mother of which— and the youngest, a two-year-old girl called Nelitchka, who spoke six languages, Louis found irresistibly comic and fascinating. At this time Russian literature was not available to British readers, and Louis knew nothing of Russians, their mentality nor their ways. The Russian sisters were equally ignorant of the Scots and found Louis a very puzzling creature: 'Monsieur est un jeune homme que je comprends pas,' said Madame Zassetsky early on in the acquaintanceship. 'Il n'est pas méchant, je sais cela, mais, après, ténèbres, ténèbres, ténèbres, rien que des ténèbres.'

He was soon on easy-going, chaffing terms with the sisters, but not before having been made scrupulously anxious about their real attitude to himself. As usual, he confided in Mrs Sitwell by letter asking her what the behaviour of Madame Garschine might imply. Either she was making fun of him, or she was trying to flirt with him —but which? If she was falling in love with Louis he thought that that would be very awkward indeed. His perturbation proved short-lived:

> The Russian difficulty—the Eastern question, so to speak — is solved. Both the ladies are very kind and jolly to me today, and this is the second without any foolishness up to now. They are both the frankest of mortals, and have complained to me, in one way or other, that I am to them as some undiscovered animal. They do not seem to cultivate R.L.S.'s in Muscovy.

These two light-hearted sisters, who could however discuss Mill and Spencer, and gladdened Louis's heart by admitting to agnosticism, provided just the mental therapy which he needed. They read his palm, played such games as the stool of repentance with him, had him photographed in a cloak, called him *Berechino* (little rascal), gave fancy-dress tea-parties and ended by absorbing him so completely that when Madame Garschine was ill in bed for only one day he was heartbroken. He promised to visit them in Russia next year, a pledge he could not in the end fulfil. This sunlit winter of laughter and high spirits formed the perfect antidote to the last tense months in Heriot Row.

All this time Louis was writing weekly budgets to Mrs Sitwell, who seems to have sent regular replies. He likewise felt well enough to experiment with his own work again, sketching out an article on his hero Walt Whitman and one on the novels of Victor Hugo. He was also reading a lot of George Sand. So far as his writing went he was still despondent about it, and thought Colvin judged his potential more highly than it deserved. The Russian ladies, too, thought him very clever — 'people will take me for being cleverer than I am ... I do say and think true and nice things; people observe that; but they cannot tell the want of *suite* and *finie*, the defect of strong continuousness, that there is behind it all.' Yet the Russian ladies understood their new friend pretty well. When he was explaining to them how very vividly most things remained in his mind, Princess Zassetsky 'with her little falsetto of discovery' announced: 'Mais c'est que vous êtes tout simplement enfant!' Princess Zassetsky, her sister and the two children sat at meals at the same end of the table as Louis, Colvin and a French painter, Robinet, known as 'le Raphaël des cailloux'. Colvin described how day after day Louis 'kept this little company in an enchanted atmosphere of mirth and mutual delight with one another and with him.' Colvin knew that, like the character of Dick Naseby in *The Story of a Lie*, Louis was 'a type-hunter' — 'He despised small game and insignificant personalities, whether in the shape of duke or bagman, letting them go by like seaweed' — but his mind was alerted by a plangent voice, or a passionate gesture, or an ambiguous smile. He thus became, as he deserved to be, the epicentre of the small, gay and cosmopolitan society of the long-vanished Hotel Mirabeau that winter of 1873 and spring of 1874.

All good things have to end, and in late April 1874 Louis tore himself away from Menton and went to Paris, with a half-formed intention of setting out to study Roman law at Göttingen University under a famous German professor of that subject. As soon as he reached Paris all his old symptoms returned, and he decided to creep home to chilly Edinburgh and abandon the Göttingen project. From now on until his death, Louis Stevenson's health was a governing consideration in all his plans. After the unhealthy, coddled childhood there had been a period of fairly normal health, when he was able to lead his own personalized version of the lives that his contemporaries led. By 1874 that period was closed.

[III]

'Quoiqu'on sache depuis longtemps que vous aimez les changements et les surprises, mon cher Stevenson—je vous avoue que celle de vous savoir déjà à Edinbourg m'a fort désagréablement surpris,' Sophie Garschine wrote to Louis from the Hotel Mirabeau in May 1874. She went on to say that had she been able to write to him in Russian—'mais, hélàs, vous avez été si paresseux élève'—she would have told him a number of distasteful truths. Madame Garschine said she was feeling lonely, that the hotel's empty corridors echoed only to the strident voice of its owner, and that she herself was in a state of 'surexcitation nerveuse des plus désagréables'. She then attacked Louis for his hatred of the rich—were not the rich and dowered also a part of humanity? This must be an echo of old conversations at the Hotel Mirabeau. Louis's socialism, emotional and generous in its roots, was currently (like his rebellion against Christianity) at full flood.

Whilst he had been at Cockfield Rectory the previous summer, Louis had helped the Churchill Babingtons in organizing an annual school-treat in the meadow beyond the moat. He had even hurt his hand by cutting so much bread-and-butter, and he had been aghast to find how stupid at simple games were the children of the rural English poor. A whole ten shillings' worth of penny toys had been distributed; but Louis felt, as he assisted at this tea-time celebration, how unjust it was that a simple tea-party, a rare treat to the children, was an unremarked everyday occurrence to his family and friends. Later, when Mrs Sitwell took a job as secretary to a London working men's college, he was delighted. 'I think you have truly a great work before you,' he wrote to her. 'You must recollect where the difficulty is: the whole crux of Society lies in the distinction of class and the iron barriers that shut off one from the other. You, one of an upper class, are now going to have an opportunity to mingle freely and kindly with those of another; if the College even fail, how much you may have done in the time to render easy the dangerous transitions toward which we now drift blindly.'

When he reached Edinburgh once more, in late April 1874, Louis did not linger in the city itself. 'We are now in Swanston Cottage, Lothianburn,' he informed Mrs Sitwell. ' ... It is very cold and sleeted all this morning. Everything wintry. I am very jolly, however, having finished *Victor Hugo* and just looking round to see what I should next take up ... My people are very nice to me indeed and I hope we shall go on well; I have had lots of talk with my mother and take much hope from what has passed between us.'

Swanston Cottage, a small residence which always seemed to reduce the tensions habitual to 17 Heriot Row, lies on the lowest slopes of the bleak Pentland Hills. Thomas Stevenson had leased it in May 1867, when Louis was seventeen. He retained the lease for fourteen years. In their domestic lives Swanston Cottage had replaced the hotels or lodging houses in which they had used to spend summer months at the Bridge of Allan or in North Berwick. For Louis himself the cottage could provide a respite from family life, since, especially in snowy winter-times, he would go and shut himself up there alone with his dog, to read and write before a blazing fire. Swanston hamlet consists of a white farmhouse, surrounded by what Louis called 'a bouquet of old trees' and a handful of cottages. Above Swanston the bare pasture of the hills rises to one thousand feet. Swanston Cottage itself, which is really a commodious small house, had been built by the Edinburgh municipality, who because of the natural springs had first erected a water-house near by, and then decided to build a little homestead as a pleasure-resort for the city fathers. The quarry from which stone for the cottage and the water-house had been hewn was made into a garden, and gradually the dell in which the cottage stood had become an evergreen thicket. The young elms and beeches had grown tall, so that, by the time of the Stevensons' tenure, they overshadowed both cottage and garden. Swanston Cottage could boast, and still retains, one peculiarity: having been erected at the time of the ruthless restoration of old St Giles, the cathedral of Edinburgh, it bears above the front doorway, on the gables, and scattered about the garden, crockets and gargoyles of medieval date.

These relics of old St Giles give to the cottage a fanciful, an almost capricious air, and make it resemble a miniature Abbotsford. In *St Ives*, one of the novels which Louis Stevenson left unfinished at his death, he described Swanston Cottage with all the nostalgia for Edinburgh and its surroundings which his voluntary Polynesian exile had induced. He wrote of the little house as having 'something of the air of a rambling infinitesimal cathedral', with its central storey two rooms high, a steep-pitched roof and sending out on all

Swanston Cottage, from a drawing by John Knight

hands 'one-storeyed and dwarfish projections'. The hero of *St Ives* (a military Frenchman who has made a spectacular escape from gaol in Edinburgh Castle) first sees Swanston Cottage in the pale grey dawn, when a shepherd is striding along the rough sides of the mountain, yelling at his dogs. Above Swanston lies the holy well of Halkerside, up to which Louis would clamber to meditate by its brink and superstitiously to sprinkle the well-water on the turf. The local old shepherd, John Todd, had at first resented the presence on his pastures of Louis Stevenson and his vivacious and devoted dog Coolin. Louis soon won Todd over, however, and would then go 'on patrol' with him as he guarded his flock of sheep and, in springtime, the bleating lambs, on the hillside. Returning in the twilight Louis would wait whilst his dog ran upstairs to fetch his slippers, and would then settle down with a novel of Dumas 'for a long, solitary, lamplit evening by the fire'. Sometimes he would get up and pull aside the blind to look out 'to see the snow and the glittering hollies chequer a Scotch garden, and the winter moonlight brighten the white hills'.

Yet even solitude at Swanston Cottage did not allay Louis's longing to see his real friends, inhabitants of the new world to which he had now been admitted. 'You don't know how I yearn today to see you all,' he wrote to his madonna from Swanston. 'I feel myself alone in the uttermost parts of the earth with ugly puppets and my heart just melts within me when I think of you, and CS, and Madame Garschine, and Bob. Any of the four of you I want to see badly; and somehow CS most, I feel as if I could be good for him and I am so vexed that he is not well. ... What a day! Cold and dark as midwinter. I shall send with this two new photographs of myself for your opinion.'

4

London Liberation

LIKE many another victim of a hopeless passion or an unrequited love, Louis Stevenson would keep trying to persuade himself, and Mrs Sitwell also, that his feelings for her were under his control. He was always apologizing for being a burden, and for having behaved as 'a poor and selfish creature'. Once embarked upon the filial tack, he stuck to this to sublimate his eroticism:

> ... I long to be with you most ardently, and I long to put my arms about your neck and kiss you and then sit down with my head on your knees and have a long talk and feel you smoothing my hair; I long for all that, as one longs for—for nothing else that I can think of. And yet, that is all. It is not a bit like what I feel for my mother *here*. But I think it must be what one *ought* to feel for a mother. That's a lie; nobody loves a mere mother as I love you, *madonna*, Before God R.L.S.

This clever woman evidently handled his feelings with supreme tact. A letter from Madame Garschine contains an arcane reference to Mrs Sitwell, and indicates that it was at the latter's suggestion that Louis came down to London in the summer after Menton. Madame Garschine writes that she is pleased to know that he will now have a few days of peaceful happiness: 'Pauvre Berechino! Espérons que tout s'arrangera puisque enfin Mme a pris l'initiative.'

Mrs Sitwell's initiative seems to have consisted in arranging for him to stay at the Hampstead cottage in which her friend Sidney Colvin was then living. Her son Bertie unexpectedly contracted measles, and she herself was unwell that June. Louis wrote to her that he had 'an unlimited desire and capacity' to be her sick-nurse and that he would most like to look after her when she was dying. This rather pre-Raphaelite sentiment was perhaps induced by the fact that he was once more feeling very ill himself: 'You do not know that I was ill last night myself; but I was; and when I hid my eyes it was that I might not see your face grow great before me, as things do when one is feverish. The terrible sculptured impassivity of a face one loved, when it is seen thus exaggerated, frightens and pains me strangely.'

To Mrs Sitwell and Sidney Colvin, Louis was a species of private discovery of their own. At Cockfield (Colvin afterwards wrote) Louis had 'sped the summer nights and days for us all as I have scarce known any sped before or since. He seemed, this youngster, already to have lived and seen and felt and dreamed and laughed and longed more than others do in a lifetime.' Colvin was twenty-eight, six years Louis's senior. In London that summer of 1874 he set about launching his young friend with the strong Scottish accent. His first step had been to put Louis up for the Savile Club, which had then been founded just five years and was in Louis's own words 'the place known by fame to many, to few by sight'. The point of the Savile Club was not that the Prince of Wales or Mr Gladstone might sometimes be glimpsed there, but that it was a recognized rendezvous for the brilliant and gifted young — 'eaglets of glory, the swordsmen of the pen'. Here Louis felt immediately at home, lunching there almost every day that he was in London during the 1870s and, according to Colvin, 'accepted and immediately surrounded as a radiatory centre of good talk, a kind of ideal incarnation of the spirit of the Society'. Edmund Gosse, then a young poet and critic working as a translator at the Board of Trade, used to lunch with Louis at the Savile four or five times a week during these London visits. Although a devoted friend of Stevenson, Gosse was uncertain whether he thought Louis's popularity at the Savile an unmitigated benefit for Louis himself. Years later Gosse described how Louis 'used to wind upstairs after lunch', enveloped in a cloud of talk 'and accompanied by anyone who would follow his piping'. The afternoon would spin away 'in rather foolish jesting' and altogether these Savile days seemed to Gosse to be about the idlest and silliest part of his friend's existence. There may well have been a kind of auto-intoxication about Louis's Savile Club chatter, but when one bears in mind his Edinburgh life and his ill-health this seems neither surprising nor open of blame.

During his stay at the Hampstead cottage in June 1874, Louis was writing busily, preparing his *Notes on the Movements of Young Children*. He had already submitted the Victor Hugo article to Leslie Stephen, who accepted it for the *Cornhill*. Later in the summer he cruised in the Inner Hebrides with Walter Simpson, and then settled down again to his studies for the Scottish bar. At the end of the year he was once more in London, and went on to stay at Colvin's rooms in Cambridge, a place which seemed to him, compared to Edinburgh University, to be almost too tame and civilized. He was now a regular contributor to the *Portfolio*, was writing reviews for the *Fortnightly* and contributing sometimes to the *Cornhill*, where he was much encouraged by Leslie Stephen's praise.

Helpful though Leslie Stephen could be to the literary young, he was a formidably silent man, with a thin, bright-red beard that was fan-shaped, a curiously flat top to his head, long hands and what Edmund Gosse called 'distraught and melancholy eyes'. Gosse has left an account of an evening in the mid-seventies when Louis Stevenson and he were asked to dine with the Stephens. They had expected to find 'a large collection of literary notabilities' and had hung around outside the house before making up their minds to go in. All that they found were the two Stephens themselves and the novelist Miss Annie Thackeray. The Stephens scarcely spoke, and both Gosse and Stevenson were reduced to most uncharacteristic silence by shyness. Miss Thackeray was forced to keep the conversation going unaided. The room was ill-lit by only two or three candles; 'her voice was heard holding a sort of dialogue with itself'. Gosse and Stevenson were overcome by a desire to giggle, but managed to survive the muted dinner-party without any such lapse.

Besides publishing his essays, Leslie Stephen, in February 1875, did Louis the singularly good turn of introducing him to William Ernest Henley, then a young invalid poet who was spending twenty months in a room of the Edinburgh Infirmary under the care of the famous Professor Liston. Louis's friendship with Henley, which lasted twelve years and ended in disaster, was probably the most stimulating and important literary friendship of his life. He collaborated with him on plays, and he wrote to him so often that the National Library of Scotland alone contains upwards of three hundred pages of R.L.S.'s letters to him, written in the four different handwritings which Louis used, and which reflected his moods.

> 'Oh!' almost incredulously; and then quite a long while after:
> 'Do you know the noise of the water astonished me very much?'
> ... I have lost the sense of wonder of course; but there must be something to wonder at, for Henley has eyes and ears and an immortal soul of his own.

Louis also lent Henley English and French books, encouraged him to go on with his French and Spanish, and enlisted Mrs Fleeming Jenkin to teach him German. In this spring of 1875, Leslie Stephen published in the *Cornhill* a selection of Henley's verses *In Hospital*. 'What do you think of Henley's hospital verses?' Louis asked Mrs Sitwell. 'They were to have been dedicated to me, but Stephen wouldn't allow it—said it would be pretentious.' Dedication or no, Henley did write some lines describing his new friend. Although these have been frequently reprinted in connection with Stevenson, and are in their way as well known as the Sargent portrait, I think that they should be quoted once again:

> Thin-legged! thin-chested! slight unspeakably,
>   Neat-footed and weak-fingered; in his face—
> Lean, large-boned, curved of beak, and touched with race,
> Bold-lipped, rich-tinted, mutable as the sea,
> The brown eyes radiant with vivacity—
>   There shines a brilliant and romantic grace,
>   A spirit intense and rare, with trace on trace
> Of passion, impudence and energy.
> Valiant in velvet, light in ragged luck,
>   Most vain, most generous, sternly critical,
>   Buffoon and poet, lover and sensualist;
> A deal of Ariel, just a streak of Puck,
> Much Antony, of Hamlet most of all,
> And something of the Shorter-Catechist.

In his turn Louis wrote a poem about Henley playing on the penny-whistle, to entertain the children in his room, and for old Kate the scrubber to dance to. One writer on Henley has seen significance in this exchange of poems, suggesting that these two young men had a common bond in tuberculosis; but even if Louis Stevenson were in fact tubercular, which has never been satisfactorily proved, he was certainly not so at the time of his meeting with Henley. Louis's verses do not need to be quoted in full. The last four lines should suffice:

> So is pain cheered, death comforted; the house
> Of sorrow smiles to listen. Once again—
> O thou, Orpheus and Heracles, the bard
> And the deliverer, touch the stops again!

More successful is the account of Henley under the pseudonym of 'Burly' which occurs in the first of two papers, *Talk and Talkers*, which Louis contributed to the *Cornhill* in the spring and summer of 1882. Contrasting Henley with Bob Stevenson (of whom he writes as 'Spring-Heel'd Jack') he says that they were of dissimilar calibres — Henley 'a man of great presence' giving the impression of 'a grosser mass of character than most men', someone whose presence you could feel in a room if you entered it blindfold. He calls Henley's talk 'boisterous and piratic'. 'He will roar you down, he will bury his face in his hands, he will undergo passions of revolt and agony.' He says that Henley 'with many changing hues of fire' burned at the sea-level, like a conflagration. W. E. Henley, who was a touchy man as well as a disloyal one, was not flattered by his portrait in *Talk and Talkers*.

[II]

W. E. Henley was born in August 1849, and was thus little more than a year older than Louis Stevenson. He was one of the five sons of a Gloucester bookseller who came of old yeoman stock and had married a descendant of the eighteenth-century clergyman-critic, Joseph Warton. At twelve he developed a tubercular disease which made him a cripple and for many years endangered his life. One foot was amputated, but when he learned as a young man that the other was likewise threatened he went up to Edinburgh in 1873 to consult Professor Liston, whose long treatment made further amputation unnecessary. He was a big, broad-shouldered man with a bushy head of yellow hair that stood straight upwards, and a copious reddish beard. Although frequently in pain he began to work at literature in the Edinburgh Infirmary, writing poems and critical articles which Stephen published in the *Cornhill*. Save for some of his poetry, Henley is scarcely read today, for he was essentially an ephemeral writer, an excellent critic of literature and art and a first-rate editor and journalist. In later life he was surrounded by a band of young disciples who revered him as a sage. He was of a jealous nature, very noisy and drank too much whisky.

Louis Stevenson's massive correspondence with Henley is naturally enough entirely different in tone to that with Mrs Sitwell. It also differs from the letters to Charles Baxter which, when they are not jocular, are entirely about urgent business affairs. To Henley he wrote constantly, often addressing him as 'dear lad' or 'dear boy'; his subjects were the progress of his own writing which he would often submit to Henley's judgment, his reading, and other literary matters generally. Because of their quantity, their length, and their detail, the letters to Henley are, for a biographer of Stevenson, invaluable.

It was on a Friday in February 1875 that Leslie Stephen, who was in Edinburgh to lecture on mountaineering, introduced his two youthful contributors to one another in the room at the Infirmary which Henley was sharing with two small boys, whom he would amuse by playing on a penny whistle. 'The gas flared and crackled, the fire burned in a dull economical way,' Louis wrote of this scene to Mrs Sitwell. 'Stephen and I sat on a couple of chairs, and the poor fellow sat up in his bed with his hair and beard all tangled, and talked as cheerfully as if he had been in a King's palace, or the great King's palace of the blue air. He has taught himself two languages since he has been there. I shall try to be of use to him.' Louis did indeed prove of immense use. He would visit Henley's room repeatedly and when the invalid was well enough to get out of bed, he brought him an armchair which he carried personally through the streets of Edinburgh from Heriot Row. When the spring came at last, and the snow had melted, Louis began to take Henley driving in the family carriage. To put him into the carriage was difficult since he could not walk, and, according to Mrs Sitwell, Louis 'half-killed himself carrying Henley on his back in & out of the Hospital'. To Louis the pleasure of these drives through the spring countryside. beneath a blue sky against which the cherry-blossom stood out as though in a Japanese print, lay in Henley's naive delight in being out in the world once more:

> The look on his face was a wine to me . I always stopped him on the bridges to let him enjoy the great *cry* of green that goes up to Heaven out of the river beds, and he asked (more than once) 'What noise is that?' — 'the water' —

[III]

Some weeks after meeting Henley, Louis Stevenson made a short visit to the artists' colonies at Barbizon, and had his first sight of the Forest of Fontainebleau, which was soon to play so imperative a part in his personal life. At about this time his restless, or at least his errant, nature was becoming more pronounced. He made journeys, excursions and walking-tours in England and Scotland as well as in France. His official biographer quotes a list Louis once concocted while he was ill about the year 1886, his idea being to find out how many towns he had slept in. The totals were: forty-six towns in England, nineteen more than once; fifty towns in Scotland, twenty-three more than once; seventy-four towns in France, nineteen more than once; forty towns in the rest of Europe, sixteen more than once. The grand total was two hundred and ten. Between 1871 and 1876 'no less than nine of his papers deal with travel or the external appearance of places known to him'. His first three books were also about places — *An Inland Voyage* (1878), *Picturesque Notes on Edinburgh* (1878) and *Travels with a Donkey in the Cevennes* (1879).

In London, after a walking-tour alone in Buckinghamshire in the autumn of 1874, he had written to his mother to warn her that she must not be vexed at his continual absences:

> You must understand ... that I shall be a nomad, more or less, until my days be done. You don't know how I used to long for it in old days; how I used to go and look at the trains leaving, and wish to go with them. And now, you know ... you must take my nomadic habits as part of me ... I *must* be a bit of a vagabond; it's your own fault after all, isn't it? You shouldn't have had a tramp for a son!

For all his restlessness he seldom found what he was looking for, a predicament he expressed in *The Song of the Road*, written in the Forêt de Montargis in 1878:

> For who would gravely set his face
> To go to this or t'other place?
> There's nothing under Heav'n so blue
> That's fairly worth the travelling to.
> On every hand the roads begin,
> And people walk with zeal therein;
> But wheresoe'er the highways tend,
> Be sure there's nothing at the end.

It is Smout's disillusion with the toy theatre all over again. In some ways Louis never wholly got rid of Smout all his life long.

Although he was now writing and reviewing prolifically, and being published regularly in the magazines, Louis still found the act itself involved him in acute stress. The *Picturesque Notes on Edinburgh*, for instance, which appeared in the *Portfolio* from June to December 1878, proved uphill work — 'The Edinburgh articles are a sore drain,' he wrote to Henley, 'and a sharp strain; they won't come right, and be damned to them; and it is important they should come right as if I and the picturists can hit it off well enough we shall sail into the book form in due time, with more coins and honour.'

Picturesque Notes was published in December 1878 by a firm in Fleet Street, in a handsome folio format with six full-page etchings and twelve engraved vignettes.

It was the second of his books to be published in 1878. The first was *An Inland Voyage*, the record of a journey made with Sir Walter Simpson by canoe from Antwerp to Pontoise. It is an agreeable, lively book, full of observation, and giving instances of the troubles, including arrest, into which Louis Stevenson's bohemian shabbiness would get himself and his dapper companion. There was always something about Louis Stevenson's appearance that immediately aroused the hostility of customs-officers, bank-managers, hoteliers and the police. It happened all over the world, from Chatillon-sur-Loire to Zurich, from Sidney to Monterey. Even when he and his companions first landed in his adored Samoa they were taken for a troupe of shiftless, out-of-work musicians. At Chatillon-sur-Loire, during a walking-tour with Simpson in 1875, Louis was actually imprisoned for half an hour, while the respectable-looking baronet battled for his friend's freedom with an obstinate Commissary of Police. Louis had only to appear in a foreign bank for the bank-clerks to refuse to believe that they held any money for him, or that his letter of credit was really his own. As a result he would make the situation worse by turning pale and nervous and speaking in a trembling voice. On some of these occasions he would get impotently furious and flash his eyes. On others he would try a few ill-judged jokes, or ridicule his interlocutor. He managed, in fact, to get on to a collison-course with any form of officialdom he happened to come upon. Bankers he held in particular horror, and one of his favourite expressions was 'a common banker', which he used as others might have said 'a common labourer'. 'Why even a common banker would renig at a thing like that!' he would exclaim, using a verb of which he was very fond. It was a verb which could actually have been applied to himself, for, having renigged at Edinburgh society and at lighthouse engineering, he was now busily renigging at the Scots bar, to which he had been admitted as advocate in July 1875, just one year previous to the canoe trip with Sir Walter Simpson.

[IV]

While he really had very little intention of practising at the bar, Louis had been unaffectedly enchanted to pass advocate. 'Madonna, Passed, ever your R.L.S.' he announced to Mrs Sitwell on a sheet of paper on which he made the 'S' of his last initial into a wild and widening whirligig. A girl cousin of his was staying at Swanston Cottage at the time, and she never forgot the day of triumph. She, Louis and his parents drove into Edinburgh to hear the results of the examination. They were using the big open barouche, and on the return journey Louis insisted on perching on the top of the carriage with his legs between his seated father and mother. He kept waving his hat and calling out to passers-by—acquaintances and strangers alike—' … just like a man gone quite mad. I often wonder what impression it made on passers-by,' Mrs Younger wrote, 'as Uncle Tom always used to have good horses, and liked them to go very fast.'

An advocate's brass plate was ceremoniously affixed to the door of 17 Heriot Row, and it seemed as though Thomas Stevenson's second plan for his son's future had come to final fruition. It had not, for his father had been counting without Louis. Years afterwards Louis's mother used to relate how, after he had been photographed in wig and gown on her insistence, she showed him her album of photos of himself from childhood. 'This is you, Louis, from Baby to Bar,' she said. 'The next will be, I suppose, from Bar to Baronet?' 'No, Mother,' the newly fledged advocate replied, 'the next will be *from Bar to Burial.*'

Nevertheless, Louis did go and strut up and down the great *salle des pas perdus* of the Parliament House, but he never managed nor, presumably, ever tried, to look like his fellow-advocates. For one thing his long hair protruded from below his barrister's wig. There is a story that one day when Louis was 'tripping' past the big fireplace, a wag, who was holding forth to an admiring throng, looked up and remarked, 'Oh, here is that gifted boy, the new Chatterton!' It is alleged that Louis was mortified and fled. During his short period in the Parliament House Louis Stevenson was offered two briefs but, to his father's chagrin, refused both. He told his family that as he was now a briefless barrister, he intended soon to retire from the law and devote his whole time to literature. He had proved to himself and his parents that he could pass a stiff law examination. There was no longer anything his father could do to prevent his becoming a full-scale author, and so, disillusioned, the old man threw in his hand. It was Louis's final gesture against the Edinburgh world of security in which he had been reared and into which he had steadfastly refused to fit. Soon he was back in France amongst the art students and their mistressed, carefree company that he relished. He was now studying the French poets of the fifteenth century, research which later produced a published essay on François Villon and another on Charles of Orleans.

The autumn of 1875 found Louis back at home, gearing himself up to face the Edinburgh winter. His health was good, but he was suffering from black depressions, and he would still drift about the law-courts. He complained to Mrs Sitwell, in a short letter written on the day following his twenty-fifth birthday, that he couldn't get away from home because of his poverty. His father had given him one thousand pounds, but it is likely that he himself gave much of this away to needy friends, as was his habit whenever he had money. He told Mrs Sitwell that his debts were 'red like crimson' and that he did not know how to clear them up, at any rate before Christmas. 'You know, I lose all my forenoons at Court!' he explained. 'So it is, but the time passes; it is a great pleasure to sit and hear cases argued or advised ... In every way, you see, but that of work the world goes well with me. My health is better than it ever was before; I get on without any jar, as if there never had been a jar, with my parents.' 'Our weather continues as it was, bitterly cold,' he wrote to her in a letter of January 1876. 'There is not much pleasure in life certainly as it stands at present. *Nous n'irons plus aux bois, hélas.*' But that was exactly where he would go in this new year of 1876. In the silvery summer-time, at the village of Grez-sur-Loing in the forest of Fontainebleau, there would be awaiting Robert Louis Stevenson the greatest surprise of all his life.

We must now momentarily leave Louis, his parents, Sidney Colvin, Henley and Mrs Albert Sitwell. We must also abandon Edinburgh and London and turn our eyes towards Paris, five years after the Commune. There, in a small, sunny apartment in the Rue de Naples, high up in Montmartre and within sight of the dome of the Sacré Coeur, there is living an American family of such straitened means that they often dine off black bread and smoked herring. The family consists of a neat, dark vivacious lady of thirty-five, from Indianapolis, her equally attractive eighteen-year-old daughter, and two blond sons, one of eight, the other, who is ill, of four. There is also a Californian governess. The name of the family is Osbourne, and they have come to Paris via Antwerp from the raw new western city of San Francisco. The two ladies of the family are studying art, and attend the *Atelier des Dames* of the painter Monsieur Julien, in a passage off the Boulevard des Italiens. Neither of them can speak French.

5

Forest Murmurs

As an eccentric and formidable old lady, Mrs Fanny Van de Grift Osbourne, by then the widow of Robert Louis Stevenson, was once asked why she had never written her memoirs. She replied that her life had been too much 'like a dazed rush on a railroad express' for her to be able to record it accurately. It is indeed true that this vivid woman's career was by no means a slow trudge towards the tomb.

Frances Matilda Vandegrift—as her maiden name was originally written—was born on March 10th, 1840, in a small red-brick house next door to a Presbyterian church in Indianapolis, Indiana. She was the eldest of her parents' seven children, a wild and swarthy little girl who was thought to resemble a tiger-lily. When she was two years old Fanny Vandegrift was received into the Second Presbyterian church at the same time as her mother, at a communal christening in the White River 'in the presence of a concourse of several thousand spectators'. Her father, Jacob Vandegrift, was a successful lumber-merchant who had moved from Philadelphia to Indianapolis as a young man and was descended from early Dutch settlers. Her mother, Esther Keen, also came from Philadelphia and claimed a Swedish military ancestry. Esther Keen was pretty and diminutive, and had passed on her looks and her small scale to her daughter Fanny. The darkness of Fanny's complexion was a burden to her as a child; she would be sent out to play with her sunbonnet sewn to her hair, in the hope that this would give her a fashionable pallor. Her grandmother, in whose bed she often slept, would beguile the child at night-time with hair-raising stories of ghosts and witches. A part of Fanny's childhood was for some reason spent in an undertaker's house, and she never forgot the excitement amongst the children as a corpse was brought in to be put on ice, as the undertaker always ordered a little extra (at the mourners' expense) to make ice-cream. At the undertaker's Fanny dramatized *Pilgrim's Progress* 'and was sent home as an irreverent little wretch'.

Fanny was a tomboy and did not care for girlish games. A member of her family described her as 'a little flashing firefly of a child'. As a teenager she was a recognized local beauty, whose initials would be cut on the trunks of neighbourhood trees by admiring swains. When she was seventeen, however, she fell in love with a young Southerner who, when first he called at the Vandegrifts' house, had found her stumping about the yard on stilts. In December 1857 she and Samuel Osbourne were married in a house furnished for them by her father. The bride wore heavy white satin with a long train and a lace-edged bertha. Her dark hair was worn in ringlets. The groom sported a blue coat with brass buttons, fawn trousers and a flowered waistcoat. He carried a white beaver hat. To a wedding-guest they looked 'like two children'. When a baby girl, Isobel, was born to them, the father was not yet twenty-one years old, and the tiny mother was once taken for her child's elder sister by an old gentleman in a railway-carriage.

When the Civil War broke out Samuel Osbourne, although a Southerner, joined the armies of the North and ended up a captain. When he came back from the war he set out for California and, impressed by its opportunities, told Fanny to join him there, which she did, travelling by sea to San Francisco via the Panama Canal. Fanny's first stay there was brief; for like many thousand others, Samuel Osbourne had been infected by the silver-mining fever, and he had gone to a new mining camp in Nevada. Fanny and her child followed him to this camp, the name of which was Austin.

Life in the camp at Austin was primitive and strenuous. The food consisted chiefly of meat without any vegetables, and young Mrs Osbourne distinguished herself by inventing fifteen different beef dishes and by making imitation honey for griddle cakes from boiled sugar and a root of alum. There were only six other women in the vicinity of Austin, and when a dance was given at a neighbouring camp Fanny and her female acquaintances set out for it in a sleigh made from a packing-case and set on runners. At this party there were fifty men and seven women; no woman danced with the same man twice. In the camp at Austin there were no mirrors; Fanny dressed herself for the dance in front of a polished tin can one of her friends held up for her. The miners were mostly young, adventurous enterprising lads and many of them were college-bred. From time to time there would be scares about an Indian attack. Ordinarily the

Indians would drift daily through the camp, peering into windows at the housework or cooking in progress within.

Mining at Austin proved unprofitable, so Sam Osbourne and his little family moved up to Virginia City on the cold, grey flank of Mount Davidson. Virginia City had been built on top of the famous Comstock Lode. It was a wild and lawless place, filled with gambling-hells and drinking saloons. Osbourne bought a small mine and, while waiting for results, took odd jobs in the town, at one time working as clerk to the Justice's Court. In those days men were often shot dead in Virginia City, and there were constant quarrels over mining claims, drunken brawls, and violent rows at the gaming-tables. The untrammelled manners of the place were exhilarating but also demoralizing. Young Osbourne quickly became demoralized, and it was at Virginia City that his wife realized, apparently for the first time, that her husband was being unfaithful to her. This nasty shock was followed by a worse one when Sam Osbourne went off on an expedition into Indian country and did not return. His wife took their child down to San Francisco, where a report reached her that Sam was dead; in fact other members of the expedition had been slaughtered by Indians, but Osbourne had separated from his companions before this massacre.

Regarding herself as a widow, Fanny Osbourne now took a place as a fitter in a dress-shop, wore deep mourning and, oddly, tried to pass herself off as a Frenchwoman. During this period she was greatly helped by a young Englishman, John Lloyd, who had been a friend of the Osbournes at the Austin mining-camp and who had fallen in love with Fanny. On Osbourne's sudden reappearance a comparatively settled family life was established. A son was born in 1868, and named Samuel Lloyd, the second name in honour of Fanny's English admirer. In time, though, Mrs Osbourne once again found out about her husband's infidelities and withdrew with her children to her parents' home in Indianapolis, only going back to San Francisco nearly a year later. The marriage was again patched up, and another son, Hervey, was born in a cottage like a bower of roses which Osbourne had bought in East Oakland, across the Bay. Fanny's mother-in-law attributed the disruption and ultimate collapse of the Osbournes' marriage to Fanny herself, and we do know from her subsequent history that she was hysterical and that her reason would, under certain circumstances, give way. Whoever's fault it was, the marriage now seemed to her to be without hope. In San Francisco she had been studying painting at the studio of Virgil Williams, an artist who took students. In 1875 Fanny decided that she could stand Osbourne's behaviour no longer, and took the very bold step of setting forth for Europe, with her daughter Belle, aged seventeen, her elder son of seven, little Hervey Osbourne, a remarkably beautiful child of three, and the governess, Miss Kate. She travelled on free railroad passes and stopped off in Indianapolis to bid her family adieu. A large area of Indiana was under flood and the roads east were said to be impassable. Undaunted, Fanny insisted on driving to New York. On one occasion a bridge spanning a flooded river was washed away fifteen minutes after the Osbourne family had been driven helter-skelter across it in an old country omnibus drawn by what Fanny called 'two stout horses'. The decision to brave the floods was in keeping with Fanny Osbourne's passionate and impatient character.

The resolution to head for Europe was an audacious one, since none of the little family knew a foreign language. The ostensible reason for travelling was so that Fanny and Belle could continue their painting under a foreign master. Probably on Virgil Williams's advice they had selected Antwerp, and here the strangeness of being abroad first came home to Fanny. Their steamer had entered the port of Antwerp at eleven o'clock at night and they ended up in an overcrowded hotel which could only provide them with one room. On the night of their arrival, as they were sitting silent in this room, the midnight chimes rang out from Notre Dame. 'I then realized that I was in Antwerp,' Fanny wrote to Mrs Virgil Williams. 'I held my breath to listen, with tears in my eyes, and my heart in my mouth. I think I felt as Mr Williams did when he first caught sight of Rome. It was a moment in my life that I shall be loth to forget.'

In Antwerp the Osbournes settled for a time in the Hôtel du Bienêtre, run by a family who treated them with affection and of whom they became fond. They next took a small house in the city, but after three months they set out for Paris, where Fanny had been told it would be easier for ladies to study painting. Here, as we have seen, they leased an apartment in the Rue de Naples, Montmartre.

[II]

For a very small woman Fanny Van de Grift Osbourne was a dramatic, even an imposing, figure. Louis Stevenson once wrote in a light, affectionate poem that she came up to the height of his heart, and in another poem he speaks of her 'eyes of gold and brambledew'. Her low, unmodulated speaking voice he described as like 'water running under ice'. Henry James once wrote of her to Owen Wister as being almost as interesting as Louis himself: 'If you like the gulch and the canyon you will like her.' On Henry's sister Alice James, on the other hand, Fanny made 'such a curious impression of a type ... From her appearance Providence or Nature, whichever is responsible for her, designed her as an appendage to a hand organ ... such egotism and so naked! giving me the strangest feeling of being in the presence of an unclothed being.' Another observer, the American writer Birge Harrison, thought her 'a grave and remarkable type of womanhood, with eyes of a depth and sombre beauty that I have never seen equalled, eyes, nevertheless, that upon occasion could sparkle with humour and brim over with laughter'. He thought her a woman of profound character and serious judgment, 'in no sense ordinary', and that she 'belonged to the quattrocento rather than to the nineteenth century'. In her second year in Paris Fanny cut her dark hair, and wore it in short curls all over her head. She rolled and smoked cigarettes incessantly, and complained that in Paris you could not get 'a good cigarette'.

In San Francisco Fanny had had one particular friend, an erudite lawyer named Edward Rearden who was Librarian in the Mercantile Bank. During the first years of her French exile she wrote him many very long letters, most of which have, fortunately, been preserved. The letters are saucy and flirtatious in tone, and suggest a certain coarseness of approach which she may have picked up in Nevada and, later, lost; but beneath the badinage they are candid and sincere. She would write freely of herself and her opinion of her own character, setting herself up as 'one of those creatures so much despised by the "strong-minded" whom they call derisively the "clinging vine". I do not want to be an oak and stand alone ... it makes me lonesome to think of the oak with no shelter nor support except what it provides for itself'. Rearden was a friend of Sam Osbourne also. He had surprised Fanny by telling her that Osbourne was missing his family; she had thought it would have been a weight off his mind to have got rid of them all once more. 'His letters quite touch my heart,' she wrote, ' ... I don't like to be selfish, and it makes me feel so if he is unhappy at our absence. I didn't know I should miss him as I do.' She shows a strong preoccupation with being ladylike ('Sally Hurt ... is not a lady in her manners') and in after years, when she never had a good word to say for her first husband, she condemned him as common and likely to be a bad social influence on their gentlemanly son Samuel Lloyd Osbourne. When Fanny took a dislike to anyone it immediately became fierce and obsessional. At this same period she would accuse Osbourne of having always been mean over money. He was in fact a poor and unsuccessful man, who wrote fond and charming letters to his surviving son. He was, anyway, keeping his whole family during their French sojourn.

In the spring of 1876 Fanny Osbourne's character was put to a severe and hideous test. Her second son Hervey, aged four, fell mysteriously ill; the doctors diagnosed scrofulous tuberculosis. The child had convulsions, his joints cracked, his bones stuck out through his skin, his eardrums were perforated, and he would lie in his bed crying out, 'Blood, Mamma!' Sam Osbourne rushed over from America and got to Paris just in time to see Hervey die early one April morning. The family could not afford to purchase a permanent grave at Père Lachaise, and the child was buried in one from which his bones would be tossed out into a communal ditch in five years' time. His mother was told that, had he lived, he would have been deaf and dumb, and probably deformed, but she found no comfort in such an assurance. 'That only makes me feel that he must be tired lying so long on his back, and that I must dig him up and turn him over. Then they talk to me of heaven ... ' she told Rearden, who had tried to comfort her with his own philosophy of life. She replied that this held no weight with her whatever: 'Because you do not find life a flower-garden, or because I have found a thorn or two, is that any reason why I should be satisfied that my child is dead?' Fanny's reaction to Hervey's death was, naturally enough, highly emotional, but it was also strictly materialistic. She was worn out. The doctors recommended a change, and urged her to take her son Samuel Lloyd to the country before he, too, fell ill. Fanny consulted a black-bearded American student of sculpture named Pardessus, who recommended the village of Grez in the forest of Fontainebleau. At Grez there was a ruined castle and, more important, a fairly cheap old inn with a garden running down to the banks of the river Loing. In summertime Grez was an artists' colony, but smaller and less noisy than nearby Barbizon. Here to the Hôtel Chevillon Fanny came with her husband and her two remaining children. The governess, Miss Kate, left them to take another job.

The village of Grez—formerly spelt Gretz—lies on the river Loing and is on the edge of the great forest of Fontainebleau, eleven kilometres from the town of Fontainebleau itself. It is a small, self-contained place, known for its twelfth-century church, which has a fine, tile-roofed tower, the ruins of its twelfth-century keep built to guard the river-crossing, and a medieval bridge of eight arches which was much painted by the artists of the summer colony. You can fish from the bridge, as well as from the banks of the Loing and from boats out on the river. In summer Grez becomes immensely lush, with splendid old trees along the river bank. The whole river-scape at Grez in June or July gives you an overpowering sense of green — the huge trees in full leaf, the shrubs and reeds along the river's brink, the deep green water of the river itself. Azure dragon-flies dart over the river. There is an atmosphere of peace but also of melancholy. This melancholy may be a case of hindsight; standing on the bridge or wandering along the river banks it is impossible not to reflect upon the gaiety and young *insouciance* described by some of those painters who congregated there a century ago, and reminders of long-dead pleasures do cast a shadow across the present scene. Each of the neighbouring towns and villages set along the Loing has a character and aspect of its own; Montigny with the weir and the old mill-house; Nemours, a larger and more bustling place. But of them all Grez, which feels shut-in and airless in summer, is the most beautiful and, so to speak, the most touching. The trees, and the adjacent forest, seem to cut Grez off and make it a private place. It is easy to see why Fanny's painter friends haunted it every summer. It would also be a good place to assuage a grief such as Fanny Osbourne's for the loss of her son.

[III]

After Pardessus had so warmly recommended the Hôtel Chevillon he began to get cold feet about it. With some embarrassment he explained to Fanny Osbourne that the manners and mode of life of the painters' summer colony might prove offensive to an American lady and her daughter. He may well have used the word 'bohemian' to explain what he meant. Fanny, with her Virginia City and San Francisco background, could, however, take any irregularities of behaviour in her stride. In some ways she resembled Mrs Winifred Hurtle, Paul Montague's American mistress in Trollope's *The Way We Live Now*. Fanny had not, of course, like Mrs Hurtle shot and killed her man, but she always travelled with her own pistol. This relic of Nevada days she had had put in order in Antwerp: 'I took my little pistol to the gunsmith to have the rust cleaned off it,' she explained in a letter to Rearden. 'The man examined it with the greatest delight saying that to see it was worth having lived a life-time.' As it turned out, there was no need at the Hôtel Chevillon either for Mrs Osbourne's protective revolver or for Mr Pardessus' apprehensions. The hotel was run on strictly moral lines. Painters' mistresses were not admitted and in the high summer Fanny and Belle Osbourne were the only females amongst fifteen or sixteen guests. The others were young painters, who prided themselves upon their bohemianism in a slightly self-conscious way, some Americans with money going so far as to pretend that they had none. One of these artificial paupers wore a quantity of rings on his fingers so that he might have the excitement of taking them to the pawn-shop.

The Osbourne contingent had gone by rail as far as Bourron, and had then travelled by rattling diligence to the little village of Grez, the church spire of which was the first sight they had of their future home. The Hôtel Chevillon was built of the same grey stone as the other houses in the village street, but instead of a door it had an archway leading into an inner courtyard; beyond this another archway opened into the walled garden which sloped down to the river. On the right was the *salle à manger*, on the left the tap-room with little tables and chairs, and a roaring wood fire, for the weather was still chilly. On the upper floor were two lines of bedrooms, with a corridor between them and a solitary bathroom at one end. The Osbournes thought it was the sight of these rather elementary living-conditions which made their Californian governess, Miss Kate, take to her heels after only two days at the Hôtel Chevillon.

This preliminary visit to Grez lasted three weeks. The family then returned to Paris, wound up their apartment, visited Hervey's grave in Père Lachaise, and then came back to Grez for the summer. Samuel Osbourne seems to have left for the United States during this short time in Paris. When Fanny and her two children were once more ensconced at Grez on their own, they found the hotel filling up with its seasonal bohemian guests. Fanny was dressed in deepest mourning, and was such a figure of maternal grief that a little Californian painter, Bloomer, complained when she gradually began to lose her 'tragic look'. Fanny wrote complacently to Rearden:

> But as I am known among the villagers as the 'beautiful American' and they crowd round to look at me, I don't care so much. Isn't it funny that they should do that? It was a long time before I could believe but that I was mistaken. Only think! Some artists came from a distant town to see me. I never dared to ask what they thought. I don't mind, on the contrary I think it is all very nice.

Mr Pardessus had warned the Osbournes that the clientele of the Hôtel Chevillon was not only bohemian but very choosey, and was quite capable of making the family's stay there impossible. In particular he kept referring to two Scottish cousins by the name of Stevenson. No one who failed to please these Stevensons would be allowed to stay a moment at Grez. In the mind of little Lloyd Osbourne, aged eight, these imagined Stevensons took on the aspect of bogies. He had spent the happiest three weeks of his life at the Hôtel Chevillon, fishing from the old stone bridge of which his mother was painting pictures. The place seemed to him a paradise — but would the dreaded Stevensons drive them out? 'We, as a family, seemed so harmless, so sad in our bereavement,' Lloyd wrote years afterwards, 'so worthy indeed of the consideration the kindly village people gave us, yet these tyrants had somehow the power to say to us: "Grez is ours. Get out!"'

The Stevenson cousins, then briefly at Barbizon, had heard tell of the two American women at Grez, and they had heard of them without pleasure. It was decided that Bob had better go to Grez to scout out the ground and to determine whether the American ladies were tolerable or not. So it came about that one summer's morning as Fanny and her boy were peering out of their bedroom window on to the courtyard below they saw Isobel Osbourne talking to a dark, roughly dressed stranger who was smiling with a mocking expression and held his hat in his hand. Lloyd remembered him as being 'as lithe and graceful as a Mexican vaquero, and evoking something of the same misgiving'. Belle had at first thought that Bob Stevenson was a Pole 'or a sort of gentleman gipsy'; but when she ran upstairs she was able to report to Fanny and Lloyd that Bob was most agreeable and entertaining, and had been highly amused by their apprehensions about him. He soon became a close friend. Fanny herself was immensely attracted by his saturnine looks and his flighty conversation, indeed she practically fell in love with him. Bob talked constantly of his cousin Louis, as did Walter Simpson, who had followed Bob to Grez. From having seemed a threat, Louis Stevenson now became a hero, at any rate in Lloyd's imagination. The other painters, who set off with their white umbrellas into the forest each morning, also spoke of Louis Stevenson with excitement as 'the most wonderful and inspiring of men', as well as the wittiest. They all cried, 'Wait till Louis gets here,' with an eager and excited air. The Osbournes were like an audience at the play, awaiting the entrance of the *jeune premier*. They did not have to wait for long.

In the dusk of a July evening, as the company at the Hôtel Chevillon were seated at dinner at the long *table d'hôte*, there was a sudden flurry at one of the high windows which gave on to the street. In vaulted a tall, thin young man, with a healthy reddish complexion, flowing light-brown hair and a small drooping tawny moustache. He was carrying a dusty knapsack. The men in the dining-room rose to their feet in clamorous welcome. Louis Stevenson had arrived. The stranger said that he had dined but would have a cup of coffee. There was an empty chair next to Mrs Osbourne and here he settled. He must have explained to her that he could only stay at Grez for a few weeks; he did not return again until the end of his canoe trip with Simpson in September. It was apparently during those autumn months that he got to know Fanny Osbourne well and that she began to pay him particular attention. In those days of high summer at Grez he was, simply, the beautiful Bob Stevenson's literary cousin.

[IV]

Nellie Sanchez, Fanny's sister, who ultimately wrote her biography, states that Louis Stevenson admitted that he had fallen in love with Fanny at first sight. Another romantic, Fanny's daughter Belle, declares in her autobiography that Louis had told her the same thing. She even adds the detail that she herself first noticed the young man at the window because her mother was staring at him 'with an odd intent gaze'. Apart from the fact that love at first sight is a fairly rare and seldom durable phenomenon, it seems likely that Louis's love for Fanny Osbourne was a cumulative, dreamy process, and that she herself was, initially, far more attracted by Bob Stevenson, whom she at this time described as 'the most beautiful creature' she had ever seen. Writing to Rearden of the 'charming, lotus eating, Brooks Farm sort of life' they were leading at Grez, she referred to Bob as 'Adonis' and as 'Apollo', stressing his 'wonderful grace and perfect figure'. 'He is exactly like one of Ouida's heroes, with the hand of steel in the velvet glove and all that.' One night, before Louis's arrival, a moralistic young man amongst the painters deliberately made Bob Stevenson drunk, hoping that his state would disgust Fanny and her daughter and put them off him. Fanny, however, was made of sterner stuff, and, when Bob had been carried up to bed, after 'a wild sort of time', she decided that she had never seen such a charming drunk before.

Soon there were endless jealous complications at the Hôtel Chevillon. Belle Osbourne, described by one young American staying there as 'a bewitching young girl of seventeen with eyes so large as to be out of drawing', was loved by Pardessus, but herself was in love with another admirer, a handsome Irish boy of twenty who carried a blackthorn shillelagh and was named Frank O'Meara. Bob Stevenson, also, was attracted to Belle, and Louis may well have been so at first. Just as he had never met Russians until his convalescent time at Menton, Louis had never met American women, and was dazzled by the contrast they offered to conventional Edinburgh girls. 'He never saw a real American girl before,' Belle wrote in a letter home, 'and he says I act and talk as though I came out of a book — I mean an American book ... He is such a nice looking ugly man, and I would rather listen to him talk than read the most interesting book I ever saw. We sit in the little green arbour after dinner drinking coffee and talking till late at night. Mama is ever so much better and getting prettier every day.'

The position of Fanny and Belle as the only women amongst a set of entertaining and very young men suited them admirably. When they were not painting, the guests at the Chevillon amused themselves on the river, trying to upset each other's canoes. In these sports Louis was the ringleader. Fanny, who could not swim but was always ready to take a ducking, wore a bathing suit with sleeves, tucked her curls up under a scarlet neckerchief, and had another knotted round her waist, while her small feet were shod in scarlet espadrilles. Her daughter remembered that her mother then 'looked like a little girl'. On rainy days they acted charades and played 'Consequences' and 'Telegrams', or a game which involved the writing of impromptu verse. In good weather they would adjourn to the garden after meals, where Fanny, who had injured an ankle in the river jollities, would lie in a hammock while everyone else sprawled on the grass at her feet. Life at the Hôtel Chevillon in that high summer was idyllic, and seemed tailor-made for romance.

Little Lloyd Osbourne began to notice how well his mother and Louis Stevenson were getting on. They would sit and talk 'interminably' on either side of the dining-room stove, when everyone else was out painting under their great white umbrellas in the forest and the fields. He began to associate his mother and Louis together, and felt strangely happy about this. Louis had long won Lloyd's heart by reading *Tales of a Grandfather* and *Pilgrim's Progress* to him, and inventing stories to tell the boy, whose secret name for Louis was 'Greatheart'. Louis obviously shared the general admiration of Mrs Osbourne, who was spoiled by everyone on the premises. She wrote to Rearden:

My chair by the fire and my chair at the table are always held

sacred. I am taken out solemnly every afternoon for exercise ...
Weekly pilgrimages are made to the city to get things to tempt
my appetite ... Then to make me more vain they paint me,
making me very beautiful, and make up sketches of my mouth,
the back of my head and my nose, and model my arms in clay,
and propose costumes for me and situations for me. Oh, I am
awfully vain I do assure you.

One day in October 1876, Bob Stevenson had gone for a forest walk
with Fanny. They lost their way and were late back, which dis-
quieted the other inmates of the Hôtel Chevillon. During this walk
Bob had told Fanny which of the young painters at Grez she should
see when she went back to Paris for the winter, and which she should
not. He particularly emphasized that she must cultivate the friendship of his cousin Louis, saying, 'You must have nothing to say to *me*
for I am only a vulgar cad, but Louis is a gentleman and you can
trust him and depend upon him.' He also thanked Mrs Osbourne for
never having laughed at Louis, who had been indulging in attacks of
hysteria and weeping, which Bob said were entirely due to bad
health. At this period, also, Louis would suddenly erupt into a fit of
laughter which he could not control. According to his own theory
these cataracts of laughter could only be stemmed if someone bent
his fingers backwards. Once in a carriage with Fanny in Paris he
began to laugh and begged her to apply the remedy. To show her
how to do it he bent her own fingers back so painfully that she bit
his hand to stop it. Both the Stevensons amazed Indianapolis-bred
Fanny by their habit of weeping and throwing themselves in despair
upon the floor : 'I do wish Louis wouldn't burst into tears in such an
unexpected way; it is so embarrassing. One doesn't know what to do,
whether to offer him a pocket handkerchief, or look out of the
window.' The Stevensons' general tone and behaviour offered a
baffling contrast to that of the student-miners of Nevada.

Even after the deaths of Louis and Fanny, her family went to
extreme pains to conceal the fact that they had been lovers at Grez.
This seems not to have taken place in the year of their meeting, 1876,
but presumably happened in the spring of 1877. In April of that
year, writing again to Rearden, Fanny gives a bizarre version of the
Stevenson cousins' lives and prospects. She describes Louis as a
'tall, gaunt Scotsman, with a face like Raphael', and added that
between over-education and dissipation he had ruined his health,
but had reformed his habits two years before. She also reported that
Louis's parents, being cousins, were threatened with insanity and

that she was 'quite sure' that their son was also mad. She added that Louis was 'heir to an immense fortune which he will never live to inherit'. This quantity of misinformation about the staid household at 17 Heriot Row seems to have been culled from the painters' gossip at Grez. She must, of course, have been trying to put Rearden off the scent, for the detached tone of the letter would not suggest that she was writing about a man she loved. She emphasized in the same missive that the two 'mad Stevensons' were men of spirits, and so joyful 'that their presence is exhilarating'. She had never heard one of them say a cynical thing nor do an unkindness. 'With all the wild stories I have heard of them fresh in my mind, I still consider them the truest gentlemen and nothing can make them anything less.' She told Rearden that she did not suppose that she would ever see the Stevenson cousins again. Unless this letter of April 1877 be misdated, Fanny was being thoroughly disingenuous with her San Francisco friend, for there is very good reason to suppose that by this spring she and Louis had recognized and accepted the fact that they were intensely in love. At some point in the late autumn or winter of the previous year crystallization, in the full Stendhalian sense, had taken place.

We have earlier noted Louis Stevenson's tendency to exteriorize even his most fleeting and trivial emotions by writing of them for the public; it was this custom which made critics of his earlier essays accuse him of crass egotism. We should thus confidently expect that an event as titanic as falling in love with the woman with whom he intended to spend the rest of his life would provoke some literary record of his state of mind. We should be correct. In February 1877, over the modest initials R.L.S., the *Cornhill Magazine* published a most remarkable article headed *On Falling in Love*.

On Falling in Love was written in November 1876 in Edinburgh, whither Louis had reluctantly gone after following Fanny and her children to Paris; where he had lingered deliciously in a winter city set aglow for him by Fanny's presence. This essay is one of the best of that particular period of his life—he was now just twenty-seven. It is sensitive and perspicacious, and perhaps one of the most brilliant analyses of its subject extant in the English language. He describes falling in love as the only 'event in life which really astonishes a man' and calls it 'the one illogical adventure, the one thing of which we are tempted to think as supernatural, in our trite and reasonable world'. He writes of 'the pang of curiosity' at the first moment of meeting, and of how future lovers begin by looking into each other's eyes. This has of course been done by each of them in the past a dozen times with no great result: 'But on this occasion all is different. They fall at once into that state in which another person becomes to us the very gist and centre-point of God's creation ... And all the while their acquaintances look on in stupor.' He imagines the lovers wandering into love step by step 'with a fluttered consciousness, like a pair of children venturing together into a dark room'. The lovers 'read the expression of their own trouble in each other's eyes' and so certain do they in the end become that no declaration is needed. It seems to the man that he has never heard or felt or seen before that moment of truth. His love illuminates every mundane aspect of life and gives a supreme pleasure to all of it—to sleeping, to waking, to moving, to breathing. The lovers are so enchanted by each other that they are convinced that 'their presence must be the best thing for everybody else.' He takes a passionate kindness as being the very essence of love, 'kindness, so to speak, run mad and become importunate and violent'. He speaks, too, of the form of retrospective jealousy which makes the lover hate to think that his idol has had any past at all before they met. The lovers fear future separation, but they also resent that form of separation which has already existed because they had not yet met. He terms Cupid 'the blind bow-boy who smiles upon us from the end of terraces in old Dutch gardens', shooting his bolts laughingly among a fleeting generation. The essay ends on a note of melancholy:

> When the generation is gone, when the play is over, when the thirty years' panorama has been withdrawn in tatters from the stage of the world, we may ask what has become of these great, weighty and undying loves, and the sweethearts who despised mortal conditions in a fine credulity; and they can only show us a few songs in a byegone taste, a few actions worth remembering, and a few children who have retained some happy stamp from the disposition of their parents.

Even when under the influence of the most splendid illusion that human life can offer, Louis looked sadly, but not cynically, ahead. If he was primarily a romantic, he was a realist as well.

The theme of kindness in relation to love recurs in a short poem, written presumably at Grez in 1877 or 1878, and inspired by taking Fanny in his canoe upon the Loing:

> Deep, swift and clear, the lilies floated; fish
> Through the shadows ran. There thou and I
> Read kindness in our eyes and closed the match.

An independent witness (if such were necesssary) to this passionate love affair of 1877 is the American painter, Will H. Low, an intimate friend of Louis and Fanny at Grez, who afterwards wrote his own memoirs, *A Chronicle of Friendships*. In a letter to the author of *On the Trail of Stevenson*, written in 1916, Low makes the point that Louis had always abstained from the promiscuity rampant in the artists' circles in Paris, because he was concentrating on learning to write, ' ... this, of course,' Low adds, 'until he met his fate.' The 'sudden and imperious passion which held him' seemed to Low and even to his most irreverent friends not destined to be merely 'episodic'. He adds that when the romance began Fanny was 'in full possession of the charm of womanhood' and that no disparity of age between the lovers was to be seen or felt. It is interesting to note that, like Mrs Sitwell, Fanny was considerably older than Louis Stevenson — ten years older, to be exact. This, of course, means nothing in a passion-ate love affair, and certainly to Louis Fanny's seniority meant nothing at all. Among several poems which he addressed to her is a two-stanza lyric beginning 'To you let snow and roses, And golden locks belong', which was published in *Songs of Travel* in 1895, a year after Louis's death. This lyric, which was first called by Louis *Dark Women*, originally consisted of six stanzas. Various manuscript versions of the poem exist; one of the earlier of these probably seemed to Louis too personal for publication. In it he praises 'swarthy women' as against the golden-haired, snow-and-roses type of beauty:

> The hue of heather honey,
> The hue of honey bees,
> Shall tinge her golden shoulder,
> Shall tinge her tawny knees.
>
> Dark as a wayside gypsy,
> Lithe as a hedgewood hare,
> She moves a glowing shadow
> Through the sunshine of the fair;
> And golden hue and orange,
> Bosom and hand and head
> She blooms, a tiger lily,
> In the snowdrift of the bed.
>
> Tiger and tiger lily,
> She plays a double part,
> All woman in the body,
> And all the man at heart.

> She shall be brave and tender,
> She shall be soft and high,
> *She* to lie in my bosom
> And *he* to fight and die.

Although, later, Louis's ill-health probably precluded much physical expression of passion and although he came to regard Fanny as an almost maternal protectress, the relationship at its beginning was emphatically not devoid of sensuality.

For the next two years, indeed until Fanny Osbourne's sudden return to California in August 1878, Louis spent as much time as he could in France, either in Paris in winter or at Grez in summer. In June 1878 he had what his parents would have regarded as an official reason for being in Paris, since he acted as secretary to Professor Fleeming Jenkin, who was a judge at an International Exhibition there. His parents resented his other long sojourns in France: '*At last* on the 21st [of December] after being more than six months away Louis came home', we read in his mother's diary for the winter of 1878. Although the *Cornhill* article on falling in love should have proved to them revealing (or perhaps because it did), his parents kept urging him to return. 'I wish you would come home,' his father wrote to him in the autumn of 1877. 'Magnus Simpson says he can't see any fun in remaining so long at Gretz [*sic*], neither can I ... I said you should come home. I now say you must come home. If you don't you will be voted a humbug and be regarded as unpopular as the Colorado beetle.'

In February 1878 Louis, who had been receiving frequent letters and telegrams from Heriot Row, wrote to ask his father to come over to Paris for talks. 'Don't be astonished,' Louis wrote to Colvin, 'but admire my courage and F's. We wish to be right with the world as far as we can; 'tis a big venture; wish us God speed.' He had already asked Colvin and Mrs Sitwell to intercede for him with his father, to what effect we do not know. All that we do know is that Thomas Stevenson did cross over to Paris and seems to have behaved kindly; it is highly improbable that he met Fanny on this occasion. (A curious sidelight is thrown on the whole situation by the fact that the elder Stevenson himself had always believed in and loudly advocated easy divorce for women who were badly treated by their husbands.) His Parisian discussions with Louis probably ended in some sort of a compromise, for it must have been the parents' hope that, given time, his passion for Fanny would evaporate in the natural course of things. Louis, on the other hand, already regarded himself as virtually married to the undivorced Mrs Samuel Osbourne. After his father's Paris visit, Louis wrote him a rather odd letter, part of which runs: 'I have taken a step towards more intimate relations with you. But don't expect too much of me. This is a rare moment and I have profited by it; but take it as a rare moment.'

Meanwhile, some months earlier, Fanny had had her first glimpse of England and, more specifically, of the London circle of Louis's friends. In the autumn of 1877, in Paris, Louis developed some infection of the eyes which seemed to be sending him blind. Fanny boldly took him into her own lodgings in the Rue Ravingnan and had her first experience of one of the roles she was to play, off and on, for the next seventeen years—that of sick-nurse to Louis. When his eyesight did not improve under her care, she tried to get Bob to come over and fetch him, but could not get in touch. She next tele-graphed to Colvin, explaining that she herself was bringing Louis across the Channel for treatment in London. Once there, Fanny took the opportunity to have her injured foot examined, and submitted to some kind of surgical manipulation of it. When convalescent she was asked by Mrs Sitwell to come and stay in her house in Chepstow Place. Fanny entertained Mr Rearden with her impressions of this intellectual London atmosphere:

> I was with very curious people in London, the leaders of the Purists, I was so out of place in their house that a corner was arranged, or disarranged, for me. They dishevelled my curls, tied up my head in a yellow silk handkerchief, wrapped me in yellow shawls and spread a tiger skin rug over my sofa, and another by me. Everything else was of dull pale blue or green, so that I had quite the feeling of being a sport of Pocahontas in my corner. It seemed most incongruous to have the solemn Mr Colvin, a professor at Cambridge, and the stately, beautiful Mrs Sitwell sit by me and talk in the most correct English about the progress of literature and the arts. I was rather afraid of them but they didn't seem to mind but occasionally came down to my level and petted me as one would stroke a kitten. They called me Fanny directly ... I had always been told that they were cold heartless people, but I didn't find them so. I wonder why people never are that to me. Perhaps because I am little and not so clever as they.

Louis had warned Fanny that whatever she did she must not smoke in Mrs Sitwell's house, but, talking one day to Leslie Stephen and Henley, who were calling on her, Mrs Osbourne became so excited that, finding a cigarette in her pocket, she began absent-mindedly to puff it. Contrary to Louis's predictions, her hostess was charming about it. Colvin went out and bought Turkish tobacco and papers, and he and Mrs Sitwell demanded lessons on how to roll cigarettes correctly. They ended by making far too many for even Fanny to consume and expressed disappointment when she wanted no more. This convalescence in Bayswater was the first time that Fanny and Henley met. It was the beginning of a very uneasy friendship which had a sad, explosive end.

[V]

Late in 1876, Henley had been given what seemed to be an ideal opportunity for trying out his talents as an editor. Robert Glasgow Brown, who had once collaborated with Stevenson on the fore-doomed *Edinburgh University Magazine*, had founded a new weekly, financed by a group of Tories. It was called *London: The Conservative Weekly Journal of Politics, Finance, Society and the Arts*. The first issue appeared in February 1877; the magazine folded in April 1879. Brown had asked Henley to take on the editorship of *London*, and Henley relied on Louis Stevenson to collaborate in the work. By doing this, Louis squandered a good deal of time, for it often happened that there was not enough copy for some issue of the magazine, and Henley, who was feverishly writing verse to fill up space, would call on Stevenson for essays, poems or — a new and significant departure for Louis — serial fiction. Earnest Edinburgh well-wishers, like Professor Fleeming Jenkin, strongly objected to Louis prostituting his gifts by 'society journalism'. '*London* is rapidly hustling me into the abhorred tomb,' Louis wrote to Baxter early in 1878. 'I do write such damn rubbish in it, that's a fac' [*sic*] and I hate doing it so inconceivably. I declare I would ten times rather break stones or — or in short do anything that didn't involve an office.' Many of his contributions were anonymous, and the magazine was run in that state of imminent crisis which seems endemic to weekly journalism. Even so, Louis declared that he was sorry at the magazine's demise after its one hundred and fourteenth number. He wrote that *London* was 'deeply regretted by none who knew it, excepting myself, its author, founder and slave'.

In the career of Robert Louis Stevenson, *London* is of interest for two reasons. In *The Suicide Club* and *The Rajah's Diamond*, afterwards published as part of the volume *New Arabian Nights* in 1882, Louis tried his hand at fiction. In the unsatisfactory allegorical tale *Will o'the Mill*, published in the *Cornhill* for January 1878, he had already, so to speak, built a bridge between writing essays and writing short stories, and now his contributions to *London* marked a distinct step forward in what proved to be his famous future line.

Secondly, he now involved Fanny Osbourne in his work, and even sought her advice. Fanny had herself vaguely dabbled in journalism in San Francisco, and like many other dedicated amateurs she cherished a firm belief in the value of her own literary views. To the day of her death she regarded herself as a sibylline literary critic, gifted with second sight. So far as *London* was concerned she told Rearden that although she did not actually write for the magazine she 'helped to choose the staff of writers for it, and examined manuscripts and accepted and rejected things'. Fanny was ever ready to counsel Louis about his writing, and even to act as self-appointed censor. In some cases, most notably that of the second version of *Dr Jekyll and Mr Hyde*, he was grateful to her for this, but on the whole he stubbornly went his own way. After Louis and Fanny were married, old Thomas Stevenson, who respected his daughter-in-law's judgment, made Louis promise to publish nothing without her consent. Henley, accustomed to be Louis's literary confidant and, in one sense, mentor, resented Fanny's influence as much as she in her turn resented his whisky-swigging and his vociferous capacity for exhausting Louis almost to extinction.

Although he finally tired of *London*, and was, in after years, rather ashamed of his contributions to it, Louis began by enjoying the novelty of instant journalism. In 1878, for a reason unknown, but most probably because her husband must have ceased subsidizing his wife and family to live in Europe, Fanny suddenly determined to go back to San Francisco, an acutely painful decision for both Louis and herself. Before embarking that August, however, she brought Belle and Lloyd to London, where they occupied dingy lodgings in Chelsea for some weeks. Louis would frequent these rooms in Radnor Street, flitting in and out like a dragonfly and full of technical talk about 'going to press', 'middles' and 'closing the formes'. Histrionic as ever, he had adapted himself to his new rôle, wore a fine double-breasted blue suit and brandished a cane weighted with steel for use 'in a tight place'. He had even invested in a stiff felt hat which he would wildly toss aside in excitement. He would rattle up Radnor Street in a cab, and then dart off to get another for the return journey to Shepherd's Bush, where Henley and his newly married wife were then living.

One evening he read the Osbourne family his tale of the Brenner

Pass, *Will o'the Mill*. From his mother's intent expression as she listened, little Lloyd Osbourne, now ten years old, could not fathom whether she liked the story or not; but when Louis had finished she was brimming over with enthusiasm. Louis's reading aloud of his own work was an experience in itself—haunting and, to the audience, incomparable. Lloyd Osbourne once wrote that he had never heard anyone read as Louis read—'the glamour he could give, the stir of romance, the indescribable emotion from which one awoke as though from a dream.' As well as *Will o'the Mill*, Louis read the *Suicide Club* series aloud on various evenings in that bleak Chelsea sitting-room. These stories provoked much merriment, but Lloyd thought that Louis attached no importance to them—they simply served to fill up the empty columns of *London* week by week, and brought him in a few necessary pounds. By this time he had long ago disposed of the thousand pounds his father had given him in the summer of 1875, when he passed attorney at the bar. It has been reckoned that of this sum he gave 90 per cent away to needy friends; it seems likely that he was also helping Fanny Osbourne.

It was late summer before Fanny and her children set off from London for Indiana and California. Neither Fanny nor Louis was in a position to make plans, even for meeting again in the foreseeable future. 'This is the last 20 days of my passion,' Louis had written to Baxter from Paris in June 1878. ''Twill then be over for good. They are steep.' It is not even known whether Fanny herself had at this point so much as begun to consider divorce. Her own Presbyterian family in Indianapolis would have been as shocked at the idea of divorce and re-marriage as the Stevenson parents, and Samuel Osbourne's father, a strict Methodist, would have been equally repelled by the idea. When Louis went to the station to see Fanny and her children off on the boat-train his personal outlook thus seemed impenetrable and obscure. He said goodbye to them all on the station platform, just in front of their reserved compartment. Lloyd always remembered how Louis then turned abruptly and walked 'away down the whole length of the platform, a diminishing figure in a brown ulster'. To Lloyd's disappointment Louis did not once glance back. Already, while Fanny had still been in Paris and he himself at Heriot Row, Louis had felt overwhelmed by a terrible loneliness. In an undated letter to Henley at this time he declared that he was not 'as black at heart' as under the circumstances he might be. 'And do I not love?' he rhetorically asked, 'and am I not loved? and have I not friends who are the pride of my heart? Oh no, I'll have none of your blues; I'll be lonely, dead lonely, for I can't help it; and I'll hate to go to bed, where there is no dear head upon the pillow, for I can't help that either, God help me; but I'll make no mountain of my little molehill, and pull no damnable faces at the derisive stars.'

Now that Fanny was gone his loneliness became unbearable. The company of friends could not exorcise it. In the month following Fanny's departure he set off all alone for a part of France that he did not yet know. This journey produced that perennially touching book, *Travels with a Donkey in the Cévennes*. 'It has good passages,' Louis wrote to Colvin as this book was going through the press, 'I can say no more ... But lots of it is mere protestations to F., most of which I think you will understand. That is to me the main thread of interest. Whether the damned public — But that's all one; I've got thirty quid for it, and should have had fifty.'

6

Damnably in Love

FANNY's departure, combined with the total uncertainty about when and even whether he should ever see her again, flung Louis into a profound depression. Writing to Baxter from France that same autumn, he confessed that it was 'damned hard work to keep up a good countenance in this world now-a-days, harder than anyone knows'. He hoped that Baxter would never have reason to feel one half as sad as he himself felt. 'I am damnably in love, a good deal in debt, and yours ever,' he added in another letter to the same friend. His last two years of happiness with Fanny, what he called 'my perfect relation', made absence all the more bitter. When he did not hear from her he became ill. He had more or less ceased writing to Mrs Sitwell, and at this period he wrote altogether fewer letters to his friends. He told Colvin that he never on principle wrote any letters to Fanny, but this was surely hyperbole, for she is hardly likely to have gone on writing to him if she received no replies; and, as we must have realized by now, letter-writing was Louis's chosen method for unloading his mind and dispersing his moods. His theory about writing to Fanny in California, though original, does not really ring true:

> For to F. I never write letters. To begin with there's no good. All that people want by letters has been done between us. We are acquainted; why go on with more introductions? I cannot change so much, but she would still have the clue and recognize every thought. But between friends it is not so. Friendship is incomplete, and lives by conversation—on bits of knowledge not on faith.

He went out of his way to assure Colvin that despite all his troubles he was 'a happy man and happier than of yore'. At the same time he presented himself in another new light—that of a solitary: 'I draw into my shell a little; I like solitude and silence; to have been a whole day and not said twenty words, refreshes me. I know it's not nice of me; I know it's an unkindly anti-social way; but the other is worse.' It is permissible to question whether so avid and luxuriant a conversationalist really managed to maintain these periods of silence for long, or whether Louis merely thought that he was doing so. In any case, a week or two after Fanny's disappearance, he set off by himself for Paris, and thence down to Monastier amongst the mountains of the Haute-Loire, where he spent a month alone before buying a small mouse-coloured donkey which he christened Modestine. With this donkey, unskilfully laden, he tramped for ten days through the Cévennes.

The Cévennes adventure was his first journey without a companion. He had hoped that Sir Walter Simpson would accompany him as he had on the canoe trip two years before, but Sir Walter was a stocky, slow, deliberate walker; on a previous walking-tour he had been quite unable to keep up with Louis's swift, jumpy stride. Louis therefore determined this time to go it alone. He told Baxter that he hoped to make a book out of his pilgrimage with Modestine.

Travels with a Donkey in the Cévennes bears a superficial similarity to the *Inland Voyage* but is better written, and both more wry and more pensive. The book has that quality of ingratiating charm which Louis himself could switch on in person whenever he chose; it is written with disarming candour and glimmers with poetic accounts of dawns and sunsets, intermingled with profiles of fellow-travellers, peasants and innkeepers. On several nights he slept out under the stars in his woolly sleeping bag, notably once in a pinewood and once in a grassy clearing by a brook. His struggles with Modestine, a slow-stepping animal, annoyed some reviewers but are in fact an integral part of the little book's charm. Louis's style was now perfected and he had learned to use words with the utmost skill, and to create the precise effect which he intended to create. Yet it is neither a gay nor a carefree book; and, as he had indicated to Colvin, the volume is possessed by the shade of Fanny Osbourne. 'Exulting' in his solitude at night, he writes in the *Travels* that he was aware of 'a strange lack'; what he sighed for was a *solitude à deux*. 'For there is a fellowship more quiet even than solitude,' he writes, 'and which, rightly understood, is solitude made perfect. And to live out of doors with a woman a man loves is of all lives the most complete and free.' Fanny's is not the only shade that haunts this book; Louis's reactions to the Trappist monastery of Our Lady of the

Snows among the hills of Vivarais were certainly such as his old nurse Cummy and his parents would have applauded. However, both in his account of his night in the monastery, and in the poem *Our Lady of the Snows*, later published in *Underwoods*, Louis shows a total lack of understanding of the practice and the goals of the silent contemplative life:

> Aloof, unhelpful, and unkind,
> The prisoners of the iron mind,
> Where nothing speaks except the bell,
> The unfraternal brothers dwell ...
>
> But ye?—O ye who linger still
> Here on your fortress on the hill,
> With placid face, with tranquil breath,
> The unsought volunteers of death,
> Our cheerful General on high
> With careless looks may pass you by.

The mountainous countryside of the Cévennes was anyway unlikely to inspire Louis Stevenson with Roman Catholic sympathies, for it used to be the stronghold of the Camisards, who, from 1702 till 1705 and sporadically for another ten years, had been in a state of armed revolt against the French Government following the Revocation of the Edict of Nantes. In Edinburgh Louis had read up material on the history of the Camisards, who seemed to him to be the French equivalent of the austere Scots Covenanters. All Louis's sympathies with a lost cause, combined with his admiration for feats of arms and for freedom of thought in general, made the Cévennes, with its memories of Protestant martyrs, take on an aspect that was almost sacrosanct in his eyes. Beside the Camisards, with their prophecies, their courage and their *théomanie*, the Cistercian monks sleeping in their shrouds at Our Lady of the Snows seemed to him wilful and unworthy shirkers who had opted out of real life.

He contrasted them with his own current and rather fevered version of the objectives of human existence:

> Thou, O my love, ye, O my friends—
> The gist of life, the end of ends—
> To laugh, to love, to live, to die,
> Ye call me by the ear and eye!

Unerringly subjective in his judgments, Louis Stevenson derided Presbyterian practices in Edinburgh, yet faced with a monastery of Trappist monks in France he resented them with an equal fervour.

[II]

Louis returned to London in the middle of October 1878. He spent some days in Sidney Colvin's rooms at Cambridge, but complained that he could not write: 'I can only write ditch-water,' he told Henley in a letter. ''Tis ghastly; but I am quite cheerful, and that is more important.' At this time he was struggling to produce a short story, *Providence and the Guitar*, a tale suggested by the plight of some strolling players he and Fanny had encountered at the Hôtel Chevillon at Grez. When finished, *Providence and the Guitar* came out in four successive numbers of *London* from the beginning of November; his fee for the story he very characteristically sent to the strolling family themselves. At this time Louis also began, perhaps even did the whole first draft of that brilliant thriller, *The Pavilion on the Links*, which Conan Dyle described as 'the very model of dramatic narrative'. He did not, however, complete *The Pavilion* until the winter of the following year. He apparently left off work on this story in order to collaborate with W. E. Henley on a play about Deacon Brodie, whose character and final fate had cast a spell on Louis Stevenson from earliest childhood. This was the first of four such efforts at dramatic collaboration with Henley, efforts which, shored up by intense optimism, never rewarded the time and trouble expended on them.

William Brodie, deacon of the Incorporation of the Edinburgh Wrights and Masons, was a respected citizen of Edinburgh in the latter half of the eighteenth century. Brodie had inherited from his father, and continued to conduct, a reputable business as wright and cabinet-maker in the Lawnmarket. Owing to losing massive sums of money at cards he was persuaded to lead a double life, and, as head of a small gang of thieves, committed by night many successful burglaries in the city and its environs during the winter of 1787. Until he was betrayed by a member of his own gang who turned King's Evidence, Brodie's activities had foxed the police; he was arrested in Amsterdam when about to embark for America, brought back to Edinburgh, tried and hanged in 1788. The contrast between Deacon Brodie's praiseworthy civic life and his nefarious nocturnal career as a successful burglar was felt by Stevenson and Henley to have a dramatic content which could not fail to fascinate upon the stage. 'We were both young men when we did that,' Louis explained to a *New York Herald* reporter in 1887, 'and I think we had an idea that bad-heartedness was strength'. He added that Henley and he now took the play 'for good, honest melodrama not so very ill done'.

In Louis's night-nursery there had stood a well-designed, elaborate cabinet which had been made by Deacon Brodie himself, and the story of the maker of this cabinet became one of the intimate legends of his boyhood. At the age of thirteen or fourteen, he composed some sort of a drama about Deacon Brodie, which he read aloud in Heriot Row to a school friend in the autumn or winter of 1864. He is said to have completed another play on the subject in 1869, when he was nineteen, and to have laid this aside. Louis described the later draft as 'a sort of hugger-mugger melodrama, which lay by in my coffer until it was fished out by my friend W. E. Henley and we started work together.' Louis and Henley concentrated on the play in London that winter of 1878: 'It's a chance thing, much of a chance,' Louis wrote to his mother from the Savile Club, where he spent three hours each morning writing the play, going in the afternoon to Henley's house in Shepherd's Bush for another three hours drafting, this time in collaboration. He told his mother that if *Deacon Brodie* did not fail it would do more for him than four years of articles. When the play seemed almost completed, Louis went home to Edinburgh. In January 1879 Henley followed him and they shut themselves up at Swanston Cottage for another week's work on *Brodie*. Colvin, and a great many other people, were asked for their views. Professor Fleeming Jenkin condemned it out of hand, telling Louis that he and Henley had 'tried to do an impossible thing, and had not even tried in a right way'. The play was offered to Henry Irving, who was extremely dilatory about answering and in the end refused it. In December 1879 Henley had *Deacon Brodie* printed whilst Louis was in California. First Louis's faith in the play, and then Henley's own, dwindled. It was finally staged at Bradford in December 1882, and later in Aberdeen, and in 1884 a number of performances were given at the Prince's Theatre in London. In the winter of 1887 to 1888 *Deacon Brodie* toured the United States with a company headed by Henley's younger brother Teddy, an untalented actor who tended to drink too much. Such is the history of the first play written by Stevenson and Henley. It should by rights have also been their last, but they harboured the unflinching conviction that a great fortune awaited them in the theatre, and that together they would revivify British drama. Read today *Deacon Brodie* seems artificial and insipid, and wholly lacking in dramatic fire.

[III]

Still convinced that *Deacon Brodie* was a good play, Stevenson and

Henley began drafting a successor, *Hester Noble*, which seems never to have been finished; the manuscript is lost, or was perhaps destroyed. They were also planning a farce, *Autolycus*. Stevenson's part in the composition of *Hester Noble* may well have ceased after he had received a stern letter about it from Fleeming Jenkin, the most outspoken of all Louis's older friends. Jenkin not only condemned *Hester* and Louis's emendations to Henley's text, but tried to dissuade Louis from attempting to write plays at all. 'I am so thoroughly convinced that while you can write admirable appreciative things ... this play business is an *ignis fatuus* — causing waste of brain and time ... I am not sure that Henley could not write a play but if so you are hindering him not helping him.' Louis may have taken Fleeming Jenkin's advice so far as completing *Hester* went, but, as we shall see, he returned to dramatic collaboration with Henley in 1884 and 1885, with very indifferent results. When Jenkin died prematurely in the latter year Louis lost his most vehement and affectionate critic.

Despite his jaded state Louis continued to work hard during the spring and early summer of 1879. After reading Professor Shairp's new *Life of Burns* that spring, Leslie Stephen asked Louis to do an article on that poet for the *Cornhill*. Already in 1875 Louis had been commissioned by the editors of the *Encyclopaedia Britannica* to contribute an article on Burns, but when it was done they had rejected it as too unorthodox and, indeed, heretical. Louis had a good deal to say about Burns as a man, most of it detrimental, and he accepted Stephen's offer with glee: 'Have written to Stephen saying briefly and candidly that nobody knew anything about Burns but me,' he explained in a note to Henley. The essay, *Some Aspects of Robert Burns*, which came out in the *Cornhill* in October 1879, is not a lenient piece, and certainly ran counter to the idolatry with which the poet was always treated in his native Scotland. 'This strong young ploughman, who feared no competitor with the flail, suffered like a fine lady from sleeplessness and vapours,' we read. Louis emphasizes Burns's squalid attitude towards women, beginning with Jean Armour, the mother of some of his bastards and whom he ultimately married. Burns is presented as perpetually desiring to be in love, grossly greedy for women and spending his life on an emotional voyage of discovery that had no end. Safely anchored by his own love for Fanny, Louis asserted that Burns's 'affections were often enough touched but never engaged', that he 'trifled with life' and paid the penalty of all Don Juans. Tracing what he termed Burns's 'downward course' to a demeaning death, Louis remarked that it was the fashion to say that the poet died of drink. Pointing out that many men have drunk more, and lived reputably to a good old age, Stevenson made a perspicacious comment: 'He died of being Robert Burns, and there is no levity in such a statement of the case; for shall we not, one and all, deserve a similar epitaph?' Writing to Edmund Gosse from Swanston Cottage in July 1879 he called Burns 'a very gay subject for study', and explained that he had made a chronological table of the poet's 'various lusts and loves', and that he had been 'comparatively speechless ever since'. He disliked to admit it, but he found in Robert Burns 'something of the vulgar, bagmanlike, professional seducer'. It is said that when, after Louis Stevenson's death, the idea of a monument to him in Edinburgh was being canvassed, the project was successfully opposed on the grounds that he had slandered Robert Burns. In the late winter of 1878, or the spring of 1879, Louis was also drafting an uncompleted and rather unattractive clutch of essays, entitled *Lay Morals*, which he put aside until he added to them in 1883. *Lay Morals* was post-humously published in the Edinburgh Edition, the first collected edition of his work.

During the spring and early summer of 1879 Louis Stevenson was understandably restless, spending time in London and in France, rather than in Edinburgh, as well as sullenly staying with his parents at the Shandon Hydropathic at Gairloch. This Gairloch sojourn was not a success: 'I think I never feel so lonely as when I am too much with my father and mother,' Louis wrote from the Shandon Hydropathic to Mrs Sitwell, 'and I am ashamed of the feeling, which makes matters worse ... F., in a letter which did me much good, sent you her love.'

In May, just after the publication of *Travels with a Donkey*, he was alone with George Meredith at Box Hill, renewing a literary friendship which he prized. They had met in March of the previous year, when Louis and his parents were lodging at the inn at Burford Bridge, a rustic green-shuttered hotel in which John Keats had finished writing *Endymion* in 1817. Meredith was living with his second wife at Flint Cottage, Box Hill, which had a little chalet for writing at the top of the steep garden.

It was probably the chance of meeting Meredith that made Louis Stevenson persuade his parents to make a rendezvous with him for a three-week stay at Burford Bridge. His publisher, Kegan Paul, had given him a letter of introduction to a newly married couple, the Jim Gordons, who lived in the vicinity and were close friends of George Meredith, then a handsome but not very well-preserved fifty. According to Gosse, Meredith was at first put off by Louis's extreme enthusiasm and 'a little bewildered at being taken by storm'. Mrs Gordon, however, remembered in later years how skilfully Stevenson exercised his power to draw Meredith out: 'They used to meet constantly in our garden,' she wrote. ' ... Their mutual liking was pleasant to see, yet I remember feeling somewhat surprised when he prophesied great things for Stevenson, and declared that some day we should all feel proud to have known him.' Louis harboured a genuine passion for Meredith's work, especially for *Harry Richmond* and *Richard Feverel*, and when *The Egoist*, on which Meredith was working when they met, was published, Louis read it six or seven times; the influence of Meredith's style is unhappily reflected in Louis's novella *Prince Otto* (1885). Once Meredith had got used to Stevenson's ebullience, and had managed to get him to listen instead of indulging in pyrotechnics, the older novelist became fond of his young disciple, referring to him as 'the dear fellow', as 'a brave spirit', and, remembering Shelley, as a 'pard-like spirit, beautiful and swift'. It seems to have been as a personality rather than as a writer that Meredith most appreciated Louis, although he wrote warmly about *An Inland Voyage*. When, on their second meeting in May 1879, Meredith read him some chapters from *The Egoist*, Louis excitedly exclaimed, 'Own up—you have drawn Sir Willoughby Patterne from *me*!' The older man replied, 'No, no, my dear fellow. I've taken him from all of us, but principally from myself.'

In a novel which he began after sending *The Egoist* to his publishers, Meredith did in fact start off on a portrait of Louis Stevenson, in the guise of 'Gower Woodseer'. This new novel, *The Amazing Marriage*, was left unfinished for fifteen years, by which time Meredith's style had become almost nonsensically elaborate, and the Woodseer of the later part of the book is not consistent with the Stevensonian youth we encounter at the beginning. Gower Woodseer, whose clothes are 'frowsty' and whose hands are noticeably dirty, is tramping through the German mountains on the way to Baden and Karlsruhe when he is discovered by the wayside with a sprained leg by the healthy heroine of the novel, Carinthia Kirby, and her brother Chillon Kirby. He is then taken up by the young millionaire Earl of Fleetwood. Woodseer is a thin and worn young man, given to 'precocious flashes' in conversation. He prefers tramping the world alone, and, like Louis himself, has a notebook in which to jot down his thoughts. To some of the people in *The Amazing Marriage* Gower Woodseer is a startling and original young philosopher, to others, who judge him only by his exterior, he is 'a dirty-fisted vagabond' and a 'nondescript'. As the novel becomes more and more enmeshed in the verbiage of Meredith's last style, any likeness to Louis Stevenson fades quite away, as Sidney Colvin has noted.

[IV]

During the summer of 1879 Louis's low spirits and his nervous state were a cause of anxiety to his London friends. Edmund Gosse, a feline personage but a devoted friend, whom Louis had met initially in 1870 on a boat tour of the Hebrides, and with whom, through Savile Club membership, he had since become intimate, protested at his Scots friend's devitalized state. 'How is it that thou art feeble?' he asked Louis in a letter of late July 1879. 'It is a paradox that you, the General Exhilarator, should feel depressed. I take you for my emblem of Life, and you talk of feeling lifeless. I am not in a fit state to bow down to your Scots passions. Out upon Burns for a fornicator.'

The source of Louis's depression was, of course, his worry about Fanny, whom he must by now have realized to be quite remarkably unpredictable. How would she feel when she saw her husband again, and was once more re-integrated into familiar Californian life? Whether she wrote many letters to Louis during their year of separation we do not know, since none of them have survived. Two members of her family, her sister Nellie, who married Adulfa Sanchez, a young Spanish saloon-keeper in Monterey, and her daughter Belle, who eloped with a young painter, Joe Strong, have left accounts of Fanny's life during the period between her return to the States and her divorce from Sam Osbourne. Nellie Sanchez published the biography of Fanny in 1920, and Belle Strong wrote her own reminiscences, *This Life I've Loved*, which came out in 1937. Both women are distinctly cagey about Fanny at this time, determined to obliterate the fact that she had been Louis Stevenson's mistress, and to make her separation from her husband and the ultimate divorce sound as smooth and as respectable as possible. A more independent witness is Samuel Osbourne's mother, who went to the Vandegrift homestead at Clayton, Indiana, to see Fanny and her children on their return from Europe. The elder Mrs Osbourne stayed several days at Clayton, and was 'mystified and grieved' to find that her daughter-in-law did not want to talk about her husband and 'didn't seem at *all* glad' at the thought of seeing him again – after the long separation.' Fanny's mother-in-law was too 'true-hearted' to suspect that some other man was involved. In their books Mrs Strong and Mrs Sanchez also concealed the state of Fanny's health after her return to America; she seems to have suffered the first of a series of breakdowns or mental collapses which reached their apogee many years later in Samoa when she became violent and had to be forcibly held down in her bed.

That what letters Fanny wrote to Louis during the months of separation must have been desperately odd seems to be shown by the fact that, in February 1879, Sidney Colvin bothers to comment on a 'sane' one. Writing to Edmund Gosse on February 6th, Colvin reported that Louis 'had been to pieces, and was together, or nearly together, again, when he went away yesterday week.' Fanny had written to him from the old Spanish capital of Monterey, in Southern California. 'He had got quite a sane letter from an intelligible address in Spanish California,' Colvin told Gosse, 'where, after wild storms, intercepted flights and the Lord knows what more, she was for the present quiet among old friends of her own, away from the enemy, but with access to the children. What next, who shall tell? Louis had eased his mind with a telegram, without, however, committing himself to anything. He won't go suddenly or without telling people. Which is as much as we can hope at present.' In October 1916, two years after Fanny's death, Colvin wrote to Louis's biographer Graham Balfour about the mistakes her family were making 'in trying to sugar and disguise the facts of Fanny's history and his and her early relations'. Mrs Sanchez had contributed an article about her sister to *Scribner's*, and Colvin thought that, while pleasant and harmless, it gave 'quite a false picture of that time of family scandal and tribulation and struggle at Monterey and San Francisco'.

Towards the close of July 1879, Louis Stevenson, vegetating at Swanston Cottage, received an urgent cable from Fanny Osbourne in Monterey. This message has not survived. Its contents have been a cause of much speculation, but it must have been some species of almost hysterical appeal. Louis at any rate took it in this sense, and secretly purchased a ticket for New York at the agents for the Anchor Steamship Line in Hanover Street, Edinburgh. Fearing opposition and certainly foreseeing a tempestuous scene, he did not tell his parents of the adventure upon which he was embarking. The Thomas Stevensons had expected Louis to go with them to a spa; 'Mr Stevenson is ordered to Gilsand to drink the water,' Mrs Stevenson wrote in her little diary, 'and we expect Louis to go with us, but he meets us at the train and tells us that he is called away on business—this is on the 30th of July and we hear that he has started for America.' The steamship ticket cost Louis eight guineas and was for the 'intermediate' class between first-class and the steerage. This entitled him to the use of a writing-table and to better food than in the steerage.

Down in London, Louis told his friends of his sudden plan, and possibly tried without success to borrow money from them. All of them were in adamantine opposition to his project and spoke of it as a 'mad plan'. Gosse called the expedition 'a mere freak' to his face, but nothing would dissuade Louis nor weaken his purpose. On August 7th Henley saw him off on the Glasgow train from St Pancras. He was soon at Greenock aboard the S.S. *Devonia*, which sailed down the Clyde on the seventh. Just before departure Louis sat down to write a note to his father, which he enclosed in a letter to Colvin to be forwarded. To Colvin he wrote that he had never been

> ... so much detached from life. I feel as if I cared for nobody, and as for myself I cannot believe fully in my own existence ... The weather is threatening; I have a strange, rather horrible, sense of the sea before me, and can see no further into the future. I can say honestly I have at this moment neither a regret, a hope, a fear or an inclination ... I never was in such a state. I have just made my will . God bless you all and keep you, is the prayer of the husk which once contained R.L.S.

To Baxter he also wrote from the *Devonia*, saying that he was in fair spirits but a little off his head and quite off food: 'I write this in a subterreanean smoking room, with a barmaid not far off also writing. I don't like it.' A further letter before he sailed was to Bob Stevenson, whom he told that Fanny seemed to be very ill and that he hoped 'to try to get her to do one of two things'. 'At least if I fail in my great purpose, I shall see some wild life in the West,' he explained. 'But I don't know yet if I have the courage to stick to life without it. Man, I was sick, sick, sick, of this last year.'

What Louis told his parents in the letter written to his father before the *Devonia* sailed, we do not know. For some strange reason he thought that his father would not feel with such 'vivacity' his son's pursuit of Mrs Osbourne to California and his determination to marry her: 'I went so completely out of my way, and his, to prepare him, that I did not imagine he could be taken unawares.' Whatever form this preparation took it had signally failed. To the Thomas Stevensons it must naturally have seemed that Louis had sneaked off to America in a cowardly and callous manner; in Edinburgh society they felt publicly humiliated and talked of leaving that city forever. Thomas Stevenson sent a desperate letter to Colvin, begging him 'for God's sake' to use his influence to secure Louis's return. 'Is it fair that we should be half-murdered by his conduct?' the distraught father wrote. 'I am unable to write more about this sinful, mad business ... I see nothing but destruction to himself as well as to all of us. I lay all this at the door of Herbert Spencer. Unsettling a man's faith is indeed a very serious matter.' Contradictorily enough, Louis's flight to California made him realize how fond he was of his father. 'Since I have gone away,' he wrote to Charles Baxter from Monterey in late September 1879, 'I have found out for the first time how much I love that man; he is dearer to me than all except F.' So far so good, but Louis seems never to have suspected that he was crucifying his parents by his lack of candour and his secretive, underhand flight.

[V]

The voyage to New York took ten days. Stevenson noticed how this comparatively brief period of time affected his fellow-passengers in the second cabin and the steerage: once out at sea they began to make friends with each other, for all, in Louis's words, now belonged 'to one small iron country of the deep'. He was at first surprised to find that the majority of the emigrants were not lusty venturesome youths but middle-aged, dilapidated paupers who were mild-mannered from adversity; yet all seemed cheerful and full of hope for their future in the United States and inclined to 'an innocent gaiety'. There were English, Irish, Scots, Germans, Scandinavians and one Russian. The Scots were the gloomiest, and confirmed Stevenson's belief that 'one thing, indeed, is not to be learned in Scotland, and that is the way to be happy'. He discovered the three main causes of emigration to be drink, idleness and incompetence. He himself was not idle, and sat each day at a desk, his ink bottle skidding about its surface as the *Devonia* pitched and rolled. In the teeth of many difficulties he completed the tale *The Story of a Lie*, which he had begun in Scotland in July, and likewise scrawled copious notes for a book on emigrant conditions. It was now, more than ever before, urgent for him to make money.

The Amateur Emigrant, which he completed in San Francisco, bored him to write, and was thought by Colvin and Henley to be inferior work. When about to be published in 1880 it was withdrawn at the request of his father, who told Louis that it was not only the worst thing he had done but 'altogether unworthy' of him. Henley called it 'feeble, stale and pretentious'. These criticisms do not seem fair to the book, which was abridged by Stevenson in Samoa in 1894, and only published after his death. Old Thomas Stevenson would have objected to *The Amateur Emigrant* as revealing to what straits his son had been reduced by voluntary poverty; Henley and Colvin were not prepared to agree that anything written by Louis in California could be good because they were anxious for his return and wished to prove that he wrote best in Great Britain. As a matter of fact, *The Amateur Emigrant* is executed in a vein of realism, quite new to Louis, which is very telling. In describing the steerage quarters, where he spent much of his time making friends and observing working-class conditions afloat, he was frank to a point which some of his Victorian readers and probably all of his friends found coarse. 'The stench was atrocious,' he writes of going down to the steerage, 'each respiration tasted in the throat like some horrible kind of cheese.' In another passage, to which Kegan Paul, the publisher, objected, Louis wrote, again of the steerage, 'all who here stewed together, in their own exhalations, were uncompromisingly unclean', while Colvin made him remove a passage stating of a fellow-passenger that 'he had been sick and his head was in his vomit'.

What his English friends refused to realize was that Louis Stevenson learned some brand-new facts about human nature during the voyage of the *Devonia* and his subsequent nightmare journey to the West aboard emigrant trains. He observed and investigated and made notes. Typically, he recorded the effect he himself had on his fellow-travellers, and discovered that because he had booked in the second cabin and wore shabby clothes, he was taken for an artisan. His education, his accent, his delicate white hands went for nothing and he was judged entirely by his outward circumstances. The ladies travelling in the first-class saloon never looked at him twice, and he was accustomed, he writes, to attention from ladies. Once before in his life ladies had ignored him, but that was when he had experimented by walking through the suburbs of London in a sleeve-waistcoat. 'In my normal circumstances,' he writes, 'it appeared every young lady must have paid me some tribute of a glance; and though I had often not detected it when it was given, I was well aware of its absence when it was withheld ... I wish someone would continue my experiment, and find out exactly at what stage of toilette a man becomes invisible to the well-regulated female eye.' We have already noticed how Louis Stevenson was much pre-occupied with his effect on others. The majority of the young gentlemen who were his male contemporaries would never have continued or even begun to make his experiment. They would have been more concerned with the effect of passing ladies on themselves.

When the officers of the ship had become used to Stevenson, they chaffed him about the assiduity with which he sat writing at his desk. The purser even offered him a fee to copy out the passenger list, since he felt that this evidently penurious young man was wasting his time scribbling. Louis's industry and his capacity for hard work under the most adverse conditions were seldom better exemplified than by his completion, on a bucking table aboard S.S. *Devonia*, of *The Story of a Lie*.

Dick Naseby, the hero of *The Story of a Lie*, is presented to us in the opening paragraph as 'a type-hunter among mankind' and has been pretty generally recognized as a self-portrait of Louis Stevenson himself. In the same way, the character of Dick's father, old Squire Naseby, has, with good reason, been taken for a portrait of Louis's own parent Thomas Stevenson. Whether Louis and his father had had another and so to speak final row in Heriot Row before Louis's escape to New York is unknown; but it is not unlikely, and it would explain the minute account of the uneasy relationship between Dick Naseby and the Squire. The latter is introduced as having 'the sturdy, untutored nature of the upper middle class. The universe seemed plain to him. "The thing's right" he would say, or "the thing's wrong"; and there was an end of it ... Apart from this, which made him an exacting companion, he was one of the most upright, hot-tempered old gentlemen in England.' In their frequent arguments, Dick always exaggerates his own point of view; and then apologizes to his father the next morning. Apart from this subsidiary interest, *The Story of a Lie* is an ingenious, workmanlike tale, which Colvin placed without difficulty with the *New Quarterly* and which was published in October of the year in which it was written. It apparently brought its author a greatly needed fifty pounds.

The *Devonia* reached New York on August 18th, 1879, in a persistent deluge of heavy rain. There Louis found ominous letters from California which determined him to push on west immediately. 'My news is bad,' he wrote to Henley, 'and I am wet to the skin. F. has inflammation of the brain and I am across the continent tonight.' This quixotic journey ruined Louis's health and almost cost him his life.

7

But Westward, Look, the Land is Bright

Louis Stevenson spent just one night in New York before setting off from Jersey City by the train for Pittsburgh on the evening of August 19th. At Pittsburgh and at Chicago he had to change trains, and again at Council Bluffs, the capital of Pottawattamie County, Iowa. He reached Oakland, California, before dawn on August 30th, crossed the bay to San Francisco by ferry and took the train to Salinas. Here he changed to the narrow-gauge line for the sleepy old town of Monterey, where Fanny Osbourne and her family were living.

The night in New York had been traumatic. He wrote to Henley that on the voyage he had lost a stone in weight and had 'got the itch ... — or at least an unparalleled skin irritation': he added, but deleted, 'very similar to syphilys [*sic*]'. He told Henley that on the ship he had been unable to eat: 'I could not eat and I could not sh– hush! the whole way: but I worked.' He spent the night in New York in a shilling rooming-house run by a friendly Irishman named Mitchell, but Louis had to sleep on the floor as the only bed in the room was occupied by a friend from the boat. In fact he spent the night sitting up naked but for his trousers, scratching himself from ten p.m. until seven the next morning. The washbasins and lavatories were across a rain-swept courtyard; the towels were crumpled and the pieces of wet soap were 'white and slippery like fish'. He used a feverish day creeping about in the rain to banks, post-offices, railway-offices, restaurants, publishers, booksellers and money-changers. He also consulted an apothecary who attributed the itch to a liver condition. He could no longer stop scratching — or as he called it 'flaying' — himself; it is possible that on the boat he had contracted that most maddening of all skin irritations, scabies — or it may have been eczema. By the end of the day his mackintosh was soaked through, and when he got back to Mitchell's Reunion House he stripped off all his soggy clothes and left them behind him, making a pool of water on the kitchen floor. During the day he had purchased the new, 1876, centenary edition of George Bancroft's *History of the United States*, which had been reduced from the original ten volumes to six stout tomes.

He set off for the ferry station at dusk, taking with him a small valise, a knapsack buckled to his shoulders, and the Bancroft history jammed into the pocket of his travelling-rug. There were four boat-loads of emigrants for the one train; they stampeded on to the Jersey Ferry and stampeded off it on the other shore. Children were trampled underfoot, luggage hurled about, and the whole operation involved 'downright misery and danger'. At Council Bluffs he waited outside Emigrant House with a hundred other travellers 'to be sorted and boxed for the journey'. They then boarded the train, which was chiefly made up of baggage-wagons with three cars for passengers — one for families, one for single men and one for the Chinese. The seats were wooden and so short you could not lie down at full length; the sleeping system was for an elderly railroad official to persuade two gentlemen to pair off together. Their seats were then turned to face each other, and two boards could be laid across them. The old man sold these boards and three straw cushions to each passenger for two dollars and a half. The stench in the cars, as they crossed the plains day after day, became unbearable, and Louis spent as much time as he could on the rear platform of the caboose, or precariously perched on the roof of a carriage. The train would make twenty-minute stops for meals; a 'newsboy' sold fruit, coffee and other commodities as he strolled along the cars.

Apart from the omnipresent itch, Louis was feeling very unwell on this nightmarish journey and, after Laramie, he became seriously weak and feverish, and could not sleep without laudanum (he had a small bottle with him). As it crossed the plains, and then plunged into the canyons of the Sierras, the train seemed to Louis 'the one piece of life in all the deadly land; it was the one actor, the one spectacle fit to be observed in this paralysis of man and nature'. Coming through Wyoming, he was even worse, and now his fellow emigrants began to jeer at him and make him physically as uncomfortable as they could. The majority of the emigrants were East-coast Americans, hoping to make a living in the West. Now the only

Europeans were some Cornish miners, a German family and Louis himself.

Louis was not only a sick man on the cars, but he had begun to lose his sense of identity. His lifelong anxiety as to what other people thought about him, perhaps in essence self-conscious and adolescent but none the less valid for that, had often made him feel that he only existed by his reflection in other people's eyes. Now, for the very first time in his life, he was totally adrift and unidentified. As the train chugged through Ohio he scribbled a note to Colvin in which he wrote that he had had no idea how easy it was to commit suicide: 'There seems nothing left of me. I died a while ago and know not who it is that is travelling.' He included in this letter a draft of a poem which was subsequently published. His ear had been caught by the name Susquehanna, a river which he had seen at sunrise — 'the beauty of the name seemed to be part and parcel of the beauty of the land ... That was the name, as no other could be, for that shining river and desirable valley.' While by no means his most brilliant poetic achievement, the opening verses indicate Louis's frame of mind on the emigrant train:

> Of where and how, I nothing know,
> And why I do not care,
> Enough if even so,
> My travelling eyes, my travelling mind can go
> By flood and field and hill, by wood and meadow fair,
> Beside the Susquehanna and along the Delaware.
>
> I think, I hope, I dream no more,
> The dreams of otherwhere,
> The cherished thoughts of yore;
> I have been changed from what I was before;
> Or breathed perchance too deep the lotus of the air,
> Beside the Susquehannah and along the Delaware.

In the same letter he told Colvin that American food was 'heavenly', and implied that he had no regrets. 'No man is of any use until he has dared everything; I feel just now as if I had and so might become a man ... I will not say die, and do not fear man nor fortune.'

A part of Louis Stevenson's account of the emigrant train journey, entitled *Across the Plains*, was first published in an abridged form in *Longman's Magazine* in 1883. In 1892 it was republished with the earlier part as a book, together with an abbreviated version of *The Amateur Emigrant*, called *From the Clyde to Sandy Hook*. They were again republished in the collected Edinburgh Edition of 1894. Old Thomas Stevenson, who had detested these two works and paid for them not to be printed, was long dead. As they now stand, the two sections of *The Amateur Emigrant*—one dealing with the Atlantic crossing, the other with the journey by train—are a great improvement on *The Inland Voyage* and *Travels with the Donkey*. *The Amateur Emigrant* is actual and arresting, yet not journalistic reportage. It presents the younger Louis at his very best—realistic, sensitive, aware and exceedingly humane.

Why did Thomas Stevenson, Henley and Colvin object to it so strongly? Colvin did admit that he found portions of *Across the Plains* humorous, but he agreed with the others that it was all inferior work, the publication of which could only do Louis harm. To my mind the answer to this conundrum is to be sought in the prejudices of middle-class high Victorian days. An outstanding feature of these accounts of rough travel is the exceptional lack of snobbery that the writer displays—his readiness to muck in with any of his working-class fellows on boat or train, his passionate and almost child-like interest in them, and his acceptance of them as his equals. In Edinburgh he had, it is true, haunted the howffs on the Water of Leith and had hobnobbed with thieves, prostitutes and beggars, but though all these accepted him readily they knew and he knew that he had the stately house in Heriot Row behind him, and that he could barricade himself into it at any time he liked. On the boat and on the trains he was without a shell, entirely on his own, with nothing but his kind, inquisitive, amiable nature to fall back upon.

To his father and to his London friends his easy tolerance of people of a lower order must have seemed embarrassing and anarchic. Only five years before, Anthony Trollope had profoundly shocked his public by producing, in *Lady Anna*, a novel with a heroine who is an earl's daughter but loves and marries a young journeyman tailor. Trollope had fully expected his readers to be affronted by an earlier novel, *The Vicar of Bullhampton*, which has as one of its central characters a little prostitute named Carry Brattle, but reviewers had surprised him by recommending that book as suitable family reading for young ladies. What was found inexcusable in *Lady Anna* in 1874 was the heresy that a journeyman tailor might be treated as the equal of an earl's daughter. In much the same way, I believe, Stevenson's parents, his cultivated London friends and even Henley himself must have found Louis's transatlantic exercise in egalitarianism unsympathetic and in questionable taste. This was probably what Henley meant when he termed the emigrant train passages 'pretentious'. Thomas Stevenson, in particular, would have resented Louis's strictures on the passengers from the first-class saloon of the *Devonia*, who treated the steerage families as if they were a menagerie, and made trips below decks to stare at them with a mocking smile on their lips. A basic and most admirable fact of Louis Stevenson's personality was that he was incapable of any form of snobbery. Fanny, with her over-developed sense of the ladylike and the gentlemanly, and her belief in her own precious descent from distinguished European settlers, harboured a very different point of view. Once her mind had grasped the amenities and the privileges of Heriot Row life, she put her memories of the classless, promiscuously jolly mining-camps in Nevada firmly behind her for good.

[II]

Fanny Osbourne was living in Monterey more or less by chance. On her return to the United States in the summer of 1878 she had spent some time with her mother, then newly widowed, in Indiana. When she finally went west she took with her not only Belle and Lloyd but her youngest sister Nellie, who was just a little older than Belle. Nellie was a pretty, studious girl, who read a great deal and wore her blonde hair in a plait down her back. In Monterey she fell in love with Adolfo Sanchez, a handsome and popular youth of old Spanish stock, reduced by circumstances to keeping one of the saloon-bars in the town. Nellie set herself to learning Spanish, and later married Sanchez. Their son was christened Louis. It was to this little boy that his godfather devoted one of the 'Envoys' of *A Child's Garden of Verses*:

> Now that you have spelt your lesson, lay it down and go and play,
> Seeking shells and seaweed on the sands of Monterey,
> Watching all the mighty whalebones, lying buried by the breeze,
> Tiny sandy-pipers, and the huge Pacific seas.

> And remember in your playing, as the sea-fog rolls to you,
> Long ere you could read it, how I told you what to do;
> And that while you thought of no one, nearly half a world away
> Some one thought of Louis on the beach of Monterey!

After Fanny's death Nellie Sanchez wrote the deliberately anodyne biography of her sister from which I have already quoted. Sidney Colvin thought the idea of such a book superfluous and misguided. 'In my view far too many people have tried already to make money out of Stevenson and his belongings,' he wrote to Graham Balfour in 1916, when he first heard of Mrs Sanchez's project.

On getting to San Francisco, Fanny and her sister, with Belle and Lloyd, had settled back into the flowery cottage in East Oakland. Belle was delighted to see her tall, golden-bearded father again, but has recorded that there was now a perceptible chill in her parents' relationship. After one of their rows, which was followed by a reconciliation, Fanny and Sam Osbourne told the family that they were going away alone together for a short time. In fact they went south to Monterey, but soon sent for Belle, Lloyd and Nellie Vandegrift to join them. Sam Osbourne, who was at the moment holding down a Government job in San Francisco, was again supporting his family. He came down to Monterey at weekends, but his children noticed that he and their mother spent hours arguing together behind closed doors. Belle later realized that their topic must have been divorce.

One morning Fanny looked at her son Lloyd, then a vigorous eleven, and murmured 'with a curious brightness in her eyes' that she had news for him: 'Lully's coming,' she announced. Louis Stevenson arrived next day and, according to Lloyd's evidence, was greeted with incoherent delight, laughter and tears. Even the small boy noticed how ill Louis was looking, with shining eyes in a thin white face, his clothes no longer picturesque but merely shabby, and hanging loosely on his emaciated body. 'There was about him', Lloyd wrote in retrospect and possibly with hindsight, 'an indescribable lessening of his alertness and self-confidence.'

Just as we do not know what was in the mysterious telegram from Fanny which triggered off Louis's visit to California, we have no idea of Fanny's reaction to Louis's sudden appearance in Monterey. It may have been awkward for many reasons: she was still seeing her husband, she had not divorced, she had had a nervous breakdown, and in early August she had been exasperated by her daughter Belle's sudden elopement with a penniless young San Francisco painter, Joe Strong, whom she secretly married. This union Belle's father Sam Osbourne appeared annoyingly to countenance, even arranging to take an apartment for the couple in the city. Fanny had invented the rather transparent fiction that Louis was simply 'a literary friend from Scotland' who had agreed to give lectures in America. 'I think it great nonsense and have written to tell him,' she told Rearden in a letter before Louis had embarked: ' ... He has a line that belongs to him alone and would be an idiot to leave it for money and flattery. Later on if he works and lives he will get both fame and money I am sure.' In another letter, however, in reply to one in which Rearden had mocked at Louis's precipitate arrival, she was more lenient: 'It is almost more than amusing to meet again the only person in the world who really cares anything for me.' Later again she wrote to Rearden that Louis was 'the only really wise person in the world'.

Louis's first interviews with Fanny, however incoherent and delightful her original greeting, seem to have been unsatisfactory and indecisive. It is not at all difficult to sympathize with Fanny in her quandary. Sam Osbourne might be a flighty husband who could not resist other women, but at least he had a position and a regular income. Louis had neither, seemed to have broken completely with his affluent parents and was now so delicate that he might quite likely die. Fanny, moreover, had her own son's future to think about. Her daughter would seem to have opposed the divorce; she only became attached to Louis towards the end of his life. The Vandegrift family in Indiana, firm Presbyterians, considered divorce scandalous and squalid and Sam Osbourne's relatives thought the same. To suggest, as it has been suggested, that Fanny was banking on the Stevenson parents forgiving Louis and welcoming her as a cherished daughter-in-law at Heriot Row, borders on the absurd; the risk would have been too great, and such calculations do not accord with all we know of Fanny's impetuous character and intense, wild loyalty to Louis. To her brother, Jacob Vandegrift jr., Louis Stevenson did write that if he died, he knew that his widow would be well cared for; but Fanny was not the woman to indulge in such hazardous and self-interested thinking. She was touched by Louis's devotion to her and she loved him, as she most amply proved in the difficult years to come. But at the moment at which he materialized amid the sands and cypresses of Monterey she was recovering from what seems to have been full-scale mental collapse, and must have been under very considerable strain.

Louis wrote to Baxter of having a broken heart, and to another friend that he had initially endured 'a week's misery' in Monterey. In his shattered state he decided to hire a horse and go camping in the pine and live-oak woods that shroud the hills behind Monterey. Here he fell desperately ill, lying for two days beneath a pine-tree in a stupor, unable to sleep for the noise of goat-bells and tree-frogs at night, and only dragging himself up to fetch water from a stream for his own coffee and for his horse. On the second day he was discovered by an old frontiersman and bear-hunter, who was over seventy and kept an Angora goat-ranch in the Coast Line Mountains. This old man took Louis to his ranch, where he and his colleague nursed the invalid for a fortnight. 'It was an odd, miserable piece of my life,' Louis wrote to Gosse, 'and according to all rule should have been my death.' The itch, that 'bitter, vile complaint', persisted; in Monterey it had alarmed landladies from whom this ragged and apparently moribund European had sought a room.

This illness was perhaps the lowest point that Louis had yet reached physically, and certainly the state of affairs in the Osbourne household was not designed to give him mental peace. He himself remained as single-minded and purposeful as ever, but in a letter from the goat-ranch, written lying down because he could not sit up, he told Colvin if only 'others' would be as persistent as himself, 'things would soon be straight'. When sufficiently recovered to return to Monterey, he was temporarily given shelter there in the local doctor's house, later moving to a small back room upstairs in an old adobe building known as Girardin's French House, which has been preserved and is now the Robert Louis Stevenson State Historical Museum.

The little town of Monterey has changed radically since Stevenson's day, when it was still predominantly Mexican in character and buildings like the present Stevenson Museum were not, as now, the exception but the rule. All through the town you can still sense what Louis called 'the haunting presence of the ocean' and hear the roar of the Pacific surf which he described as dwelling 'in the clean, empty rooms of Monterey as in a shell upon the chimney'. The smell of the sea, then as now, dominated the sunlit streets, together with the scent of cypress trees and pine resin. Up in the forests behind the township the trees are swathed in Spanish moss, which hangs from every branch. The surviving old adobe houses are made of unbaked brick, with very thick plastered walls. Louis liked to walk along the deserted beaches, where the bones of whales lay whitening in the sunshine; in the town the jawbone of a whale might be found like an inverted V framing a garden gate, while some thrifty people used the mammal's vertebrae to pave garden-paths and to replace the street sand or the wooden platforms outside shops. In Louis's day you could still distinguish fashionable townsfolk by the silver mountings on their saddles and by their jingling silver bridles and spurs. They would go at the gallop up and down the main street named after Cortez's lieutenant Alvarado, the street on which Girardin's lodging-house stands. The interior of this house, where the ailing Louis worked so hard at his writing, is cool and shadowy, protected from the heat by its strong, deep walls. Louis's own room gives on to an outer stairway of wood.

Once Louis Stevenson had come back to live in Monterey, he soon collected a small circle of intelligent though by no means intellectual friends. Chief of these was an old restaurant-keeper, Jules Simoneau, with whom he ate those meals he did not take at the doctor's or at Fanny's cottage. Simoneau had once been a well-off merchant at Nantes, but he had left France thirty-five years before; with him Louis would talk about French literature and play chess. Others who frequented Simoneau's cafe included Italian fishermen, Spaniards, and Mr Bronson, the editor of the local newspaper, *The Monterey Californian*. Louis's poverty soon became so evident to his new friends that a group of Simoneau's habitués secretly agreed to contribute two dollars a week to his upkeep. This was doled out to him by Bronson in return for a few articles which Louis believed the editor to be commissioning him to write as part of the staff of the *Californian*. Louis's expenses in Monterey amounted to under ten pounds a week, and at the end of September Baxter forwarded him a letter of credit for fifty pounds, from a small stock of money which had been left in the attorney's office. Louis's parents, from whom he heard nothing as he had only given them a general delivery address in New York, despatched twenty pounds but he received neither this money nor any letters from Heriot Row. He felt that his friends at home were treating him curtly for he received only six letters from them in the first three months of his Monterey exile. Every letter urged him to come home again, but he staunchly replied that he would not desert his wife—for so he regarded Fanny Osbourne, whose divorce was not yet an established fact.

At Girardin's French House Louis was hard at work, but he felt that he was getting on too slowly. He finished and despatched to London *The Pavilion on the Links*, and was now working simultaneously on *The Amateur Emigrant* and on a Californian novel to be called *A Vendetta in the West*. This *Vendetta* was never completed, and presumably Louis threw the manuscript away. On some date in October Fanny and her children, Louis approving, went back to their little house in Oakland on San Francisco Bay, and he was left alone at Monterey until December. Before they left Monterey, Louis took young Lloyd Osbourne for a walk, which, unlike their usual wanderings, proved swift and silent. Suddenly Louis told the boy that he was going to marry his mother: 'You may not like it, but I hope you will,' he remarked. Lloyd remembered that he was stricken too dumb to answer. Instead of speaking he slipped his hand into that of his future stepfather, and felt flooded by 'a rapturous sense of tenderness and contentment'. 'It was thus we returned, still silent, still hand in hand,' Lloyd wrote years afterwards, 'still giving each other little squeezes, and passed under the roses into the house.' Belle Strong, who favoured her father in the marital dispute, seems to have behaved with hostility towards Louis; he confessed to Colvin in the autumn that she had 'hurt' him – 'more hell with that young lady' was his comment.

In late October he assured Colvin that 'by or before the end of January there is some chance of *all being well in the fullest sense and the most legitimate.* Of course dealing with such cattle as I know of [referring to Samuel Osbourne, who may have been trying to screw money out of Louis by the divorce] there may be many a slip. But at least there is a piece of hope. The move hither has been blessed in every way.' To his friends in London the move cannot have sounded very blessed, if they judged by his letters. In December he was very ill with pleurisy, and heard from San Francisco that Fanny had nearly died. At the same moment a cable from Edinburgh summoned him home on account of his father's illness, a summons which Louis refused to obey: 'He would be better or dead before I got there anyway,' he wrote to Henley.

Except for his own health, and the uncertainty about the timing of Fanny's divorce, Louis was rather enjoying Monterey: 'This is a lovely place and I am growing to love it.' He found the lure of the woods compelling, and went for long lonely rambles, on one occasion light-heartedly setting alight some dry tree-moss to test whether it would start a forest fire, which it immediately did; Louis took to his heels in fear of being caught out and lynched. Having recovered from his attack of pleurisy he went ninety miles north to the brash new city of San Francisco, where he found a cheap lodging on Bush Street leased by a friendly Irish family named Carson. He wrote to Colvin in an undated letter of December that the divorce should take place in ten days: ' ... but then months must elapse. If we continue to be well treated we shall act back in kind.' He added that so far as his parents were concerned all looked 'dead and black'.

[III]

The six months that Louis spent in San Francisco, from his arrival up from Monterey in mid-December 1879, until his marriage and honeymoon in May 1880, are well documented by his letters to Colvin, Baxter and Gosse. Louis's habitual egotism makes these letters lively, if sometimes lugubrious. It is noticeable that, intent on chronicling his day-to-day life, his troubles about money, his ill-health and his own writing efforts, he asks for news of the recipients of his letters in a merely cursory manner. Like those from Samoa towards the end of his life, Louis's San Francisco letters are really elaborate bulletins on his frame of mind and wry reports on the impression he thinks he is making on his neighbours. While not precisely filled with self-pity, these epistles did not spare his friends the minutiae of his illnesses and of his enforced economies:

> Why do you write such letters to wring my heart? [Edmund Gosse inquired in late December 1879]: Here am I, who though determined that nothing signified to such an old party as me, as nearly as possible disgracing myself with crying over your letter just received. It is too bad of you … I cannot bear to think of you all alone in the midst of strangers, fretting and tiring yourself to pieces. Do come home …
>
> Are you really so bad, dear child? I try to persuade myself that it is only that you are lonely and out of spirits. You must not lose your pluck …
>
> Whether you live or die, you will live for ever in our hearts and in the roll of men of genius. Nothing that anyone can say or do can darken the bright name that you have made for yourself …

The theme of Louis's return was a fairly constant one in the letters from his English friends, who utterly failed to take the romantic view of his thraldom to Mrs Fanny Osbourne, and thought he was wilfully endangering his health, living in a state of quite artificial penury, and, worst blow of all, not writing as well as he had used to do. Louis did not at all care for these minatory letters. 'I was a little morbid a month or two ago, being far from well,' Louis confided to Charles Baxter, from Bush Street, in February 1880, 'and in receipt of a correspondence that would have taken the starch out of Mark Tapley. People rolled letters on to me like boulders, and then ran away and pelted me with notes like road metal. I feared to open an envelope.'

'You may expect that Louis will resent our criticism of his last three works,' Henley wrote to Colvin in February 1880, ' … but I think it right that he should get them … Monterey will never produce anything worth a damn.' Henley also wrote that he did not believe that their protests would divert him from marrying Fanny: 'He has gone too far to retract; he has acted and gushed and excited himself too nearly into the heroic spirit to be asked to forbear his point.' These views held by his English intimates—and, what is more, expressed in writing—can only have increased Louis's sense of loneliness in San Francisco. He spent Christmas Day forlorn and on his own, since Fanny, who customarily crossed the bay to dine with him at some little bistro twice a week, was engaged on seasonal festivities with the Osbourne family.

That Christmas of 1879 was for Louis a singularly gloomy one. Writing to Colvin on Boxing Day he told him that for four days he had spoken to no one but his landlady or landlord or to waiters in restaurants. He told him that Fanny was now divorced, but that Sam Osbourne had lost his Government appointment and could no longer support her and the children. This meant that Louis had at once to dream up enough money to keep two establishments—his own little room on Bush Street and Fanny's cottage in East Oakland. He was finding the second portion of *The Amateur Emigrant* uphill work, and declared to Colvin that he himself was 'made to be generous, and good, and an egoist, and a damned idler, and a very indifferent literary gemman'. Although the divorce by mutual consent was smoothly over, Louis's spirits were at a very low ebb.

Moved by Louis's account of his own penury, Colvin wrote offering to lend him money. Louis replied that Colvin had quite misunderstood. 'This is a test,' he explained. 'I must support myself, at what rate I have still to see.' In the same letter, which is as usual undated, but was postmarked January 18th, 1880, Louis described his daily routine. Between eight and half past nine in the morning 'a slender gentleman in an ulster, with a volume buttoned in the breast of it' could be observed leaving 608 Bush Street, 'and descending Powell with an active step'. His goal was a branch of the Original Pine Street Coffee House, where he had a cup of coffee and ate a meagre roll-and-butter breakfast for ten cents. Half an hour later, back in his room, he was to be seen by the inhabitants of Bush Street splitting kindling wood with a hatchet and breaking coal on the windowsill of his room. This was followed by three to four hours writing.

For lunch Louis went to Donadieu's Restaurant, where he indulged in 'a copious meal, half a bottle of wine, coffee and brandy' which cost fifty cents; the wine was served in a full bottle and he had had to learn to measure out exactly half of this into his successive glasses. During luncheon he read. He would then go for a walk in any direction, but sometimes straight to the 'debarkadery' of the Oakland ferry for a tryst with Fanny Osbourne. At half past four he would be back in his 'den' on Bush Street, light the lamp and work or write letters. About six o'clock he went back to the coffee-house for another cup of coffee and a roll, home to work and then at eleven or half past eleven to bed.

'The mere contemplation of a life so vile is more than enough for a professing Christian,' Louis remarks. Such accounts of his daily routine can only have exasperated Colvin and the other fond friends at home who thought the whole Californian adventure futile and wrong-headed. What Mrs Osbourne herself felt about Louis's sacrifices is unknown. Flattering it must have been to find oneself the object of so selfless a passion, but it may well have been frightening, too. Fanny herself had been ill again, and had discovered that not only did her former husband not intend to give her back the money she had brought him on her marriage, but that her own lots of land in Oakland were held by him *pro indiviso*. 'That is one of the drawbacks of being a fool; and we are a pair, real bad ones,' Louis assured Sidney Colvin. In another letter he sent a better report on Fanny's health, saying that she had got back to painting and was working herself 'dead tired every day with huge moral advantage'. In most of Louis's letters at this time he voices a stoical determination to go it alone: 'My concern is to see how I can do best *for myself*; I have taken my own way and I mean to try my best to walk it.'

The divorce was recorded on December 18th, 1879, but the marriage to Louis Stevenson still held fire. Fanny's sister back in Indiana had herself now developed some species of mental illness, and so far she and their widowed mother had not been told of the fact of the divorce, and certainly not of an imminent remarriage. Even at this late stage Sidney Colvin had advised against marriage. His attitude irritated Louis, who wrote back that Colvin's remarks left him 'in wonder': 'I marry her certainly. What else should I do? Do I not want to have all rights to protect my darling? Perhaps you think there has been some scandal here; none. We have to be darkly circumspect, I can tell you. But indeed I don't understand you about that; p'haps I'm stupid.' Yet however much he might determine to be so, Louis was no longer master of his fate, for his body refused to forgive him the emigrant train, the subsequent illness in Monterey and the self-neglect and semi-starvation in San Francisco. It was at this time that he first drafted the *Requiem*, and sent it with his own epitaph to London.

In the very early spring of 1880 his landlady's younger boy, Robbie, who was four years old, nearly died of pneumonia. Characteristically, Louis gave up his own work to help nurse the child, who recovered; but the strain had been such that Louis fell ill and seemed to be dying himself. A doctor finally diagnosed malaria. To be able to nurse him properly, Fanny now took him across the ferry to a hotel in Oakland. The hotel turning out to be too expensive, Louis was moved into the Oakland cottage, with his future sister-in-law Nellie as chaperone. Louis had once described Nellie as 'conscientiously selfish' and seems to have used her as a prototype for his character of Arizona Breckenridge, the heroine of the abortive Western novel, *A Vendetta in the West*. It was here at Oakland that a real danger-signal most ominously flashed—Louis had his first haemorrhage from the lungs.

In San Francisco Louis had been almost expecting consumption. After his first bout of illness there he had written to Gosse that 'it was not consumption this time, though consumption it has to be some time, as all my kind friends sing to me, day in, day out. Consumption! how I hate that word; yet it can sound innocent, as, e.g. consumption of military stores.' After this first haemorrhage Louis Stevenson lived for the rest of his life under the threat of recurrence, a threat in fact of sudden death. In his exhaustive and reliable book on Stevenson, *Voyage to Windward* (1952), Mr J. C. Furnas has explored the question of whether Louis was genuinely tubercular or suffered from some other ailment of which lung haemorrhage might be a symptom. It is at any rate known that Louis's premature death in Samoa was not due to tuberculosis but to haemorrhage of the brain. 'In 1880,' writes Mr Furnas, 'modern means of exact diagnosis of tuberculosis did not exist, but the tragic series of haemorrhages that began in Oakland leave small room for reasonable doubt.' Doctors in San Francisco, Edinburgh, Davos and at Saranac Lake were in agreement that Louis was consumptive, though Dr Trudeau, the world-renowned specialist at Saranac, said after Stevenson's death that his case had been an arrested one. At all events, after the Oakland bleeding, Louis had to live his life as if he were tubercular, greatly aided by Fanny, who combined a morbid interest in illness for its own sake with a pronounced gift for nursing it. She had developed a private theory that colds were caused by germs and were therefore contagious, and later made herself unpopular with such friends as Henley by trying to protect Louis from contagion and from exhaustion brought on by over-excitement and late nights. Hers was now a future from which many women would have flinched, but she had decided to take Louis on for life; and did so.

In April 1880 Thomas Stevenson, who had by now been persuaded to approve a marriage he could in no wise prevent, cabled to Louis that he could rely on an allowance of two hundred and fifty pounds a year. The old man had always been well known for his liberal views on divorce, and his obsessional belief that an unhappy wife was invariably in the right. He and his own wife had probably objected to Louis's marriage for other reasons—the difference in age between the couple, and the fact that Mrs Osbourne was an American and a stranger and had obviously been Louis's mistress in France. They resented Louis's secret departure to New York bitterly, and suffered from it both publicly and privately. Perhaps justifiably, Louis's mother wrote to him two months before the marriage:

> We cannot understand why you have never attended to our request for information as to your plans. I must repeat again what we have said over and over before that *we can tell nothing because we know nothing.* We do not even know the names of any of your friends in San Francisco. So for any favour give us a story to tell ... You have behaved like a fool ever since you left us, running risks which you were not fit for and you have surprised and disappointed me much for I had thought you had learned to take care of yourself.

At the Oakland cottage, Louis was recovering from his grave attack. To Baxter he wrote that, owing to it, they had nearly been married already, and to another friend, a year later, he called the actual union 'a sort of marriage *in extremis*'. 'If I am where I am,' he wrote in this letter to P. G. Hamerton from Pitlochry in July 1881, 'it is thanks to the care of that lady who married me when I was a mere complication of cough and bones, much fitter for an emblem of mortality than a bridegroom.'

[IV]

Fanny Osbourne's sister Nellie has recorded how gay and youthful Louis Stevenson seemed at the Oakland cottage, no matter how ill he might be feeling. He read aloud to the others, sometimes in English, sometimes in French, of which he did an impromptu translation as he went. Louis also dictated the beginnings of his tale *Prince Otto* to Nellie. He had always showed a great admiration for the practical gifts of American women, and now would watch Fanny and her sister cutting out from patterns and then making up new dresses. One night, when they all had new clothes, Louis suggested a celebration, and they spent the evening in San Francisco seeing a performance of *The Pirates of Penzance*. Louis, who had been suffering intermittently from toothache due to rotten teeth, could now afford to have these replaced by a San Francisco dentist. Spring was in full bloom in the Oakland garden. A date was chosen for the wedding ceremony: May 19th. Nellie, in her *Life* of her sister, asserts that Fanny 'took this step in the almost certain conviction that in a few months at least she would be a widow' and that the most she hoped for was to make Louis's last days happy and comfortable. Too much notice need not, I think, be taken of this statement, for Nellie Sanchez's whole aim in her book was to present Fanny as a heroine and an angel of unselfishness. We may assume that Fanny married Louis because she loved him.

For superstitious reasons, or because of Fanny's strong sense of etiquette, Louis returned to San Francisco before the marriage. On that spring day Fanny Osbourne took the ferry across the Bay alone, without Nellie or Lloyd. At the landing stage she was met by Louis and their friend, the painter Mrs Virgil Williams. They proceeded to the house of a Scots Presbyterian minister, the Reverend W. A. Scott, who was the patriotic President of the San Francisco St Andrews Society. Fanny recalled that there was no one else present beyond herself and Louis, the minister and the two witnesses – the minister's wife and Mrs Williams. There was also present, Fanny mentions, 'a *cat* that had followed Mrs Scott into the room, no other living creature was there'. After the brief wedding service, Mr and Mrs Robert Louis Stevenson took Dora Williams to dine with them at the Viennese Bakery, 'a good restaurant in those days'. From the Bakery the married couple went to stay for two nights at the Palace Hotel, seeing no one they knew but Mrs Williams. Nellie Vandegrift then brought Lloyd over from Oakland, together with a dog named Chu Chu. Fanny, Louis and the dog set off for the Napa Valley, where they had planned to spend the strange romantic honeymoon later immortalized by Louis in *The Silverado Squatters*. Once again he was offering the reading public a share in his private experience.

On the advice of their friends the Virgil Williamses, who had a small ranch thereabouts, Louis and Fanny had decided to go first to Calistoga, a new small spa-township lying in the exquisite vineyard country of the Napa Valley, which is dominated by rugged heights of Mount St Helena. In spite of old Thomas Stevenson's generosity – 'my people as good as gold,' Louis wrote to Mrs Sitwell during the honeymoon – money remained a sharp problem for the newly married couple. They had been led to believe that they could find empty old houses in the Calistoga neighbourhood, dwellings left over from former silver-mining activities. After some initial disappointments they found what they were looking for at the old Silverado mine, high up on the flanks of Mount St Helena with a view over the Napa Valley to the distant sea. Silverado had at one time been a thriving community, with shops, hotels and many miners' houses; when the silver shaft was worked out, the miners and the townsfolk had moved on in true Californian fashion. Most of the houses had moved on too, being dismantled and trundled down into the foothills of the mountain. All that was left marooned at Silverado was a three-storied wooden structure, full of rubbish such as old mining boots, and situated on a natural platform at the mouth of the deserted silver-mine with rails and an abandoned truck beside it. Today the view from the site of this house is much obscured by tall trees; in the Stevensons' day these were only five or six feet high — madrona, manzanita, buckeye, maple and firs. The old redwood forest had long been destroyed to provide timber for houses and fencing. It was a place haunted by the rustling sound of rattlesnakes, and by the cries of a few birds.

The Silverado shack, which had no windows left, and let in sunlight and moonlight through the chinks of its planks, would not have seemed to many people an ideal site for a honeymoon. It suited Louis and Fanny perfectly — the resinous air was a great change from the fogs of San Francisco, the isolation was delightful, and the circumstances almost accorded with Louis's longing, expressed in *Travels with a Donkey*, to camp out of doors with the woman he loved. After the first six days at Silverado Fanny and her son, who had by this time joined them, caught mild diphtheria, and the whole party was forced to withdraw to Calistoga to get the services of a doctor. Fanny had also smashed her thumb carpentering and was suffering from sleeplessness.

After these first setbacks, the little party, which was at times joined by Nellie Vandegrift or by Belle and Joe Strong, passed two thoroughly happy months, which the pages of *The Silverado Squatters* recapture. It was at Silverado that the resourceful Fanny really came into her own, fitting calico windows into the broken window-frames, making doors with leather hinges (strips cut from old mining boots), cooking, organizing the supply of water from the well and the collection of firewood for the stove. She refused to let Louis work, made him take sunbaths and rubbed his body with oil twice a day.

By a paradox this marriage, which had seemed to his family and friends so wayward as to be almost demented, provided Louis with exactly the careful and efficient nurse and devoted companion he required and had hitherto lacked. He himself was completely impractical, being what the Scots then called 'a handless man'; Fanny's bent, developed by her varied experience of life in Nevada and elsewhere, was for making a home in unexpected places, and for looking after other people. As so often in the fourteen years to come, she salvaged Louis's health and gave him instinctive protection against the world and, most important of all, against himself. 'As to my dear boy's appearance, he improves every day in the most wonderful way,' Fanny wrote from Silverado in July, in her first letter to her mother-in-law. '... Taking care of Louis is, as you must know, very like angling for shy trout; one must understand when to pay out the line, and exercise the greatest caution in drawing him in.' The San Francisco doctor, she told Mrs Stevenson, had declared that her nursing had saved Louis's life, but she could not quite concur in this opinion herself. She believed that, in San Francisco, Louis's soul had been purified by 'the atmosphere of the Valley of the Shadow' and that his parents would now take more comfort in their son than ever they had done before. In point of fact, as we have seen, Louis had never been a comfort to his parents at all.

Fanny's first letter to her mother-in-law is candid, disarming and clever. It was not at all an easy letter to write, and Fanny must have been acutely aware of her parents-in-law's doubts about her. 'You know it is all very much against the grain with me,' Mrs Thomas Stevenson had written to her son in April of that year, 'and I cannot attempt to do more than make the best of it to the public. You know that you have my best wishes and most earnest prayers for your happiness in all circumstances and if you have God's blessing all will be well.' Fanny went so far as to confide in her mother-in-law her own exasperation at the way Louis's London friends had kept writing him carping letters when he was in reality desperately ill. She also warned Mr and Mrs Thomas Stevenson not to be deluded by her photograph, which had been sent them. She wrote that photographs always flattered her, and explained that Louis believed her to be the most beautiful creature in the world, but that was because he loved her and so it made her very glad. 'Louis is, as I know, a mother's boy,' she added, 'and I am sure he looks like you.'

She also explained that unfortunately she herself was no more businesslike than Louis. She referred to her husband as a genius and earnestly hoped that his parents would like her. It was an altogether reassuring letter and spoke of their return to Europe in the near future. Further reassurance came from an Edinburgh friend of Maggie Stevenson's who told her that she had heard from San

Francisco that the new daughter-in-law was 'pretty and clever and nice and good'. Louis's mother took Fanny's photograph out to dinner-parties with her to show to guests. 'I hope you both understand that I don't care for ancient history at all—I know nothing about it,' she wrote prudently to Louis in late June. Towards the end of July 1880, the Robert Louis Stevensons, together with Lloyd Osbourne, left the Napa Valley; on August 7th they sailed from New York for Liverpool.

Although Louis Stevenson and his wife never did return to Mount St Helena or the Napa Valley, their presence there can no longer be forgotten. In the little town of St Helena, among all the vineyards, and where I have myself spent halcyon days, there is now the Silverado Museum, meticulously kept, and devoted to letters, manuscripts and first editions of Robert Louis Stevenson, as well as to family portrait-crayons that were once at 17 Heriot Row, a painting by Fanny of the bridge at Grez-sur-Loing, Samoan scenes by Fanny's son-in-law Joe Strong, and many other relevant items. From St Helena you can drive into the foothills of the mountain of the same name, and then take a steep path up to the mouth of the mine where the honeymoon shack once stood. This is a silent and evocative place of intense natural beauty, and here it is easy to picture the Stevensons on their unconventional honeymoon. It is quiet and wild and solitary, and they seem to haunt it still.

8

A Wolverine on the Shoulders

ON August 17th, 1880, the Robert Louis Stevensons and little Lloyd Osbourne reached Liverpool. To Louis's surprise, Sidney Colvin had the previous night taken a sudden decision to meet his friends at Liverpool, had caught the night mail, and now boarded the liner from the harbour tug. He later told Henley that, on re-flection, he might not have travelled to Liverpool had he known that the Thomas Stevensons—'the old folks', as he called them—were coming down from Edinburgh to welcome their son and his new family. Louis's parents did not venture to the quayside, but remained in their hotel. Colvin reported that Louis was looking better than he had expected, and that his face was much improved by his new teeth. He seemed, however, weak and 'easily fluttered ... and so small you never saw, you could put your thumb and finger round his thigh'. Colvin stayed to lunch with the Stevenson contingent and found that when he was later talking alone to Louis in the smoking-room it was 'quite exactly like old times'. About Fanny, whom we may remember he had already known in London, Colvin expressed reservations, although he found Louis peaceful and happy in his newly married state. ' ... Whether you and I will ever get reconciled to the little determined brown face and white teeth and grizzling (for that's what it's up to) grizzling hair which we are to see beside him in future—that is another matter,' he wrote to Henley. Colvin thought, looking at Fanny and her mother-in-law, that the elder Mrs Stevenson seemed 'the fresher of the two'.

The first luncheon seems to have gone off well. Mrs Thomas Stevenson noted in her diary that she had found Fanny certainly very amusing. It was arranged that, after a brief stay in Heriot Row, the whole family, including Lloyd, were to settle for some weeks at the Ben Wyvis Hotel at Strathpeffer, far up in the Highlands.

Louis's mother wrote that they had chosen Strathpeffer so that her son 'might have more mountain air'. Both Louis and Fanny were by now tired of travelling, but Louis at any rate disliked both Strathpeffer itself and the guests at the hotel. 'This is a beastlyish place, near delightful places, but inhabited alas! by a wholly bestial crowd,' he explained in a letter to Charles Baxter. In this same letter he included doggerel verses *On Some Ghastly Companions at a Spa*. These lines begin:

> That was an evil day when I
> To Strathpeffer drew anigh,
> For I found no human soul,
> But Ogres occupied the whole.

> They had at first a human air
> In coats and flannel underwear.
> They rose and walked upon their feet,
> And filled their bellies full of meat.
> They wiped their lips when they had done—
> But they were ogres every one:

Fanny found the Highlands beautiful but cold, yet she was warmed by the attitude of her parents-in-law to herself and to her son: 'They are the best and noblest people in the world, both of them,' she wrote to Belle, 'and I can hardly write about them without tears in my eyes. Every day, almost, I come upon fresh proofs of their thought for our comfort or pleasure.' We have already seen how well old Thomas Stevenson got on with his new daughter-in-law; she was soon addressing him as 'Master Tommy' and he would call her 'the Vandegrifter' or, when she was in her most pessimistic mood, 'Cassandra'.

More unpredictably, perhaps, Fanny also became genuinely fond of her mother-in-law. Writing to Dora Williams from Strathpeffer she analysed Maggie Stevenson as 'a much more complex creature' than her husband—'much more like Louis'. She observed that Mrs Stevenson senior was 'adored by her husband' who spoiled her like a baby, and that both parents had evidently combined to spoil Louis. The régime the elder Stevensons imposed on their son and daughter-in-law was the very reverse of bohemian. 'Louis has to be brushed every morning, which is a great cross to him,' Fanny told Mrs Virgil Williams, 'and I have to dress properly and wear fallals and things, which is something of a cross to me, though not so much.' In another missive to Dora Williams, written some months later, Fanny asserted that she was never allowed to do 'any useful work'.

She was constrained to painting a dessert service for her mother-in-law's mission bazaar and to doing 'some high art embroidery ... A change from old times, that, is it not? A maid darns my stockings while I do high art embroidery in a silk gown. Well, there's nothing like a change, especially a change for the better.' To Belle Strong her mother wrote that she felt guilty that she and Lloyd were taking so much from the old Stevensons, and were unable to give them anything in return. 'Aunt Maggie', as Fanny soon began to call her mother-in-law, had opened up her wardrobes in Heriot Row and had showered presents of silks and sealskins on her son's wife.

Fanny was by nature adaptable, and soon fitted into staid Edinburgh living. She was at first amazed at the plumbing—or rather the lack of it—in 17 Heriot Row. Some years afterwards she confessed to her mother-in-law that she had not been able to lift the heavy ewers with which every bedroom was equipped, and had supposed that Heriot Row lacked wash-basins and running water because her parents-in-law could not afford such normal transatlantic comforts. She also began by having misunderstandings with the Heriot Row staff. A housemaid told her that she spoke English very well for a foreigner, while two others judged, from her swarthy complexion that 'Mr Louis' had 'merrit a black woman'. But by and large, Fanny's own good nature and her desire to please seem to have made a potentially awkward situation an easy one. Nor should we overlook the great and kindly efforts of Louis's parents to accept his marriage as an accomplished fact which would never have been of their own choosing. Nor, again, that the peace and comfort of Heriot Row, and even the boredom of the spa hotel at Strathpeffer, must have proved for Fanny a very welcome change from the neurotic wrangles with her former husband at Oakland and in Monterey. For Louis, too, who had staked everything on a desperate gamble, there was the vital satisfaction of having achieved, against all odds, his heart's desire.

With the beginning of the autumn, the Stevensons left the ogres of the Ben Wyvis Hotel and retreated to Edinburgh, but, for his health's sake, Louis did not dare to face a winter in that cold and windy city. He and Fanny toyed with the idea of going to Menton, but on the advice of Louis's uncle, Dr George Balfour, they finally decided to try Davos in the Swiss Alps. Dr Balfour, who approved of Louis's choice of a wife, and referred to Fanny as 'a besom'—Scots for a broom or bundle of twigs—was an up-to-date physician, and he had heard excellent reports of Davos as the new Mecca for consumptives, and of Dr Ruedi, who had a tubercular sanatorium there. The overall plan was that the Robert Louis Stevensons and Lloyd should travel slowly through France, but they began this peaceful project by a heady week in London, where they overspent entertaining Louis's friends at the Grosvenor Hotel. This week was really Fanny's first complete confrontation with Louis's London friends; her reaction to them was one of immediate disapproval since she thought that they dissipated Louis's strength and endangered his health. She wrote to her mother-in-law about these metropolitan jinks:

' ... we leave London tomorrow and glad enough I shall be to get away ... For no one in the world will I stop in London another hour after the time set ... Louis knows far too many people to get a moment's rest ... Company comes in at all hours from early morning till late at night, so that I almost never have a moment alone, and if we do not soon get away from London I shall become an embittered woman ... '

She complained that she was 'all the time furtively watching the clock and thirsting for their blood because they stay so late'. Thus was set up a pattern of disapprobation on the part of his wife, which, in after years, Louis's intimate friends began to resent. As Fanny grew older she became more and more possessive and protective. There was clearly an element of jealousy in her attitude and it goes far to explain her happiness once she had got Louis, so to speak, stranded with herself on a tropical island in the South Sea.

[II]

'Davos in 1881,' Lloyd Osbourne wrote in one of his prefaces to Stevenson's collected works, 'was a small straggling town where nearly all the shops were kept by consumptives. It possessed a charity sanatorium and three large hotels, widely separated from one another, in which one died quite comfortably. It was the "new Alpine cure for tuberculosis".' Davos is high up, with resinous pine-woods and brilliant winter sunshine. For five months of the year it is under snow: 'Snow, snow, snow,' wrote Lloyd. 'Icicled trees; a frozen little river; a sense of glinting and sparkling desolation.' The hotels were mainly filled with English guests, many of whom were dying; but the life they led was gay and hectic, and the dead were deftly and unobtrusively removed to the cemetery.

Louis did not enjoy this first of the two winters he was compelled to spend in Davos. He soon found, as others have found and do find, that a Swiss mountain valley has what he called 'a certain prison-like effect on the imagination'. The glittering snow-covered mountains began to seem to him a trap. He did not care for the English people in the hotels, his room was too small for real work, he lacked all incentive for writing, was weak and ill and very, very bored. His stepson noted the first Davos period as the only one in Stevenson's life in which he had seen him display mental inertia. At a thoroughly loose end he now began to depend on Lloyd for amusement, joining in battles with the boy's tin soldiers and writing little booklets for Lloyd's miniature printing-press.

It was in these vacuous winter months that Louis exerted an ever-increasing influence on his eleven-year-old ward, whom he came almost to regard as his own son. It was his firmly held theory that a boy of Lloyd's age should read anything he wanted to read, and further he hoped that Lloyd would overhear remarks which some English people then thought unsuitable for children. To an interfering Englishman who remonstrated with him over the way he was bringing Lloyd up, Louis replied that 'a child should early gain some perception of what the world is really like—its baseness, its treacheries, its thinly veneered brutalities'. He added that he had no patience 'with this fairy-tale training that makes ignorance a virtue', that he had himself been reared on this false principle and that it had cost him 'bitter misery'.

The Stevensons had with them in the Davos hotel another personage besides Lloyd. This addition to their party, whom they all came to regard as a fourth member of the family, was a very small, pretty and intelligent Skye terrier which Louis, who wrote about him two years later in an essay called *The Character of Dogs*, describes as 'as black as a hat, with a wet bramble for a nose and two cairngorms for eyes'. He had been given to Fanny in Edinburgh by Sir Walter Simpson, and was at first called 'Wattie', then 'Watty Woggs', and, finally, 'Bogue'. About the same time as the gift of Woggs, Walter Simpson's sister Eve had presented Fanny with a Manx cat. I have already quoted from the spiteful books which Eve Simpson wrote after Louis Stevenson's death about his Edinburgh life, and it is more than probable that she had hoped to marry Louis herself. He had even thought of proposing to her at some remote time in his youth: ' ... when I remember,' he wrote to Baxter from Samoa in 1892, 'that I once seriously dreamed of marrying that underhand virago my heart wells over with gratitude'. The gift to Fanny of the young cat may have been well intentioned, but it was not a success, as 'Manxy' was by no means house-trained, was so delicate that she had to be fed wholly on milk, and was left behind in London when Fanny, Louis, Lloyd and Woggs set off for Davos.

The Skye terrier seems also to have been indifferently trained at first, and made messes all over French hotels. 'The dog has bogged more upon this hostile soil,' Louis wrote from Troyes, 'with a preference for hostile carpets, than could be believed of a creature so inconsiderable in proportion ... Yet we all adore that dog.' Initially the dog was Fanny's special favourite, but soon they all three grew to dote on him equally and to adjust themselves to his intricate and neurotic character. He was subject to alarming fits, in which he lay as though dead; a doctor in Davos pronounced him too excitable and put him on bromide at night.

Once, when Fanny was watching some tobogganing in which Louis was taking part, the little dog on her knee gave what she described as a human cry on seeing Louis going down the slope. It buried its head in Fanny's shawl and would only occasionally peer out to see if Louis had or had not had an accident. Fanny returned to the hotel, carrying in her arms the dog, which was trembling too much to walk, and which seemed likely to have another fit—it had already had two of these. It lay insensible in her lap until Louis had reappeared safe and sound. 'Wasn't that an intelligent Woggs?' Fanny inquired of her father-in-law in a letter reporting the incident: ' ... Woggs is not a good Woggs; he is ill-tempered and obstinate, and rather sly, but he is most loveable and intelligent, I am afraid it is with dogs as with people; it is not for their being good alone that we are fond of them.'

Woggs—or rather Bogue—was a fighting dog, and often turned into a biting one as well, until he died as the result of a fight in Bournemouth six years after his first experiences at Davos. Bogue bit Colvin and then once bit Fanny. He was never a particularly healthy dog and suffered agonies from ear-canker. But, such as he was, he seems to have fitted well into the highly strung and peripatetic family he had involuntarily joined in Edinburgh in 1880. It seems improbable that a dog like the wise and ponderous though affectionate Coolin, another Skye terrier which was the joy of old Thomas Stevenson's life at Heriot Row, would have suited either Louis or Fanny at all.

Although Louis, in the six long months of their stay there, grew very tired of Davos, he could not deny being gradually affected by that species of artificial exhilaration that a sojourn in the Alps inevitably produces. He would set off for a walk with Woggs in the early morning, before the sun had irradiated the valley, and would watch the dawn upon the mountain-tops. The heady, crystalline air was irresistible, but he discovered that its very exhilaration hindered him from writing well. Just as he observed that after some weeks perched up at Davos everyone became immensely talkative and used the longest words they knew, so he perceived that his own attempts at work were producing long-winded, elaborate and over-loaded prose. With Fanny, who was upset by heights, Davos did not agree in another way, and in their second winter there she fell seriously ill and took to her bed. Their first incarceration at the Swiss resort did, however, confirm her in one conviction—that of Louis's lovable nature. 'I cannot tell how, aside from my love for Louis, my admiration for him grows,' she wrote from the Hotel Belvedere to her San Francisco confidant, Edward Rearden. 'I have seen wise men, past their youth, proud to be his disciples; how much more proud am I to be his wife. I believe his life to be as holy as any man's may be. He returns good for evil like the lowly Nazarene and he surrounds himself with a pure and clean at-mosphere that no mean thing can exist there.' No more than Louis himself did Fanny have any doubts or regrets about their marriage.

In April, at the end of their six months at Davos, Dr Ruedi gave Louis permission to leave, on condition that he returned for the next winter, at the end of which 'the cold-hearted leech,' as Louis called him, more or less promised that Louis's would prove to be a really arrested case of tuberculosis. Before they left they were made even more aware of the illusory quality of life at Davos by the death, that same April, of Mrs Sitwell's surviving son, Bertie, who had developed consumption at the age of eighteen after leaving school at Marlborough. His mother was advised to take him out and place him under Dr Ruedi's care. Fanny and Louis shared in Mrs Sitwell's alternate moods of hope and despair. The boy was not aware that he was dying and, by Davos standards, he seems to have had an easy death. It was in memory of Bertie Sitwell that Louis Stevenson wrote the once-famous verses, 'Yet, O stricken heart, remember, O remember', in which he urged the mourning mother to reflect on how much knowledge of evil Bertie had been spared by an early death. The argument is much the same as that which had enraged Fanny when Rearden wrote to her of her little son Hervey's death in Paris in 1876. Two of the quatrains became particularly well known to the Victorians, whose thinking was always much absorbed by early death:

> Doomed to know not Winter, only Spring, a being
>   Trod the flowery April blithely for a while,
> Took his fill of music, joy of thought and seeing,
>   Came and stayed and went, nor ever ceased to smile.
>
> All that life contains of torture, toil and treason,
>   Shame, dishonour, death, to him were but a name.
> Here, a boy, he dwelt through all the singing season
>   And ere the day of sorrow departed as he came.

To Colvin Louis wrote that Bertie's death had 'helped to make me more conscious of the wolverine on my own shoulders'.

At the close of April 1881, Louis, Fanny and Woggs began to drift homewards through France, Lloyd having been despatched to an English boarding-school. The Stevensons spent some days at Barbizon, and some more at St Germain-en-Laye, where Louis rather inexplicably, heard his very first nightingale, and where they ran into trouble with the hotelier for being short of money, Louis's shiftless manner of dress arousing the worst suspicions. Bailed out by his parents, they reached Edinburgh on May 30th, and proceeded to a rented cottage at Pitlochry, and then on to another at Braemar near Balmoral. Though almost fatal to Louis's newly regained health, this wet Scottish summer produced in him, doubtless as a reaction from the dreariness of Davos, a veritable explosion of writing. It is to the Braemar cottage that the world owes that supreme and deathless story *Treasure Island*.

[III]

Fresh from the claustrophobia of Davos, Louis Stevenson had stipulated to his parents that he would not at any price stay in a hotel in the Highlands, but wished to live in a house, and that this house must be near a running burn, with heather and fir trees within reach. His father had therefore leased, through an Edinburgh agent, Kinnaird Cottage at Pitlochry in the Vale of Atholl. The cottage was modern, conveniently divided into two flats, and had a long garden, the wooden gate of which gave access to a burn and to the glen. It was lit by oil lamps at night and contained no bath. 'Both Louis and I enjoy getting above the pomps and vanities for a little,' Mrs Thomas Stevenson wrote in a complacent letter to Baxter praising the discomforts of their holiday home. The cottage, which stood high above Pitlochry, was owned by a widow lady, Mrs Sim, who did the cooking while her daughter, Helen Sim, waited.

The dining-room was so small that when the family were seated at table Helen could not hand the dishes round it. Thomas Stevenson came up intermittently from Edinburgh, bringing boxes of books and some fresh fish. They stayed at Pitlochry two months, leaving it at the end of July when with Lloyd (who had joined them) they went north to Braemar.

Everything about Kinnaird Cottage was ideal, except for the weather. Fanny one day thoughtlessly asked her mother-in-law when the spring would begin? 'This *is* the spring,' Mrs Thomas Stevenson stoically replied. Fanny next inquired when the summer might be expected, and was told that that depended on St Swithin's Day. On St Swithin's it poured, and the elder Mrs Stevenson confessed that the summer was now over, and that they could expect no more good weather. Maggie Stevenson never got up before eleven, when she and Fanny would take a walk along the burnside under umbrellas with Woggs, who had been savaged by Scottish dogs, on a leash. Hitherto Woggs had had it all his own way, since the Swiss dogs at Davos were all muzzled, and the dogs he had encountered in France always ran away when they were confronted by this alien, black creature with hair falling all over its sharp eyes.

At Pitlochry Louis was obliged to spend almost every day shut in the house, brooding over a fire in the small stuffy sitting-room, and writing. In their hostess Mrs Sim, however, Louis discovered a real Highland gift for telling traditional tales of ghosts, Resurrectionists, burials of suicides and other gripping topics, and on wet afternoons he would coax these out of her. Influenced by the rain, by the forbidding Highland scenery, and by Mrs Sim's ghoulish stories, Fanny and Louis themselves began writing tales of the supernatural and reading them aloud to each other. This was the genesis of Louis's brilliant and eerie short story *Thrawn Janet*, which, although it was in broad Lallans, was accepted for the *Cornhill* by Leslie Stephen, and which Henry James called 'a masterpiece in thirteen pages'. Louis also wrote *The Body-Snatchers* at Pitlochry, and began work on another, longer tale, *The Merry Men*, which deals with the terrors of living on an island off the west coast of Scotland. It was during the Pitlochry period that he applied for the Chair of Constitutional Law and History at Edinburgh University which was about to become vacant and which—not at all surprisingly, given his lax academic past—he did not obtain. The Highland climate did no good at all to Louis's health, yet the very downpours of rain were useful in keeping him indoors where he was forced to write. When he read *Thrawn Janet* to Fanny in their bedroom, by

'Down went Pew with a cry that rang high into the night!' (From the first edition of *Treasure Island*)

the light of a dim candle they had forgotten to snuff, with shadows in the dark corners and the rain hammering on the roof, they frightened each other so much that they crept downstairs like a couple of children, hand in hand. On another night Mrs Sim and her daughter were alarmed to hear 'screams and yells coming from upstairs'. Mrs Sim rose to find out what catastrophe had occurred, but Fanny reassured her, calling out, 'It's only Louis and I reading ghost stories to each other, and that last one was too terrible. It got on our nerves.'

The move northwards to Braemar was, strangely enough, made on doctor's advice. Here the weather was worse than at Pitlochry, and Fanny satisfied her curiosity by watching Queen Victoria driving through the rain with two ladies-in-waiting seated back to the horses. But once more the cold and wet outdoors kept Louis at home, and seems in some way to have stimulated his imagination.

Dating from Davos, his quasi-fraternal attitude to Lloyd Osbourne, who was now on his holidays, persisted in the Highlands. Indirectly it produced *Treasure Island*, the first burst of which, comprising fifteen chapters, was written at Braemar in only as many days. Louis regarded it as his 'quickest piece of work', and the rapidity with which the tale flowed from his pen is indeed astounding. In the sixteenth chapter he suddenly stuck, or as he himself described it, 'ignominiously lost hold'—not an unusual experience for any writer, but in this special case very perplexing, for it was Louis's first attempt at a sustained novel, and he had already corrected proofs for the serialization in *Young Folks*, which was beginning on October 1st. Later, *Treasure Island* picked up again, and was completed in another bout of fifteen days at Davos.

We have three accounts of the genesis and progress of *Treasure Island*—Fanny's, Lloyd's and Louis's own. By the time that Fanny wrote her version of events she was deeply committed to her role of noble widow of a world-famous genius, and thus seems to have forgotten that at one time she had disapproved of *Treasure Island*. On occasion—*Dr Jekyll and Mr Hyde* is a case in point—Fanny's criticisms were helpful to her husband; but by and large they were pretentious and aglay. Before she realized that *Treasure Island* was to bestow on Louis an immense popularity, she wrote of it disparagingly from Davos to Edmund Gosse's wife, 'I am glad Mr Gosse liked "Treasure Island" (in Young Folks). I don't. I liked the beginning but after that the life seemed to go out of it and it became tedious.' She added that she was opposed to its ever appearing in book form.

Decades later, when she and her own family were living fatly on Louis's posthumous royalties (amongst which those from *Treasure Island* bulked large), Fanny changed her tune. She described with reverence the sessions at Braemar when Louis read the chapters of the novel, then called *The Sea-Cook*, aloud each day, his voice 'extraordinarily thrilling and sympathetic, with a fine dramatic quality'. She wrote that the story, first thought of as an amusement for her son, began, under the influence of their two appreciative visitors, Gosse and Colvin, 'to be regarded seriously as a possible novel'. Both she and Lloyd are, in their accounts, insistent that Louis began the book as a mere amusement for Lloyd, who was bored at Braemar — Lloyd's recollections of the book's genesis agree with those of Louis, in so far as Louis was inspired to write it by a water-colour map of a mysterious island. Lloyd, however, says that it was he who drew and coloured the map, and Louis who, watching him, added to it: 'Had it not been for me, and my childish box of paints, there would have been no such book as *Treasure Island*,' he writes. Louis, who was after all the author of the book, says that it was he himself who drew the map.

The question of who first drew the map seems irrelevant, but Louis's memories of how he started the book illuminate his personal creative processes. He had always retained a child-like pleasure in small things — at seventeen he was still building houses with toy bricks in his study at Heriot Row, at thirty he was still playing avidly with toy soldiers. In thinking of him it is essential to keep in mind this touching trait. Writing of *Treasure Island* he describes how his imagination was first ignited by a flat piece of paper on which an amateur map had been painted by himself:

On one of these occasions I made the map of an island; it was elaborately and (I thought) beautifully coloured: the shape of it took my fancy beyond expression; it contained harbours that pleased me like sonnets; and with the unconsciousness of the predestined, I ticketed my performance *Treasure Island* ... as I pored over my map of Treasure Island, the future characters of the book began to appear there visibly among imaginary woods; and their brown faces and bright weapons peeped out upon me from unexpected quarters, as they passed to and fro, fighting, and hunting treasure. The next thing I knew I had some paper before me and was writing out a list of chapters. How often have I done so and the thing gone no farther! But there seemed elements of success about this enterprise. It was to be a story for boys, no need of psychology or fine writing; and I had a boy at hand to be a touchstone. Women were excluded.

Stevenson soon found that he had not one but two boys as commentators, for his father was as delighted with the story as was Lloyd Osbourne himself. Thomas Stevenson had indulged in a lifelong habit of inventing unfinished stories to lull himself to sleep at night. In *Treasure Island*, Louis explains, the old man 'recognized something kindred to his own imagination; it was *his* kind of picturesque'. Thomas Stevenson not only enjoyed each instalment of the tale as it was read out to him, he actively collaborated in it, making out, for instance, a careful list of the contents of Bones's chest at the Admiral Benbow Inn, and insisting that Flint's ship should be called the *Walrus*.

'A story for boys, no need of psychology or fine writing'—this is surely the key to the eternal vitality of *Treasure Island*, a book which fascinated Gladstone and was compared by Andrew Lang to *The Odyssey* and to *Tom Sawyer*. Besides being in no way precious, Stevenson's novel shows evidence of great dramatic sense—a sense which, as we have noticed, his own play-writing so outstandingly lacks. Louis himself regarded parts of *Treasure Island* as influenced by Washington Irving and Defoe, as well as by Captain Marryat and Edgar Allan Poe. This may indeed be true, but the finished product is entirely original. In describing Jim Hawkins's nightmares of the man with one leg, Louis was reverting to the hideous dreams of his own childhood. The episode of Hawkins hiding in the apple barrel recalled a similar incident in his own father's childhood one day aboard Captain Souter's *Regent*. An interesting psychological fact is that the character of John Silver was deliberately based on that of his friend W. E. Henley: 'Henley was John Silver,' Louis wrote to Lloyd in 1890. To Henley himself he wrote, 'It was the sight of your maimed strength and masterfulness that begot John Silver.' Henley was lame, genial and crafty; what he thought of the identification we do not know.

Treasure Island was Louis Stevenson's first really successful and popular book. Despite Fanny's counsel he agreed to its being published as a volume when serialization should have ended. He was dazzled by the publisher's offer of one hundred pounds—'A hundred jingling, tingling, golden-minted quid. Is not this wonderful?' he wrote in elation to Henley. Soon the book was being reprinted. In his lifetime it was appearing in tens of thousands. Louis had his first taste of fame.

' "One more step, Mr Hands," said I, "and I'll blow your brains out," ' (From the first edition of *Treasure Island*)

[IV]

The conditions under which the Robert Louis Stevensons lived during their second winter at Davos, that of 1881 to 1882, were in every way more sympathetic than those of their first six months. They no longer stayed in a hotel, but took the little châlet belonging to one. This gave them space and privacy. The sun caught the châlet an hour earlier than it did the fronts of the big hotels, and the daylight lasted an hour longer. There was a veranda on which Louis could restlessly prowl. A Swiss maid, with whom Fanny had at first many difficulties, cooked for them and looked after the house. In an attic the toy soldiers were given floor space to themselves, and Louis and Lloyd organized complex and exciting war-games, according to rules drawn up by Louis himself. The Châlet Stein was secluded, had a fine view down the valley, and seemed to the family like home. Fanny was suffering from a liver complaint, and was much in bed. The doctor forbade her to do any work in the kitchen, and she was reduced to supervising the surly Swiss cook. The menus at the Châlet soon became a problem, as Louis had taken it into his head that he only cared for beefsteak or curried beef; lamb he would not touch. Years later, their friend and neighbour, John Addington Symonds, described the Stevensons' visits to his own household where they would apparently stay for some days, ruining the sheets 'with haemorrhages, ink and cold mutton gravy', and sleeping in the same bed, Louis with his back to the light and Fanny facing it.

Louis's new friendship with John Addington Symonds, to whom in the first Davos winter he had carried a letter of introduction from Edmund Gosse, was a great solace to him. They walked together almost daily: 'Beyond its splendid climate,' he wrote at this time, 'Davos has but one advantage—the neighbourhood of J. A. Symonds. I dare say you know his work, but the man is far more interesting.' All the same, Louis found Symonds had first come to Davos as a consumptive patient in 1887. He, his wife and their daughters settled down there, and he built a house, deciding to make Davos their permanent residence. He was at the moment working on his seven-volume *History of the Italian Renaissance*, as well as translating Michelangelo's sonnets and Benvenuto Cellini's *Autobiography*.

It was perhaps by Symonds' example that Louis himself decided to write a serious biography, choosing Hazlitt as his subject. He was already hard at work on his description of his honeymoon, *The Silverado Squatters*, as well as on a variety of essays, including the first *Talk and Talkers*. He negotiated with the London publisher Bentley about the Hazlitt project: 'You know I am a fervent Hazlittite', he wrote to a friend in the autumn of 1881, 'regarding him as *the* English writer who has had the scantiest justice. Besides which, I am anxious to write biography; really, if I understand myself in quest of profit, I think it must be good to live with another man from birth to death.' Louis was making preliminary studies for the Life of Hazlitt, but then gave it up, perhaps, as has been once suggested, from distaste for the *Liber Amoris*. A subsequent commission to write a short biography of the first Duke of Wellington also proved abortive. He never tried his hand at biography again.

Louis Stevenson devoted some pages of the first of the essays in *Talk and Talkers* to John Addington Symonds, who rather resented its high-faluting tone. Louis chose for him the pseudonym of Opalstein, and described his friend's 'troubled and poetic talk': 'He sings the praises of the earth and the art, flowers and jewels, wine and music, in a moonlight, serenading manner, as to the light guitar; even wisdom comes from his tongue like singing; no one is, indeed, more tuneful in the upper notes.'

9

The Last Years in Europe

IN the spring of 1882, to the Stevensons' delight, Dr Ruedi announced that Louis was now well enough to leave Davos for good. He sanctioned his living in the south of France, provided that he was fifteen miles from the sea and near a pine forest. Fanny and Louis left Davos with relief, but did not immediately follow the doctor's instructions. It was April when they left the Alps, but they spent the next three months in London and Edinburgh. Then there was the pull of Louis's parents, who expected their son and daughter-in-law to spend the later summer with them in rented quarters in the Scottish countryside — this time at a house near Peebles called Stobo Manse. Later they went on to Kingussie. The elder Stevensons never lost their incurable faith in the therapeutic effect of a wet Scots summer. As usual, neither Stobo Manse nor Kingussie suited Louis's health. The weather was bad, he began haemorrhaging again, and most of the good of the long months under Dr Ruedi's intelligent care at Davos was undone.

In March of this year Louis had published *Familiar Studies of Men and Books*, which is simply a collection of nine essays already published in the *Cornhill* and other periodicals from 1874 until 1881, with a preface in which Louis describes the contents of the volume as 'but the readings of a literary vagrant'. In August appeared the *New Arabian Nights* which had a mild success. The stories in this book, including 'The Suicide Club' and 'The Rajah's Diamond', had already been printed in the defunct magazine *London*, and were all artificial in style and tone. It is an indication of Louis's serious ill-health at this time that he should republish old magazine material rather than try his hand at anything new. Whilst at Stobo Manse, which was dank and shut in by trees, he did indeed begin *The Treasure of Franchard*, in which he drew on recollections of his summers at Grez-sur-Loing, but his health worsened and after a fortnight he went down to London to consult Dr Clarke. He then proceeded to Kingussie in the company of Colvin; the rest of the Stevenson family joined him there. Kingussie, however, did not answer, and after further medical consultations it was decided to follow Dr Ruedi's advice at last and to house-hunt in the south of France. Fanny was herself too ill to go with him, so he set off with Bob Stevenson. On reaching Montpellier Louis was floored by another violent haemorrhage. Fanny rushed out to meet him in Marseilles. When he was better they found and agreed to lease a rural property, the Campagne Defli, five miles outside Marseilles in the suburb of St Marcel.

At first, the Campagne Defli seemed to offer everything that could be desired. The valley was lovely, the hills wooded. The house itself had a noble salon, the bedrooms were good and two of them even had dressing-rooms, the kitchen was capacious, the house was full of cupboards, out of doors was 'a large, large olive yard, culti-vated by a resident *paysan*' as well as a rockery and pine shrubbery. Here at last was a home in which they would settle for years: 'The tragic folly of my summers is at end,' wrote Louis. They engaged a good cook, and Fanny set about teaching her to clean the knives and other utensils. The only aspect of the Campagne Defli which aroused Louis's parents' suspicions when they heard of it was that, for so charming a house, it was unbelievably cheap.

They settled into the Campagne Defli in October. By Christmas their delight had turned to dust and ashes. Louis was perpetually ill, and it became clear to Fanny that St Marcel was a most un-healthy place. When an epidemic of fever broke out in December, Fanny bundled Louis off on his own to Nice, while she struggled with the problem of giving up the house. After some misunder-standings due to lack of communications, Fanny joined Louis at Nice, returning alone to St Marcel. In the railway carriage she was exasperated by an Englishman who had seen Louis at Nice, pro-nounced him at death's door and asked Fanny if she intended to have him embalmed. By February they had wriggled out of the Campagne Defli lease, and optimistically set about house-hunting once more. This time they tried Hyères.

More than a decade later, Louis Stevenson wrote to Colvin, 'I was only happy once, that was at Hyères. At Hyères the two of them in fact led an existence which, but for Louis's severe hemorrhages, sciatica and his attack of Egyptian ophthalmia, would have been idyllic. At the bottom of the steep hill which is crowned by the castle ruins, and just on the edge of the winding *vieille ville* of Hyères, there then stood, and there still stands today, a rather astonishing small and toy-like building—a tiny Swiss châlet made of bricks and wood, with elaborate Swiss gables and balconies, behind it a very romantic garden with thirty-five large olive-trees and with paths cut into steps. The châlet had been designed for a Paris exhibition in 1878, had been bought there by an admirer and rebuilt at Hyères-les-Palmiers. The owner had named it *Châlet de la Solitude*. The Stevensons fell in love with it. Once again it seemed that they had found a perfect and lasting home. They leased it for nine years, but after only nine months Louis's ill-health and Fanny's medical fads drove them out of Hyères. It was as though Fate was not going to let Louis settle permanently anywhere until he finally reached his journey's end in the South Seas.

Although the châlet was so minute that you could hardly turn round in the rooms, and that Fanny, cooking, was in constant danger of being scorched by the kitchen stove or impaled on saucepan hooks, La Solitude suited them perfectly. In the moonlit garden nightingales nested in the twisted olive trees. The air was aromatic with thyme and wild flowers. Louis declared that it was just like living at Silverado all over again. He began to work hard for the greater part of the day, and again in the evenings. He had, wrote Fanny to Mrs Williams, taken it into his head that he wanted to get rich, and Fanny thought play-writing the surest and quickest way towards this uncharacteristic goal. Life at La Solitude was like a second honeymoon.

'You may tell Rearden that Louis is not tired of me yet,' Fanny wrote to Dora Williams. 'In fact he has got so used to me now that he seems quite miserable when I am away from him. And if my looks have gone off I am not conscious of it when I know that I am the prettiest woman in town.'

Obviously, for Louis, his rediscovered ability to concentrate on writing was a main source of his happiness at La Solitude. At the Campagne Defli he had had, in Fanny's view, 'a volcano raging inside him' because he could not work. He was still playing with the idea of a biography of Hazlitt, which as we have seen proved abortive. He did, however, complete his novel *Prince Otto*, which he had been polishing and repolishing for a long time, and which is both sprightly and Meredithian. He also continued with the verses which, first entitled *Penny Whistles*, ended by becoming *A Child's Garden of Verses*. The idea for this famous volume had originated in the Highlands in 1881, when his mother had shown him Kate Greenaway's

'I was kept busy all day in the cave, packing the minted money into bread-bags.' (From the first edition of *Treasure Island*)

Birthday Books for Children, which had what he called 'rather nice' rhymes. He had been writing his verses desultorily at Nice in the early spring of 1883, and the bulk of them at Hyères in 1884. Many of them were written during his illnesses, when he could not write prose. At Hyères an almost fatal haemorrhage had confined him to bed, with his right arm tied to his side. Later he developed sciatica, through dancing round a bonfire to celebrate Edmund Yates's conviction for criminal libel. Next came an epidemic of Egyptian ophthalmia, which ran through the *vieille ville* like lightning and to which of course Louis instantly succumbed. Undefeated and resolute, he lay there in the dark scribbling *A Child's Garden of Verses* with his left hand. Louis's determination not to die was as potent as ever.

While he was laid up in his darkened room, Louis requested Fanny to go for a walk each day and invent a story to repeat to him on her return. This was the period of the Fenian outrages in London, and Fanny thought up a series of dynamite tales. When Louis grew better these were forgotten, but later they surfaced as the only novel written in collaboration with his wife, *The Dynamiter*. Fanny's literary pretensions still flourished. *The Dynamiter* is not a happy example of that most precarious of feats — literary collaborations.

Lloyd, who was now sixteen, and whom they had not seen for a year, joined them at Hyères. He found Louis disappointingly aloof at first, and even his mother seemed to the adolescent to be in some way changed towards him. These self-conscious anxieties gradually evaporated, but Lloyd afterwards remembered the period at Hyères as the only time in his life when his stepfather and he were 'not delightfully intimate'. Louis may have found sixteen an awkward age to deal with, and Lloyd, who was a snob all his life, had, through his time at an English school, taken on the imprint of a little English gentleman. This was not a prototype that Louis Stevenson admired or liked.

Apart from his seeming coldness Louis was looking very well, much better, Lloyd thought, than he had done a year ago. He wore what Lloyd called 'presentable clothes' — 'at a little distance, in a straw hat, he might have been mistaken for an ordinary member of society'. He had grown a little imperial on his chin, and wandered about Hyères in a black *pelerine*. 'Louis is getting quite good-looking again, which for a time he certainly was not,' Fanny assured her parents-in-law in February 1883. She was making him take cod-liver oil, which had such 'a beautifying effect' on him that the

French-Swiss girl who was their new maid asked if she could not have some too.

In Valentine Roch Fanny had tumbled on what used to be called a treasure. They treated the girl as one of the family, and she devoted herself to them for six years, only leaving them when Fanny dismissed her for suspected theft at Honolulu in 1888. Valentine soon mastered the variations in Louis's health, understood what to do should he have a haemorrhage when she happened to be alone with him, and could be left in charge if Fanny went out by herself. One night at Hyères Louis had the worst haemorrhage he had ever had in his life, and took a longish time to recover.

In the spring of 1883 the invalids of Hyères began to make a general exodus away from the Mediterranean shores. Louis seemed too ailing to be moved, but in July Fanny took him up to Vichy, which they did not like, and then to Clermont-Ferrand. From there she and Lloyd scouted round the countryside looking for somewhere to settle for a month or two, and ended up by selecting the pretty new spa of Royat, near the Puy-de-Dome, a watering-place recently made fashionable by the Empress Eugénie. Royat suited them so well that they persuaded Louis's father and mother to come out. Old Thomas Stevenson, although not yet seventy, was already showing signs of breaking up, or as his wife in her anodyne way noted in her diary 'far from being well' — 'His father was far from being well this summer and was recommended to take baths, so we arranged to go to Royat.'

The waters at Royat were what Fanny called 'more or less arsenical'. They were carefully administered on doctors' orders. The patients were carried downhill to the baths in sedan-chairs, which were brought right into your bedroom to pick you up and carried you either down a precipitous street, the legitimate route, or down a street of stairs, which was forbidden. As you were shut into your sedan-chair by curtains, you could only guess by the jolting whether your chairmen were taking you the proper way or by the stairs short-cut which had been the cause of many accidents. The Stevenson contingent distinctly liked Royat, and it was here that Louis continued a tale begun at Hyères and inspired by a book that was his favourite bedside reading, *The Paston Letters*. This new story, of which Fanny strongly disapproved, was called *The Black Arrow, a Tale of Two Roses*, and was set in the troubled reign of Henry VI.

The Black Arrow, which is, despite an excess of medieval expletives such as 'forsooth!', in itself an exciting adventure story, had been undertaken in order to earn money and to give Mr James Henderson of *Young Folks* another serial by the author of *Treasure Island*. Fanny has recorded that despite its later phenomenal success as a book, *Treasure Island* had never caught on amongst Mr Henderson's juvenile readers in serial form. There was one simple test for this: part of the paper was devoted to *Questions and Answers*, a correspondence column in which the boy and girl readers would sign their inquiries under pseudonyms taken from the current serials in the magazine. Fanny writes that she and Louis looked in vain for the names of Jim Hawkins or John Silver. This seemed to Louis a challenge, and he volunteered to write a tale of the Wars of the Roses for Mr Henderson, whom he genuinely liked. He triumphed. During the serialization of *The Black Arrow* 'numbers of questioners signed themselves John Amend-All, Dick Shelton, or Joanna Sedley'.

After a month at Royat, the Louis Stevensons returned joyfully to Hyères for the autumn and winter, a winter which saw the publication of *The Silverado Squatters* and of *Treasure Island* in book form. In January of the new year, 1884, Baxter and Henley came out to see their friends in Hyères. They and Louis went on a jaunt to Nice, where, after they had left, Louis fell so ill that the doctors thought he was dying. Bob Stevenson was sent out from Edinburgh to help Fanny and in the end, by the very skin of his teeth, Louis survived. Fanny, who felt that she knew Louis better than any doctors, had never despaired, but she had this time been very gravely frightened. Thenceforth she began to have serious doubts about the south of France as a safe place for Louis, and according to her son, when cholera broke out in the *vieille ville* of Hyères, she 'fell into a panic'.

Lloyd afterwards thought it a pity that Louis ever left Hyères, which he had found so congenial and so suited for his work. Part of the trouble was that Fanny, who was always intrigued by anything medical, had subscribed to *The Lancet*, a technical journal for the medical profession not usually consulted by laymen. From its pages she harvested a whole crop of new health-fears. Salads carried tapeworm eggs. Vinegar was dangerous. Salt induced arteriosclerosis and an early death. She probably took the journal in good faith, hoping to find hints about Louis's disease in its pages. However that may be, she became obsessed by the perils around them, and finally managed to dislodge the reluctant Louis and make him leave Hyères for good and all. They went back to Royat, where once again the elder Stevensons joined them. Valentine seems to have gone with them, and of course the fierce little terrier Bogue.

To her parents-in-law Fanny described this adored animal as

more aggressive than ever in Hyères: 'Bogue waits like a fat spider just inside his own gate, and pounces suddenly upon any unwary dog that passes. He lies close and never makes a sound. One poor dog I saw stop for a long time before he ventured to pass, and then he had to take his courage in both hands and make a rush for it; but Bogue was there.' He was no doubt soon at work terrorizing the poodles and other smart dogs of the newly fashionable Second Empire spa of Royat.

[II]

Having uprooted Louis from Hyères, where he had been so very happy, Fanny returned with him to England after a month at Royat. For some reason — probably at his parents' suggestion — they settled on the West Cliff at Bournemouth. It was also at Bournemouth that Lloyd Osbourne was at school. For the first few months they lived in lodgings called Wensleydale, one of a tall row of buildings overlooking the beach and with what Lloyd Osbourne has described as 'a gloriously sparkling view of the Needles and the Isle of Wight'. The pine woods of Bournemouth vaguely reminded Louis of Scotland, and the sunny summertime Channel perhaps reminded him of the Mediterranean. However that may have been, it was at Bournemouth that he spent his last three years in Europe.

Wensleydale was cheap and comfortable, run by a landlady in rustling bombazine, who produced illegible weekly accounts. Stevenson was particularly gay at this moment, and his stepson has recorded that Louis

> was never afterwards so boyish or so light-hearted; it was the final flare-up of his departing youth. The years that followed, however full of interest and achievement, were greyer; it was a sobered and more preoccupied man that lived them. ... Stevenson is to be envied that he retained his youth as long as he did. But he left it at 'Wensleydale'.

During a few days in London before moving to Bournemouth, Louis and Fanny had been to a matinée of *Deacon Brodie* at the Prince's Theatre, which was received by London critics with what Louis's official biographer calls 'interest'. Louis and Fanny were encouraged by the notices to persist in their theory that play-writing was the best way to easy money. Henley, now a major literary figure in London, genial and authoritative, brought his young wife down to Bournemouth, and the collaboration between him and Louis began again. *Beau Austin*, which is set in Tunbridge Wells in 1820, was rattled off in four days, and is about as poor a play as *Brodie*. This was followed by *Admiral Guinea* and by *Macaire*. Henley never lost his faith in these works, but Louis, possibly under Fanny's guidance, soon ceased to believe that they had any dramatic power. When Henley was back in London Louis would happily resume his own tasks. 'R.L.S.', writes Lloyd Osbourne, 'lost not only the last flicker of his youth in "Wensleydale", but I believe also any conviction that he might become a popular dramatist.'

Louis and Fanny had intended to go back to the Continent after a few weeks in Bournemouth, but, although his health was at its nadir, they lingered on, moving from Wensleydale to a furnished house at Branksome Park. Their decision to stay in England was partially founded on the advice of the doctors, but far more strongly influenced by the state of old Thomas Stevenson, who had retired from his business and was failing rapidly. 'Uncle Tom wanted us to stay in England,' Fanny wrote in reminiscence. 'He was so pathetic about it that we concluded to do so, though we knew it was not best for Louis. The dear old man tried to bribe me with a house. I refused the house, saying that there wasn't a house in Bournemouth that I wanted. The old man made me go and look at several, and then became convinced, with me, that they were all too hideous in their showy bad taste.' On another day, however, when out walking by herself, Fanny discovered a villa she liked, called Seaview. Seaview stood on the edge of Alum Chine, was built of yellow brick with blue slates and had an acre of garden. The only drawback was that the house belonged to a retired naval officer and was not for sale. Some days later she and old Mr Stevenson took her mother-in-law to look at Seaview, and, by one of those coincidences which may be presumed to show the importance of will-power, the house had a notice on it saying it was indeed for sale. Thomas Stevenson bought it at once and presented it to Fanny as a delayed wedding-present. He took Fanny for a week up to London where they bought a quantity of furniture in various antique-shops. The name of the house was changed, and it was given that of Skerryvore 'in commemoration of the most difficult and beautiful of all the lighthouses erected by the family'. Although their tenure of Skerryvore coincided with the longest and worst period of Louis's ill-health, he was delighted by the house. Afterwards, in the midst of his physical renaissance in the South Seas he used to say that he had lived like a pallid weevil in a biscuit at Skerryvore.

From Skerryvore you could only view the sea from one of the upper windows, but the house had a coach-house, a pigeon-house, a drive to the sunken porch of the front door, flower-beds, a good lawn at the back, a shrubbery, a kitchen garden, and a wild rhododendron garden cut into steps running down Alum Chine to a stream at the bottom. The yellow bricks of the house itself were hidden by ivy. 'I cannot tell you what a lovely luxurious little nest Skerryvore looked when we first came home,' Fanny wrote to her parents-in-law after an autumn absence in 1885. 'I wouldn't change it for the Queen's palace.' Fanny had her own ideas of interior decoration, and she made the interior of Skerryvore light and pretty, ignoring the dark colours which William Morris had made fashionable. In the drawing-room, which was light blue, she installed three oak chests as window seats, putting on top of them mattresses covered in yellow damask, with yellow pillows standing in a row. There were convex mirrors on the walls, and a small statuette of St Cecilia, and a cabinet to which Louis had lost his heart. After all their years in hotels and furnished houses they both relished the sense of having their own home. In *Underwoods* Louis wrote of the new house:

> *My house*, I say. But hark to the sunny doves
> That make my roof the arena of their loves,
> That gyre about the gable all day long
> And fill the chimneys with their murmurous song:
> *Our house*, they say; and *mine* the cat declares
> And spreads his golden fleece upon the chairs;
> And *mine* the dog, and rises stiff with wrath
> If any alien foot profane the path,
> So too the buck that trimmed my terraces,
> Our whilome gardener, called the garden his;
> Who now, deposed, surveys my plain abode
> And his late kingdom, only from the road.

The one fly in the ointment was Louis's deteriorating health. 'I hope England is not a fatal mistake,' Fanny wrote to Baxter in the autumn of 1885. That August they had gone on a jaunt to see Thomas Hardy at Dorchester ('What very strange marriages literary men seem to make,' Fanny had written of Mrs Hardy). On their way back Louis fell ill and delirious in the hotel Exeter, and Fanny had had to lift him out of bed ten times in one night.

Among the positive advantages of Bournemouth was the presence there of an excellent medical man, Dr Bodley Scott, who has left an account of his distinguished patient's courage:

On his bad days, and they were very frequent, he made a fine fight to be cheerful, but, as he expressed it, his brain was in a condition of dry rot and it seemed to him always that it would never produce again, so the world became very dark; but this mood rarely lasted ... Again and again his buoyant spirit brought him up to the surface, and his mind triumphed over his defective body ... He valued any kindness shown to him, even from the most obscure and humble folk.

[III]

Whilst Louis and Fanny were unpacking their objects from Hyères, and all the new furniture that had been bought in London, they received a visit from two Bournemouth residents who might have been classified as obscure, if not precisely humble. These were a Mrs Boodle and her daughter Adelaide. The afternoon call had been Adelaide's own idea, for she had been immensely excited by the news that a writer and his wife had bought a house on the Alum Chine. Could it really be 'R.L.S.'? She persuaded her mother, who was of a less wild and more retiring nature, that it was their duty to call on the newcomers. Years afterwards, as an elderly spinster, Miss Adelaide Boodle wrote down and published her memories of the Stevensons at Bournemouth. A passionate admirer of both of them, she called her useful book *R.L.S. and His Sine Qua Non.* Her friendship with the Stevensons was by far the most important happening in Adelaide Boodle's long life, and her testimony to the daily round at Skerryvore is, despite its hero-worshipping tone, invaluable.

Something had gone wrong with the door-bell at Skerryvore, and there was at first no answer to their ring. Mrs Boodle, who was in a highly nervous state already, burst into tears, but had recovered herself by the time that Valentine tardily opened the door and let them in. The Stevensons were expecting nobody and had apparently instructed Valentine that they were not at home, information which the Swiss girl had misunderstood. The Boodles found Louis, dressed in his velvet jacket with a dark red tie, and Fanny, wearing a painter's apron, stooped over cases and crates. There was only one chair in the room, which was allotted to Mrs Boodle, whose nerves were calmed by 'the radiant cordiality' of their hosts' welcome. From that first day on, Adelaide Boodle became a kind of daughter-of-the-house to the Stevensons, and could call in whenever she liked. She saw them in all their moods and troubles and even mutual disagreements, and she has recorded all she saw.

To Miss Boodle, Louis seemed to have the character of St Christopher. She noticed that he was entirely dependent on Fanny — 'almost like a child', and that he hung upon her judgment of his work and would publish nothing that she had condemned. Skerryvore she describes as in itself 'hopelessly commonplace', but at the same time, because of the Stevensons and what they had done to it, it seemed to her unique. 'There never was, and there never will be, another place like Skerryvore,' Miss Boodle writes. 'Think of it under what aspect you will, that little home was wholly unlike any other; just one of the villas innumerable that have laid waste all the poetry of Bournemouth, there was something about it which caught and held one's imagination.' Over the empty stables a little weather vane flashed in the sunshine. The court was murmurous with doves. 'Foreign-looking' hydrangeas bloomed lavishly in Fanny's garden. Once you had passed the gate, 'the little place took one's heart by storm'. Louis, who, although he had been briefly apprenticed to an Edinburgh timber-merchant in his extreme youth, knew nothing whatever about trees, asked Adelaide Boodle to teach him, but he never succeeded in identifying bark or leaves correctly and the lessons were given up.

What most impressed Adelaide in Louis Stevenson were his gentleness, his courage and his compassion. His health was precarious at Skerryvore, he was easily tired by people like Henley and even by his own parents, and his bleeding from the lungs was frequent. In Fanny it was the eyes that attracted Miss Boodle at first — 'unfathomable eyes. No other eyes were ever at all like them; you could gaze, and gaze and gaze (as I did with a sense of fascination) and each depth that you reached was clearer, clearer, clearer, full of yearning kindness that one's heart might draw from inexhaustibly in time of need.' These eyes seemed to her both deep and tender. Miss Boodle was also struck by what she called the quiet heroism of Fanny's 'daily and hourly self-restraint'. She spent her time in protecting Louis from others and even from himself, but she would quietly make her remonstrance, say her say, and then take refuge in silence: 'she could not bear to add even a feather's weight to the burden of his infirmities.'

Adelaide Boodle became specifically a disciple of Fanny's. She learned much from her and her private views on life. One day, not finding Mrs Stevenson in the Blue Room, the girl went up to Fanny's bedroom, which she was privileged to do. She found her sewing, with a look of profound sadness, and felt that she had intruded. She had wanted Fanny's opinion on a story she herself was writing. Fanny held out her arms in welcome and Adelaide was soon seated on the floor at her feet, and reading her story. Feeling 'a sense of mental distance', however, she soon gave her story up. Fanny took her hand, held it, and began a strange soliloquy, which Miss Boodle describes as 'a milestone in my moral pilgrimage'. 'I have made everybody miserable,' Fanny muttered, continuing passionately, 'I could not help it: I should do it again. I had to do it. They were all seething. What is seething? It is evil-speaking; it is the discussion of another person's wrong-doing; it means talking over a scandal and letting it grow and grow and grow.' She continued with a sermon on 'the hideousness of gossip on subjects better let alone'. It was probably on a conversation of Henley's that she was brooding.

In Adelaide Boodle we have an enthusiastic amateur observer of the Stevensons and their life at Skerryvore. In late April of 1885 one of the great professional observers of all time came on the scene — an American novelist of forty-two who became one of Louis's most intimate and rewarding friends. This man was Henry James.

[IV]

James and Stevenson had first become acquainted in the summer of 1879, just before Louis's flight to California. They do not seem to have impressed each other at the beginning. James described Louis as 'a pleasant fellow, but a shirt-collarless bohemian and a great deal (in an inoffensive way) of a *poseur*. But his little *Inland voyage* was, I thought, charming.' At Bournemouth they speedily discovered how much they had in common.

In September 1884, exasperated by an article on the novel by Walter Besant, Henry James had published in *Longman's Magazine* 'an individual manifesto' contradicting it, and entitled *The Art of Fiction*. His theme was that any real work of imaginative fiction must be in direct competition with life itself and was, in fact, history. At the end of the article he praised 'the delightful story of *Treasure Island*', contrasting Stevenson's tale with Edmond de Goncourt's *Chérie* to the detriment of the latter. The article deeply interested Louis, who wrote a reply to it which *Longman's Magazine* printed in December 1884. This was called *A Humble Remonstrance*.

Louis began by objecting to the very phrase, 'the art of fiction', which Besant and James had both made use of. He wished it to be replaced by 'the art of narrative', and denied that art could compete with life. 'The novel', he wrote, 'is not a transcript of life, to be judged by its exactitude; but a simplification of some side or point of

Wensleydale
Bournemouth
Oct 3rd 1884

Dear Mr Chatto.

I have an offer of £25 for 9tts from
America. I do not know if you mean to have
the American rights; from the nature of the
contract, I think not; but if you understood
that you were to sell the sheets, I will either hand
over the bargain to you, or finish it myself
and hand you over the money if you are pleased
with the amount. You see, I leave this quite
in your hands. To parody an old Scotch story of
servant and master: If you don't know that you
have a good author, I know that I have a good
publisher. Your fair, open and handsome
dealings are a good point in any life and
do more for my crazy health than has yet
been done by any doctor.

Please send a copy of the Inland
Voyage, the Travels with a Donkey, Virginibus
Puerisque and the Studies to the following
address

Mrs Ben Thomas
Danville
Indiana
U. S. A

and believe me
very truly yours
Robert Louis Stevenson.

Facsimile of a letter from R.L.S. to Andrew Chatto of Chatto and Windus Ltd

life, to stand or fall by its significant simplicity.' That he disagreed with James on the nature of the novel did not mean that Stevenson did not admire his work, which, with the single exception of *The Portrait of a Lady*, he did immeasurably. Both men believed with passion in the overpowering importance of good writing, despised carelessness, 'and both', in the words of Janet Adam Smith, 'felt the degradation of public taste'.

Henry James was delighted with Stevenson's rejoinder, and wrote to him as soon as *A Humble Remonstrance* appeared. 'It's a luxury, in this immoral age, to encounter some one who *does* write—who is really acquainted with that lovely art.' He thanked Louis for so much in the article that was 'suggestive and felicitous in your remarks—justly felt and brilliantly said ... the current of your admirable style floats pearls and diamonds ... The native *gaiety* of all you write is delightful to me, and when I reflect that it proceeds from a man whom life has laid so much of the time on his back (as I understand it) I find you a genius indeed.'

Stevenson was enchanted by James's letter. In his reply he complained of the lack of 'thoughtful interest in the art of literature' and that those who tried to practise it with any deliberate purpose ran 'the risk of finding no fit audience'. He wrote that he was delighted and surprised by James's praise—'I seem to myself a very rude left-handed countryman; not fit to be read, far less complimented, by a man so accomplished, so adoit, so craftsmanlike as you.' The two men were made for each other; James brought an element of perfectionism which complemented Stevenson's own, and an atmosphere which neither Henley nor Colvin nor Gosse could provide. It was perhaps the most satisfying friendship of Louis Stevenson's life.

In this, his first letter to Henry James, Louis adumbrated a visit by James to Skerryvore:

> As you know I belong to that besotted class of man, the invalid; this puts me to a stand in the way of visits. But it is possible that some day you may feel that a day near the sea and among pine-woods would be a pleasant change from town. If so, please let us know; and my wife and I will be delighted to put you up, and give you what we can to eat and drink (I have a fair bottle of claret).

In a postscript Louis added that having re-read his own paper he could not judge it 'either veracious or polite'.

When Henry James's visiting-card was handed to the Stevensons by Valentine he became their very first London visitor at Skerryvore. He enjoyed the talk so much that he asked if he might come the next evening. 'I call that very flattering,' Fanny wrote to her mother-in-law. 'I had always been told that he was the type of an Englishman, but, except that he looks like the Prince of Wales,* I call him the type of an American. He is gentle, amiable and soothing.' Henry James had taken lodgings in Bournemouth to be near his ailing sister Alice, who was there with a maid and a nurse. He soon formed the habit of dropping in at Skerryvore each night after dinner, sitting in the armchair that had belonged to Louis's grandfather and was soon now known as 'Henry James's chair'. 'An old acquaintance of mine is ripening into a new friend,' James wrote in a letter at this time. At Bournemouth he was engaged in finishing *The Bostonians* and preparing himself to write its successor, *The Princess Casamassima*.

In *Underwoods*, his collection of verses written at Bournemouth and published in 1887, Louis wrote a sonnet to Henry James and some of the feminine characters in his novels:

> Who comes to-night? We bar the door in vain.
> My bursting walls, can you contain
> The presences that now together throng
> Your narrow entry, as with flowers and song,
> As with the air of life, the breath of talk?
> Lo how these fair immaculate women walk
> Behind their jocund maker; and we see
> Slighted *De Mauves*, and that far different she,
> *Gressie*, the trivial sphinx; and to our feast
> *Daisy* and *Barb* and *Chancellor* (she not least!)
> With all their silken, all their airy kin,
> Do like unbidden angels enter in.
> But he, attended by these shining names,
> Comes (best of all) himself—our welcome James.

In these verses Louis used a certain poetic licence, for by no stretch of the imagination could Olive Chancellor, the bleak Sapphist of *The Bostonians*, be called 'fair immaculate' or silken, or airy.

In February 1886 Henry James sent them as a present a Venetian mirror, about which Louis wrote, in March, another set of verses, ending (the mirror speaks):

> Now with an outlandish grace,
> To the sparkling fire I face
> In the blue room at Skerryvore;

* James was still sporting a beard in 1885.

> And I wait until the door
> Open, and the Prince of men,
> Henry James shall come again.

Quite aside from the recognition of the hard work which they both knew good writing to be, Henry James was fascinated, and at times appalled, by the quantity and quality of Robert Louis Stevenson's circle—from the parents who seemed to James 'ponderous' and quite oblivious of the sheer physical trial their company was to Louis; to Lloyd Osbourne, Bob Stevenson, his wife and family, his sister, the unhappily married Katherine de Mattos, and her children, Henley and other friends. 'They are a romantic lot—and I delight in them,' he wrote when the Stevensons left England for America in 1887; but he thought Louis too beset by obligations, relatives and friends, and wished he could be spared more time to himself. Fanny, as a type of American he did not know well, fascinated him. Louis would sometimes write to James about her in a tone of comic criticism:

> She is a woman (as you know) not without art: the art of extracting the gloom of the eclipse from sunshine; and she has recently laboured in this field not without success or (as we used to say) not without a blessing ... she tackled me savagely for being a canary-bird; I replied (bleatingly) that there was no use in turning life into King Lear; presently it was discovered that there were two dead combatants upon the field, each slain by an arrow of the truth and we tenderly carried off each other's corpses ... Well, here is luck, and here are the kindest recollections from the canary-bird and from King Lear, from the Tragic Woman and the Flimsy Man.

James never in point of fact used either of the Stevensons as material for a novel, but he might well have done so. When they left for the United States, and then for the South Seas, never to return, James was the only one of their friends who did not blame them, did not denigrate Louis, or join in the chorus of Colvin, Gosse and others who, from pique, used to declare that his writing had deteriorated outside of the United Kingdom. James remained thoroughly loyal, deeply affectionate, and infinitely inquisitive about their lives in Samoa. Louis's death in 1894 was a blow from which he did not recover. He wrote at the time to Edmund Gosse:

> Of what can one think, or utter or dream save of this ghastly extinction of the beloved R.L.S.? It is too miserable for cold words—it's an absolute desolation. It makes me cold and sick ...

One feels how one cared for him—what a place he took; and as if suddenly *into* that place there had descended a great avalanche of ice. I'm not sure that it's not for *him* a great and happy fate; but for us the loss of charm, of suspense, of 'fun' is unutterable.

[V]

In the summer of 1885 Fanny Stevenson wrote to Colvin a letter in which she complained of the 'wearing company', both in Skerryvore and staying in 'dependencies', which she and Louis had been enduring for some time. It had been a difficult party and she said that she quite broke down under the strain:

> Through it all the dear Henry James remained faithful, though he suffered bitterly and openly. He is gone now, and there is none to take his place. After ten weeks of Henry James the evenings seem very empty, though the room is always full of people ... We have started more or less an intimacy with the Taylors—that is, with the daughters, Sir Henry himself being almost too beautiful and refined and angelic for ordinary people like us.

The poet who had in his youth written the play *Philip Van Artevelde*, first produced in 1847, Sir Henry Taylor had been born with the century and was now eighty-five years old. As Mrs Cameron has photographed him, he was a noble-looking old man with a long white beard and thick white hair. He was sixteen years older than his wife, whom he had married in 1838 when she was twenty-two. Alice Spring-Rice was southern Irish, born in a country-house on the leafy banks of the river Shannon. Her husband came from a grave Northumbrian family of scholar-squires who had lived for generations in an old grey keep at Witton le Wear. Sir Henry had worked all his life as an influential clerk in the Colonial Office, dealing with such urgent matters as colonial prison reform, and always refusing promotion. He and his wife had discovered Bournemouth in 1861 when it was still a tiny fishing village. In the next years they had built their villa, christened 'The Roost', as a summer retreat from their house at Sheen; by the time the Stevensons arrived in Bournemouth it had become, in Sir Henry's old age, their permanent home. He died in 1886.

The Henry Taylors had a surviving son—one had died in child-hood—and three daughters. The most bewitching member of the

whole family was Lady Taylor herself, then in her sixties and re-
taining what Louis, who adored her, called 'the eternal beautiful
evidences of her beauty'. She was certainly the Bournemouth
friend whom he most revered, loving her 'for her high mind and
hot impatient heart'. She was a woman of great erudition, devoted
to German poetry but also to mathematics. Louis thought she had
'a way of superiority' which belonged exclusively to her generation :
'There was', he wrote, 'a charm in her hardness for those who were
inside.' Fanny respected her also, though no two women could
possibly have been less alike. 'She sits with an eager hand on each
of her chair arms,' Fanny recorded, 'sharpening her tongue between
her lips—whose favour one longs for and once gained trembles for
fear of losing.' She called Lady Taylor 'one of the women that I
most admired and loved in the whole of my way through life.'

By way of the Taylors, Louis and Fanny made firm friends with
another charming old couple, Sir Percy (the poet's son) and Lady
Shelley, who lived in a rambling comfortable house called Boscombe
Manor. Writing one day from Skerryvore to Mrs Thomas Stevenson,
Fanny told her that after a recent call on them, Lady Taylor,
speaking of Louis,

> said with a sigh 'I wish he were mine'. You will have to contest
> your maternal rights with more than Lady Shelley it seems …
> It is not often that a wife gets three mothers-in-law at once
> and three such very delightful ones. I think I should begin to
> look about for adopted fathers-in-law for Louis, could you
> recommend me one? There doesn't seem to be the same sort of
> eager struggle for the position.

The reference to Lady Shelley dates back to an incident when
Mrs Thomas Stevenson had been staying at Skerryvore. The
Shelleys, a fanciful couple who had a private theatre in their house,
had convinced themselves that Louis was a reincarnation of Sir
Percy's father. Hearing that Lady Shelley was in the house, Maggie
Stevenson, who did not yet know her, tidied her hair in a mirror
and went smiling downstairs, 'ready', she said, 'to be adored as
the mother of the man her visitor and Lady Shelley flattered and
praised'. To her surprise, when she introduced herself, Lady
Shelley refused her proffered hand and rose in indignation, accusing Mrs Stevenson of having robbed her of her son—the Shelleys
were childless—and suggesting that 'by some perverse trickery' her
hostess had borne a child who was really Percy Bysshe Shelley's
grandson, and who should have been born to herself.

Besides mounting plays in the private theatre at Boscombe Manor, and carpentering all the stage accessories himself, Sir Percy was a good amateur photographer. He took a series of photographs of Louis, one or two of which Fanny thought 'really very good'. These photographs seemed to show two sides of the sitter's personality. 'It is very odd', Fanny wrote to Colvin, 'that while one represents an angel, the devil must have posed for another, so ghastly, impishly wicked, and malignant is it. Plainly Jekyll and Hyde'.

Besides being photographed at Bournemouth, Louis was twice painted there by John Singer Sargent, who had been commissioned by Charles Fairchild, an American millionaire admirer who wanted a portrait of Stevenson for his private collection. The first picture was painted when the Stevensons were living in a furnished Bournemouth house; the second, and more famous, one, at Skerryvore. This shows Louis walking about the blue room pulling his moustache; part of Fanny, seated in a chair, is visible to the right of the picture. Louis liked it very much, but feared that it was too original and eccentric for public exhibition. Both he and Fanny became very fond of Sargent, who stayed with them while painting each portrait. Louis's friends regarded the second picture (which the Stevensons kept and hung at Skerryvore) as the most vivid likeness of him that they knew. Writing to Louis, Sargent, who was a noted wit, wrote of it as 'the picture of the caged maniac lecturing about the foreign specimen in the corner.' One of Sargent's friends had thought it excellent but 'paradoxical'. In the same letter Sargent wrote that his stays at Bournemouth were among his pleasantest souvenirs, and that he would like to come often 'but I fear that our prolonged and frantic talks would rather wear you out at the time and how could we avoid them?'

[VI]

Virtually imprisoned in Skerryvore by ill-health, Louis none the less, by a major effort of will, managed to turn the Bournemouth period into one of very great literary industry. *A Child's Garden of Verses*, to which he had been gradually adding poems for months, was finally published in March 1885. In April of the same year *Prince Otto* began to run in *Longman's Magazine*. He had already begun writing *Kidnapped* that March; it took five months. *Markheim* and several other short stories also belong to the Bournemouth period. So does the work that caught the imagination of every reader, from Queen Victoria downwards—*The Strange Case of Dr Jekyll and Mr Hyde*. This came out in January 1886, was reviewed in *The Times*, made the theme for church sermons, was three times dramatized by playwrights, and sold forty thousand copies in the first six months. 'The art is burning and intense,' Symonds wrote to its author, ' ... I know now what was meant when you were called a sprite.'

We have seen that the inspiration for Louis Stevenson's work at times came to him in dreams. *Jekyll and Hyde* is an example of this subconscious process. During a lull in the hectic play-writing collaboration with Henley, Louis had a nightmare during which he screamed so loudly and with such horror that Fanny woke him up. 'I was dreaming a fine bogey tale,' he told her reproachfully. He had in fact dreamed the story up to the first transformation of Jekyll into Hyde, including the draught made from the white powder. He began writing it the next morning. For three days the house was hushed as he lay in bed working furiously. When he got up for meals he was silent and preoccupied. In that brief period he completed the tale, and triumphantly read it aloud to Fanny and her son. Lloyd Osbourne was amazed at Fanny's unusually reticent reaction. She finally blurted out that Louis had missed the point of his own story, and that it was an allegory that he should have written, and not a straight piece of sensationalism. Louis was enraged, and there ensued a row which drove Lloyd from the room. When he came back he found his mother alone, seated before the fire and brooding. After some time Louis came downstairs again, but instead of resuming the scene he announced that Fanny was quite right. He threw the manuscript, which was nearly forty thousand words, into the fireplace and they all watched it burn. For another three days he worked at full tilt, rewrote the whole tale as an allegory and then read it to his delighted wife. For six weeks more he polished it, and then sent it off to his publisher.

Living as he was a life in which medical draughts played a vital role, it is easy to see how the notion of Dr Jekyll's mixture erupted naturally into Louis's mind. There had been, too, a time in his early youth in Edinburgh when he had been haunted by a series of sequential dreams night after night. In these dreams he was leading a double life which seemed absolutely as real as his actual daytime activities. He dreamed that he worked by day in a horrible surgery, and lived by night in one of the tall lands of the Old Town. He became so obsessed by this double life that he consulted a

'The man . . . leaped up, and caught hold of the bowsprit.' (From the first edition of *Kidnapped*)

doctor who gave him an opiate. The dreams stopped. At the time that *Jekyll and Hyde* came out some people criticized Jekyll's use of the powder as being too materialistic, or, as Henry James called it, 'too explicit and explanatory'; to our own generation, which takes the change or control of personality by drugs for granted, Jekyll's nostrum does not seem to be especially far-fetched. The true novelty of the story lay in the physical transformation of Dr Jekyll into Mr Hyde, and it was presumably this that gave the book its universal appeal. In classical mythology, as in German fairy-tales, people could transpose themselves to look like birds or animals; only Stevenson conceived the process by which one human being became physically, mentally and spiritually another. He had observed the dreadful changes which alcohol could make in such a man as his once distinguished friend Walter Ferrier. At Davos he had seen the dreaded alteration which disease can bring about. But it was the idea of the total incarnation of a good man's evil nature into a Caliban figure which fascinated his Victorian readers, who were as preoccupied with good and evil as they were with death itself.

Today Dr Jekyll's predicament does not seem as awesome as it did to Louis Stevenson's contemporaries. Perhaps by familiarity, and by becoming common phrase in the English language, *Jekyll and Hyde* seems to me to have lost its bite. *Markheim*, the story of a murderer who redeems himself and confesses, is somehow more alarming but neither story has the terror and the pervasive evil which Henry James evokes in *The Turn of the Screw*—a book, published in 1898, which Louis did not live to read. Henry James has written of *Jekyll and Hyde* as an example of Stevenson's 'heartless independence' from the necessity of introducing female characters into his stories. 'The gruesome tone of the tale', he suggested in an article for the *Century Magazine*, written in 1887, which he showed Louis in proof, 'is, no doubt, deepened by their absence; it is like the late afternoon light of a foggy Sunday, when even inanimate objects have a kind of wicked look.' He quotes with keen approval the account of Mr Utterson the lawyer's visit to Jekyll's house when Jekyll himself, now and for ever irretrievably Hyde, is locked in his laboratory. The butler tells Utterson, 'Well, when that masked thing like a monkey jumped from among the chemicals and whipped into the cabinet, it went down my spine like ice.' 'That is the effect', according to James, 'upon the reader of most of the story. I say most rather than all, because the ice rather melts in the sequel.'

At Skerryvore Louis wrote the *Memoir* of his old friend Fleeming Jenkin, who had died suddenly in Edinburgh in June 1885 of blood-poisoning following a trivial operation on his foot. This, Louis's sole biographical effort, was published by Longmans in 1887 as the introduction to a collection of Jenkin's scientific papers, and was written at his widow's behest. It is a workmanlike and not un-interesting book, and Louis took his usual scrupulous care in the writing of it.

We have seen that Fanny Stevenson actively influenced the writing of *Dr Jekyll and Mr Hyde*; she likewise played a role in the commencement of *Kidnapped*. During the days of the dramatic collaboration with Henley, he and Louis had invented a number of titles for plays that were never written. One of these, *The Hanging Judge*, appealed to Fanny and she asked her husband if he would mind her having a go at it. She laid the plot in the eighteenth century and sent for a quantity of Old Bailey trials from Louis's London bookseller. Both Louis and Fanny became absorbed by these trials. Sometimes the bookseller would send records of trials held elsewhere than at the Old Bailey. One of these which fascinated Louis was the trial of James Stuart in Aucharn in the Duror of Appin, for the murder of the factor of the forfeited estate of Ardshiel, Colin Campbell of Glenure, known as the Red Fox. Louis had once thought of writing a novel about this murder and its reper-cussions. Its narrator was to be a boy of his mother's family 'who should travel in Scotland as though it were a foreign country, meeting with various adventures and misadventures on the way'. He already had the character of David Balfour in his head; the Appin murder trial evidence gave him a complete description of Alan Breck Stuart. By March 1885 he was busily writing *Kidnapped*.

The new novel was a more accomplished and ambitious project than *Treasure Island*, and less artificial than *Prince Otto*. The opening scenes of David Balfour's journey to the House of Shaws and his reception there by his uncle snatch at the reader's imagination. While writing it Louis drew on his own early memories of the Highlands, in particular of the island of Mull and the isthmus called the Isle of Earraid. He had known the coast of the High-lands during his own abortive efforts to become a lighthouse engineer, and now he recalled those experiences in the seclusion of his sick-room at Skerryvore. Of the characterization of Alan Breck and of David Balfour it is hard to speak too highly; they stand four-square. Writing in 1887 Henry James called *Kidnapped* Louis's best book to date, saying that it was worthy to stand beside *Henry*

Esmond and was superior to the work of Louis's own favourite author, Alexandre Dumas. He called Alan Breck a masterpiece, but criticized the beginning and the end of the book—withholding belief from Uncle Ebenezer of Shaws, and complaining that David Balfour's 'history stops without ending, as it were'. James suspected that in the beginning Louis was over-conscious of the fact that the book would initially he serialized in a paper for boys, and had wanted to give these the kind of thrills they would be expecting to find in the magazine. He praised as 'magnificent' the chapters of *The Flight in the Heather*, and again used the word 'genius' to describe Louis's work. It seems to me likely that Louis Stevenson was less influenced by the prospect of a juvenile audience than by his own innate taste for adventure, which was in itself boyish. The theme of pursuit and escape, the fear of being caught, keeps reappearing in his novels—in *Treasure Island*, in *Prince Otto* and in *St Ives* for example. The descriptions of David Balfour's illness and exhaustion seems to be a reflection of Louis's own frequent state of physical debility, and is one of the best accounts of such a state in English fiction.

During the latter part of his time in Bournemouth, Louis had discovered Tolstoy and was intensely under the Russian's influence. He would talk to his stepson about 'the area of suffering', and seemed to have manufactured for himself a philosophy indistinguishable from that of the Sermon on the Mount—'Christianity without Christ—that was about what it amounted to,' Lloyd Osbourne wrote in later years. An alarming idea was connected with Ireland, then once again in a state of ferment, with murderous attacks aimed at those who had rented farms from tenants evicted by the British. Louis's plan, which Lloyd characterized as 'nightmarish', was that the Stevensons and Lloyd himself should troop over to Ireland, rent one of the farms, and so get themselves murdered. Louis was convinced that the sacrifice of 'a distinguished English literary man and his family, thus engaged in the assertion of human rights', would 'arrest the whole civilized world'. The crazy scheme was only dropped when it was clear that Thomas Stevenson was dying. The family from Skerryvore hurried up to Edinburgh in May 1887. There Louis was much shocked to find not the father he had known, but a mindless zombie:

> Once more I saw him. In the lofty room,
> Where oft with lights and company his tongue
> Was trump to honest laughter, sat attired

'He cursed me once more in Gaelic and took himself off.' (From the first edition of *Kidnapped*)

A something in his likeness. 'Look!' said one
Unkindly kind. 'Look up it is your boy!'
And the dread changeling gazed on me in vain.

After his father's death Louis was at first assailed by 'ugly images
of sickness, decline and impaired reason' but these passed away
with time. 'He now haunts me,' Louis wrote to Miss Boodle,
'strangely enough in two guises: as a man of fifty lying on a hillside
and carving mottoes on a stick, strong and well; and as a younger
man, running down the sands into the sea near North Berwick,
myself—*aetat* 11—somewhat horrified at finding him so beautiful
when stripped.'

From Edinburgh Louis and Fanny returned to Bournemouth.
The doctors now declared that Louis could no longer stay in Great
Britain with safety and should, for his health, go to a species of
Davos for consumptives in Colorado. Save in his mind's eye he
never saw Edinburgh or Scotland again.

10

Westward Ho!

FANNY STEVENSON was distraught at leaving what she called her 'little nest' at Skerryvore. Louis, although he burst into a flood of tears on his last morning in the house, seemed not to mind going away at all. Lloyd Osbourne noticed that in Samoa Louis would never speak of Skerryvore. Lloyd even wondered whether the scheme for being murdered by the Landleaguers had appealed to Louis because it would have formed, at least, an alternative to Bournemouth. Apart from his perpetual illnesses there, life in a bourgeois seaside villa must very soon have palled on a being of his romantic views. He was soon obsessed by the prospect of living in Colorado or New Mexico, and wrote to Lloyd of their future life in the wilds, with rifles on the walls and bearskins on the mud floors, of mustangs and silver spurs. In his new mood there was little sign that he had lost his youth in Bournemouth, as Lloyd alleged. In truth he never lost it to the day of his death.

There was one pressing problem about the American adventure, and that was what to do with Louis's mother? Struthious though she was by nature, Maggie Stevenson had been through an appalling time with her dying husband over the last few years and was told by her medical advisers that she needed a complete change of scene. Louis and Fanny decided that she must come with them to America, and when she protested that she would only be an encumbrance, they declared that should she not come they themselves would not go at all. So began the astonishing odyssey of this staid but gay Edinburgh lady, who was fifty-eight years old and from now on invariably wore, through thick and thin, the starched cap of white organdie with streamers which was the symbol of the Victorian upper-middle-class widow. She wore the caps in the forests of the Adirondacks, she wore them when strolling on a South

Seas beach with a naked cannibal chief. She had a great store of these caps, taught outlandish domestics how to launder and starch them, and in consequence survived the worst tropical heat looking crisp and fresh.

On August 22nd, 1887, the Stevenson party set off from London in the S.S. *Ludgate Hill*. There were five travellers, Fanny and Louis, his mother, Lloyd and the Swiss maid, Valentine. The journey took seventeen days and the sea was as tempestuous as in winter-time. They had decided against travelling up to Liverpool to board one of the luxurious ocean liners there because it was judged the long rail journey would be too strenuous for Louis. Their boat turned out to be full of valuable stallions and of monkeys, and Louis was intensely happy during this voyage: 'I had literally forgotten what happiness was, and the full mind ... My heart literally sang,' he wrote to his cousin Bob.

Before sailing, they had all stayed at a family hotel in Finsbury and here their most intimate friends came to bid them adieu, including Henry James, who had sent a case of champagne to the boat. Edmund Gosse went to see them on the very night before they sailed and found Louis looking much better and less emaciated than he had feared. Louis was in mourning for his father and was, Gosse reported,

> quite stylishly dressed in a black velvet coat and waistcoat, a black silk necktie and dark trousers, so that instead of looking like a lascar out of employment, as he generally does, he looked extremely elegant and refined, his hair over his shoulders, but very tidy, and burnished like brass with brushing. He prowled about the room in his usual noiseless panther fashion ... as charming as he ever was, but with a little more sadness and sense of crisis than usual.

Louis asked Gosse to be one witness to his will, the hotel landlady being the other.

It was this somewhat rough passage aboard the *Ludgate Hill* that convinced Louis that what suited him best was a life at sea. Much to her family's surprise his mother liked the sea-life too. 'Mrs Stevenson has turned out a regular sea bird !' Fanny wrote to Colvin from the steamer. 'We call her Mother Carey's chicken, the stormy petrel, etc. We have had to watch her lest she should be washed overboard, or take it into her head to mount the rigging.' Mrs Stevenson actually bruised her spine on the voyage, due to leaping into a hammock with 'a lot of giddy young things'. She lay for some time where she fell (the hammock strings had collapsed) with Valentine beside her reading *Daisy Miller* aloud. Louis found it 'very funny to hear it read in Valentine's accent'.

Louis and his family approached New York in a private and guileless mood. They were astonished by their reception. In his secluded life at Bournemouth Louis had had no inkling of his transatlantic fame. The first hint of this was the arrival on board the *Ludgate Hill* of two pilots, one of whom went by the sobriquet of Mr Hyde, whilst the other was called Dr Jekyll because he was easier going and better natured than his partner. A stage version of *Jekyll and Hyde* was about to play to full houses in New York. Newspaper reporters swarmed aboard the *Ludgate Hill*, and Louis soon found himself giving what we should now call a press conference. He tried to dismiss it all as a nine-days' wonder, but it proved to be far more durable. Not only was he enjoying newspaper fame, but he was approached by several publishers who offered him what seemed extravagant sums for weekly or monthly articles. He finally settled with Mr Burlingame, editor of *Scribner's*, to supply a monthly article for twelve months at three thousand five hundred dollars a year—about seven hundred pounds. The subjects of the articles were entirely up to him, and the results, though he found it hard going, were some of the best of his essays. At first startled, then tantalized by his fame, Louis soon had a healthy reaction against it all. He retired to the Fairchilds' mansion at Newport: 'I am much happier here, where I see no one and live my own life.' He was even embarrassed by the size of the sums of money offered him. 'I tell you I do dislike this battle of the dollars,' he wrote to Burlingame. 'I feel sure you all pay too much here in America; and I beg you not to spoil me any more. For I am getting spoiled; I do not want wealth, and I feel these big sums demoralize me.' To Gosse, who knew the eastern seaboard of the United States, Louis wrote that he had had 'some experience of American appreciation; I like a little of it, but there is too much ... I like myself better in the woods.'

[II]

The woods to which Louis was referring were those of the Adirondacks, and specifically those of Saranac, which lies twenty-seven miles into the forests, and not far from the Canadian border. After taking advice, the Stevensons had decided that the long journey to Colorado would prove too taxing for Louis's health. They had compromised on Saranac Lake, in the Adirondacks, a place of pine-trees and wild bears. At Saranac a young and already well-known doctor, Edward Livingston Trudeau, himself a consumptive, was established as a recognized expert on tuberculosis, and patients flocked to him from the east coast. Saranac was then—and out of season still is—a rather isolated hamlet in upper New York State. Its inhabitants represent the grass-roots of American life; they are friendly and welcoming to strangers. The lake, now called Lake Placid, is a small and beguiling piece of water; and, despite an airstrip, and on its margin, motels, it has changed little in aspect since Trudeau's day.

New York and his sudden, vocal fame had exhausted Louis, so, leaving him with the hospitable Fairchilds in Newport, Fanny and Lloyd made an expedition up into the Adirondacks to look for winter quarters. These they found in the wooden house of a guide named Baker, who conducted visitors into the woods for shooting and fishing excursions. He and his wife ordinarily took in boarders at Baker's Cottage, but Fanny persuaded them to let off a good part of the house to the Stevensons. The Bakers lived in the rest, shut away behind double doors. Baker's Cottage—or, as it was usually called, 'Baker's'—is a house of small dimensions, largely constructed on one floor. It was, and it is to this day, painted white, with green shutters, a red tiled roof and commodious veranda. The entrance to the Stevensons' part of this establishment was through the kitchen. Thence you penetrated into a fairly large sitting-room with an open fireplace for log fires. Further on still you reached Fanny's and Louis's rooms, and beyond that a little room which Louis commandeered as a study. Mrs Thomas Stevenson's bedroom was further on still, and up a steep staircase was Lloyd's room and a slip-room for Valentine. The house stands on a knoll above the river, which can be both seen and heard from the house, with the village ten minutes' walk away. The Adirondacks were flamboyant with the vivid colours of the Fall. Louis declared that this brilliant foliage corresponded exactly to that depicted on Skelt's Penny Plain and Twopence Coloured theatrical scenes of his childhood, and in which he had never hitherto completely believed. He said that the whole setting thus reminded him of Leith Street and home, while his mother called Saranac 'very highland'. Even in Samoa Louis and his mother sought out or invented parallels with the scenery of Scotland.

In October 1887 Louis wrote a long letter to Henry James, thanking him for the article in *The Century*, which had just appeared. 'It may be from natural partiality, I think it the best you have written.' He described 'Baker's' as being on a hill with a sight of the river but none of the lake. This lack he did not regret: 'I like water (fresh water I mean) either running swiftly amongst stones, or else largely qualified with whisky.' He wrote that the sun was shining in over his shoulder and that from the next room he could hear the bell of Lloyd's typewriter as his stepson pattered off the first chapters of what later became, with Louis's collaboration, *The Wrong Box.*

[III]

Louis, with his mother and Valentine, had followed Fanny and Lloyd so soon as the lease of the rooms at Baker's Cottage was confirmed. They travelled by the railway to Loon Lake, which reminded the elder Mrs Stevenson of Perthshire as it might have been two centuries earlier. From Loon Lake they went by a buggy in the rain to Saranac. In Baker's Cottage they found Fanny in petticoat and apron busily cooking their dinner. At Saranac she was once more in her pioneering element, struggling against the difficulties of housekeeping, aided by her mother-in-law, by Valentine and by a young Irish maid who had been engaged for them by the Lows in New York. The chief culinary standby at Saranac was venison. The cottage kitchen lacked a coffee-pot and a teapot (because the locals made both coffee and tea in saucepans) and they were unable to buy an egg-cup in Saranac. For shopping in the village they used a buckboard, a long elastic board on wheels, with a seat in the middle of it which could just hold two people if necessary.

The routine soon established at Baker's Cottage was spartan; Louis was very intent on their cottage being run as a 'Hunter's Home' and would not even allow a table-cloth on the stained deal table. When his mother complained of the draughts round her feet and wished for a footstool, she was only allowed to have sawn-off logs to put her feet upon. She had her fire lit at half past six in the morning, and remained in the 'very bright and cheery room' reading and writing letters. Louis and Lloyd were at work in separate rooms, and, rather than disturb them, she would squeeze out of the house by one of her diminutive windows. They all lunched at twelve-thirty, and then two of them went for a drive. Louis usually took a solitary walk, and very much disliked meeting any of the inhabitants. He was not popular in Saranac.

As winter set in, the advantages of Baker's Cottage became less apparent. In mid-November the thermometer dropped to twenty-five below zero. Louis had slight frost-bite on the ears, and Valentine found one morning that her handkerchief under her pillow was frozen into a ball of ice. The kitchen floor, as soon as it was washed with hot water, became a sort of skating-rink. By the end of January the temperature had dropped again, this time to forty below zero. Louis's buffalo-skin coat was frozen fast to the kitchen door, and the edge of Valentine's dress, having got damp from the kitchen floor, was frozen hard all day. All the same the climate seemed to suit Louis, and so, to some extent, did Dr Trudeau.

Although proclaimed a genius in his own lifetime, Dr Edward Livingstone Trudeau seems not to have realized till much later in life that Robert Louis Stevenson was another. Louis's untidy and slovenly habits and his constant use of cigarettes seem to have alienated the doctor; and although they kept on friendly terms, they had frequent arguments which ended in quarrels. These arguments turned upon such trivia as the different ways of sending luggage on the American and European railway systems. Louis did not like the use made of guinea-pigs by Trudeau, who infected them with tubercular bacilli in his laboratory. Louis would neither hunt nor fish at Saranac, and was always shocked by cruelty to animals. One day he left Trudeau's laboratory abruptly when the doctor began exhibiting living and dead specimens of diseased guinea-pigs. After Robert Louis Stevenson's death Trudeau, who had by then realized exactly who his distinguished Scots patient had been, took the trouble to verify that Louis had not died of consumption. In Trudeau's opinion, however, it was wrong to say that Louis had never had the disease. At Saranac Trudeau judged that Louis's tuberculosis had been in an arrested state. While there Louis had had no active symptoms such as haemorrhage, fever or tubercular bacilli, but Trudeau was convinced that his patient had undoubtedly had tuberculosis, and that it may have become active again after he had left the Adirondacks. Although he found that Adirondack life had soon palled and he could not wait to get away, Louis gave the place its due. 'Saranac, if not deliriously delectable, has not been a failure,' he wrote to Colvin: 'Nay, from the mere point of view of my wicked body, it has proved a success.' From the point of view of his writing, Saranac had proved a success, too.

[IV]

The monthly articles for which Louis was under contract to

Scribner's stimulated him. He had been given *carte blanche* in his choice of subjects and he now produced some of his best and, in their day, his most famous essays. For some of these, like *The Lantern Bearers* and *Random Memories*, he drew on his own childish or youthful souvenirs. In *A Chapter on Dreams*, which we have discussed near the beginning of this book, he also indulged in personal reminiscence. In others—*Pulvis et Umbra, A Christmas Sermon*—he returned to his old didactic vein. But on Christmas Eve, 1887, he announced in a letter to Colvin that he had 'fallen head over heels into a new tale, *The Master of Ballantrae*'. He wrote that he had now no thought apart from it, and had already got up to page ninety-two of the draft. 'It is to be a most seizing tale,' he assured Colvin.

In *The Master of Ballantrae*, Stevenson was once more exploring the subject of evil, which he found so fascinated him. The origins of this book, which begins with such brilliance and peters out to a weak and unconvincing end, went far back in Louis's life. In January 1876, when he was twenty-five, he had gone on a tramp through Carrick and Galloway, and had passed through Ballantrae; the name struck him, and he stored it away in his memory for future use. In August 1881, when travelling between Pitlochry and Strathardle, on his way to a dreary, wet summer visit, he had invented a story which was 'conceived in the Highland rain, the blend of the smell of heather and bog-plants', but he seems not to have carried this conception far. And then one winter's night in Saranac in 1887, wrapped in his buffalo-skin overcoat, he was gliding up and down the veranda of Baker's Cottage, thinking. It was a dark night, with the air extraordinarily clear and cold, and smelling of 'the purity of forests'. He had just completed his third or fourth reading of Captain Marryat's *The Phantom Ship*, a book he much admired and wished to emulate. He tells us that pacing up and down the veranda of Baker's he addressed himself to his 'engine'. ' "Come," said I to my engine, "let us make a tale, a story of many lands and countries, of the sea and the land, savagery and civilization".' The tale was to take place in Scotland, India and the Adirondacks. He then remembered the name of Ballantrae, and the story he had thought up on the way to Pitlochry. Down below Baker's Cottage he could hear the river 'contending with ice and boulders'. A few lights shone in the distance far away. He experienced a total sense of isolation—'for the making of a story here were fine conditions'.

In the next days, in Fanny's absence, Louis repeated his ideas to his mother, in those efforts at clarification in which his wife customarily participated. He relied greatly on the Pitlochry story for his projected novel — 'So long ago, so far away it was, that I first evoked the faces and the mutual tragic situation of the men of Durrisdeer.' As in *Treasure Island* and in *Kidnapped*, Stevenson resorted to narrative in the first person, but in the new book he had two narrators; Ephraim Mackellar, the ancient factor of the Duries of Durrisdeer, and the Chevalier de Burke, an Irish supporter of the Jacobite cause. The story of *The Master of Ballantrae* opens in a year which had always absorbed Stevenson, that of the Jacobite defeat at Culloden, 1745.

The story of *The Master* is as well known to lovers of Robert Louis Stevenson as that of *Kidnapped* itself. It concerns the two sons of the aged Lord Durrisdeer; the elder of them is the old man's heir and uses the title of Master of Ballantrae, the other is plain Henry Durie, who is as good as his brother is irrevocably bad — almost, indeed, diabolic. In 1745, by a family arrangement not then uncommon, the Master of Ballantrae goes to join the Jacobite rebels, whilst his brother stays at Durrisdeer in public support of King George, thus ensuring that, whichever side wins, the estate of Durrisdeer cannot be sequestrated. While at Saranac, Louis had twice met the widow of General Custer, who voiced the usual inquiry as to why Louis never had girls or women in his novels. After some argument, Louis promised Mrs Custer a heroine for his next book. Whether he remembered this pledge or not, *The Master of Ballantrae* does indeed contain a form of heroine in the insipid Alison Graeme, an heiress destined for the wicked Ballantrae, whom she loves. However, after the false reports of his death at Culloden she allows herself to be wooed and won by the younger brother.

The Master of Ballantrae was written under circumstances which Fanny thought conducive to strain. Louis sold the first chapters, and promised the remainder, to Burlingame for serialization by *Scribner's*, a prospect that made him feel under pressure. When the Stevenson contingent left Saranac he took the manuscript from Saranac to Manasquan, New Jersey, but did little work on it. During the voyage of the yacht *Casco* from San Francisco he went on plugging away at *The Master*, and at last completed it in Honolulu in 1888 to 1889, by which time the book was, according to Fanny, 'beginning to get a little on his nerves'. Louis had long had the odd habit of turning from an uncompleted work to something new, picking up the threads of the former tale whenever he felt so inclined. His serialization agreement for *The Master* precluded his exercising this habit, and the last quarter of the book indisputably shows the author's boredom with the whole family of Durrisdeer. Even at Saranac Louis was also writing the *Scribner's* articles, re-writing *The Wrong Box*, reading, studying music, receiving visitors and concocting from twenty to thirty-five long letters a day. Once the first burst of energy was over, he was inclined temporarily to shelve *The Master of Ballantrae*. To Mr Burlingame of *Scribner's* he wrote from Saranac that winter that he had to 'leave aside' the new Jacobite novel as he was 'quite worked out'. To the end of his life Louis followed this curious system of leaving things aside, with the result that when he died both *St Ives* and his masterpiece, *Weir of Hermiston*, have come down to us in an uncompleted state.

As Saranac got colder and colder, the shivering family in Baker's Cottage turned their minds more and more to a voyage in tropic seas. A literary impresario, Sam McClure, who had tried without success to capture Louis with a princely offer of ten thousand dollars a year for a weekly column in the New York *World*, encouraged the idea of an exotic voyage in a chartered yacht, to be paid for, he suggested, by monthly letters from Louis on their experiences, letters which McClure undertook to syndicate. Sam McClure was then a rising star in his profession, a slight young man in his twenties, with ash-blond hair which he constantly ruffled. A born enthusiast, he was forever suggesting projects to Louis, whom he several times visited at Saranac, skating with him on the frozen lake. Louis customarily tried to bring Sam McClure down to earth, but over the question of chartering a yacht he himself became enthusiastic too. Mrs Thomas Stevenson herself was much tempted by the project, Fanny was acquiescent, Lloyd Osbourne was mad about it, and Valentine Roche agreed to go. Evenings at Baker's Cottage were now excitedly spent poring over maps of the Pacific and Indian Oceans, and consulting Findlay's *Directories of the World*.

McClure sought in vain for a suitable yacht on the Eastern sea-board. Fanny set off alone for San Francisco to see her sister Nellie Sanchez and her own daughter Belle Strong and to make inquiries about private yachts there. After her departure in March, Saranac seemed more and more depressing to Louis, so he, his mother, Lloyd and Valentine precipitately left Baker's Cottage for New York in April, and then went on to Manasquan, New Jersey. Here Louis became enamoured of catboats, with which he and his painter friend from the old days at Grez-sur-Loing, Will Low, experimented. The manuscript of *The Master of Ballantrae* went to Manasquan too, but proved incapable of competing with this new interest in catboats and received scant attention from its author.

Fanny had been gone six weeks, and there was still no news of a San Francisco yacht. Then suddenly a telegram from her arrived at Manasquan: 'Can secure splendid sea-going schooner yacht "Casco" for seven hundred and fifty a month with most comfortable accommodation for six aft and six forward. Can be ready for sea in ten days. Reply immediately.'

Louis did reply immediately: 'Blessed girl, take the yacht and expect us in ten days.' So began Louis's South Seas venture, which only death was to end.

[V]

Hardly had Fanny left Baker's Cottage for California than Louis received a letter from London which totally shattered his peace of mind, gave him palpitations by day and insomnia by night, and rendered him at first furiously angry and then soused him in despair. To Baxter he wrote that this letter made him wish that he had died at Hyères when 'all was well' with him. 'The dreadful part of a thing like this is that it shakes your confidence in all affection and inspires you with a strange, sick longing to creep back into yourself and care for no one.' Who was the author of this letter and what were the horrors it contained?

The letter, dated from Chiswick on March 9th, 1888, was from Louis's old crony and intimate friend, William Ernest Henley. The letter was marked 'Private and Confidential', and was chiefly concerned with regrets for Louis's absence in America — 'Why the devil do you go and bury yourself in that blood country of dollars and spew?' — and also enlarged upon Henley's own exhausted state of mind. It was a long letter, such as Henley and Louis had often exchanged in the course of their thirteen years' friendship. But the letter contained one passage which stabbed into Louis's brain like a stiletto. I will quote this paragraph at once, and try to consider its purport afterwards. To Louis it constituted the gravest insult to Fanny and, through Fanny, to himself:

I read *The Nixie* with considerable amazement. It's Katharine's; surely it's Katharine's? The situation, the environment, the principal figure — *voyons!* There are even reminiscences of phrases and imagery, parallel incidents — *Que sais-je?* It is all better focussed, no doubt, but I think it has lost as much (at least) as it has gained; and why there wasn't a double signature is what I've not been able to understand.

Now *The Nixie* was a story by Fanny Stevenson, published in the March number of *Scribner's*. It was a story about a young man on a railway train who meets a Nixie (or Fairy) in his compartment. It was not a particularly skilful story, and was probably published by Scribner merely because it was written by Robert Louis Stevenson's wife. It was more or less derived from an unpublished tale by Louis's first cousin, Katharine de Mattos, Bob Stevenson's sister, who had made a disastrous marriage, lived in Chelsea, was given financial aid by Louis and was prominent in the circle surrounding Henley, on whom she had a paramount influence. Fanny and Louis had been present when Mrs de Mattos' story had been read, or any rate discussed, at Henley's house. In the de Mattos manuscript the girl is not a fairy but an ordinary human being newly escaped from a lunatic asylum. Fanny, who relished interfering in other people's literary efforts, immediately urged that the girl should be not a mad person, but a fairy. Katharine had demurred and had stuck to her original theme. The story was finished and was hawked round the magazines by Henley. There were no takers, and Mrs de Mattos then wrote to Fanny to say that she could now try to do anything she liked with it, turning the girl into a Nixie. The authoress of the first version even asked Fanny to send her a copy should it ever be published. In Louis's eyes Henley and his clique were accusing Mrs Robert Louis Stevenson of literary theft and plagiarism. At this distance of time the quarrel over *The Nixie* may sound like a storm in a tea-cup. To Louis, Henley's letter was an outrageous act of disloyalty from an old friend whom he had frequently helped when Henley was hard up for money.

The Nixie row was not by any means the first time Henley and Louis had quarrelled; but hitherto Louis had always forgiven the friend to whom he was devoted, and they had been several times reconciled. Henley was notoriously difficult to get on with, whilst Louis himself had a high temper and was very thin-skinned. It is clear that Henley, who was still impoverished and was drinking too much whisky to bolster himself up, was piqued at Louis's growing fame and riches. It is likely, also, that he resented the financial aid which Louis was always liberally doling out to him, for few people like receiving charity even from old friends. Then, Henley had always taken umbrage at Fanny's brevity of manner to him in the Bournemouth years, when all she was trying to do was to protect her husband from his insensitive and bibulous friend. Henley also suspected what was indeed true, that Louis's heart had never been in the play-writing collaboration; while Louis saw himself as doing his best to give Henley a leg-up by a collaboration which Louis himself found very tiring and in which he did not personally much believe.

W. E. Henley's younger brother, a ham actor, was then in the States taking the lead in *Deacon Brodie*, which, vaguely successful in Chicago, went on tour and proved a failure. When she was alone in New York in the winter of 1887, Fanny had seen Teddy Henley, who had asked her for money. He had recently distinguished himself in Philadelphia by becoming publicly involved in a bar brawl; in New York he was staying at a much more expensive hotel than the Stevensons themselves could afford. 'The drunken whoreson bugger and bully living himself in the best hotels, and smashing inoffensive strangers in the bar! It is too sickening,' Louis had written to Baxter from Saranac in December 1887. 'The violence of this letter comes from my helplessness: all I try to do for W.E. (in the best way) by writing these plays is burked by this inopportune lad. Can nothing be done? In the meanwhile I add another £20 to W.E.'s credit.'

After six or seven drafts, Louis did manage to reply to Henley's letter in a halting and agonized manner. Charles Baxter, to whom Louis confided the whole affair at great length, wrote him an admirably fair letter in which he said that he refused to believe that Henley, notoriously tactless as a friend, had 'wilfully' intended to hurt either Louis or Fanny. He attributed Henley's attitude to irritation over the plays, and thought that the recent gifts to the Henley family of money, 'which it gave you so much pleasure to suggest, and me to carry out, may have carried a certain gall with them'. Baxter added that 'the presence of pecuniary help' might emphasize the 'bitter contrast between success and failure'. He suggested that Louis and Henley should not correspond for a strict six months.

Although Fanny Stevenson was, so to speak, safely out of earshot in San Francisco, Louis made what seems the unnecessary mistake of telling her of Henley's accusation. She wrote off at once to Baxter, to say that Henley and his circle had now nearly murdered Louis, and that she herself felt like taking morphia or arsenic, both of which she kept by her bed. She could do without their English friends, she emphasized, although it was very bitter. 'I gave up my own country and my own friends for Louis, and God knows I was sincere ... I loved them all.' 'The injury can never be condoned,' she wrote in another letter to Baxter, 'nor do I ever wish to see England again.' Fanny may have earnestly believed that she was telling Baxter the truth, but in fact she had never really loved Louis's English friends at all. Henley, in particular, she disliked, although she wrote him a long letter on moving into Baker's Cottage at Saranac. This she signed 'ever affectionately yours—Fanny V. de G. Stevenson.'

Over the coming months Louis and Henley patched up their differences until Louis finally broke with his old friend in December 1890, because Henley, who then lived in Edinburgh, had lacked the grace to so much as call on Mrs Thomas Stevenson, then again at Heriot Row during a temporary return home from the South Seas. In 1917, writing to Louis's biographer Graham Balfour, old Sidney Colvin summed up Henley's relationship with Louis Stevenson:

We know that Henley's disloyalty to Louis in later years was chronic and due to a combination of causes—bad blood bred of scrofula and whisky counting for much, jealousy of Louis's successes won out of collaboration far more, resentment of Fanny's short (and necessary) ways with him at Bournemouth far more yet, and the blind flattery of his own bodyguard, including some foolish women, far most of all.

[VI]

The Stevensons' eighth wedding anniversary fell on May 19th, 1888. Louis was still catboating on the Manasquan River, and Fanny was in San Francisco. He wrote to her that he did not dwell so much on that particular day, and that if he had had the dates he would prefer to celebrate other anniversaries—the day when he looked through the window at the Hôtel Chevillon at Grez and saw Fanny for the first time, or the day when he came back to see her in Paris after his first absence. He agreed that the marriage day had been a mightily good one for himself—'for you, I wish I was sure, it would have been better if my health had been so. The longer I go on, the more the worst of me is my health.' Fanny, who once averred that she hated all anniversaries, had no reason to dislike that of her marriage. In protecting Louis she had found her vocation in life and she can have had few or no regrets.

After the receipt of Fanny's telegram about the *Casco*, Louis, his mother, Lloyd and Valentine left Manasquan for New York. They found the city weather close, and hastened to entrain for Chicago, where there was a wait of eight hours. This part of the transcontinental journey was almost luxurious; the second leg, on another train across the plains and over the mountains to Sacramento, provided accommodation that was cramped. The party's noses bled on crossing the Sierras, and they were relieved to reach Sacramento on June 7th. Here Fanny met them, 'looking', wrote her mother-in-law, 'so pretty in a new hat'. It turned out that the hat in fact belonged to Belle, who had been in Honolulu but had come back to San Francisco to bid Louis and her mother godspeed. Louis, whose health had been an intermittent anxiety on board the train, was put to bed under a doctor's care in the Occidental Hotel, while Fanny completed the arrangements for hiring the yacht. This proved more tricky than her cable to Manasquan had suggested, for the *Casco*'s owner, an eccentric millionaire named Dr Merritt, distrusted literary men generally, and had seen paragraphs about Louis in the local newspapers which led him to conclude that the Scots writer was a crank. He was also dubious about allowing an old lady on board. At interviews with him, however, both Louis and his mother passed muster, though Dr Merritt gave private instructions to his skipper, Captain Otis, to be prepared to bury Louis Stevenson at sea. 'The yacht is the apple of my eye,' he explained to Fanny. 'You may think your husband loves you, but I can assure you that I love my yacht a great better.'

The *Casco*, which was to be the Stevensons' home for the next six months, was a topsail schooner, ninety-five feet in length and with a seventy-ton burthen. With its white sails and white decks, and its gleaming brasswork, it was a beautiful little vessel. Although in the past it had been used for cruising, it was originally designed for racing in Californian waters. From the deck you stepped down into the cockpit, which was used as 'an open-air drawing-room' and had cushioned seats all round. The compass and the wheel were in the cockpit and, in early days, Fanny Stevenson exasperated the Captain (who was initially hostile to his passengers) by talking to the man at the wheel, which Captain Otis declared to be distracting. From the cockpit the companion stairs led downwards; to the right at the bottom was the Captain's cabin, and straight ahead was the after-cabin, a place brightly lit from a skylight and with four portholes. A table fastened to the floor of the after-cabin had a tablecloth of crimson Utrecht velvet, and the four sofas were upholstered to match. Above and behind these sofas were bunks, hidden by white lace curtains that run on brass rods. These berths were allotted to the three women of the party. Beneath the sofas were clothes lockers. A mirror was let into a wall, and on either side of this mirror was a door—one leading through a small dressing-room with a fixed basin to Lloyd's cabin, and beyond this again to the dining-room. The other door gave on to a second small dressing-room and beyond this to Louis's spacious cabin. Doors from the dining-room led to the pantry and the galley, and then on to the crew's quarters. It was a well-appointed if slightly gaudy little ship.

While Louis rested in the Occidental Hotel, his family busied themselves with buying stores for the voyage. Fanny chose everything herself, from 'whisky to the sailors' tabocco'. She sent her mother-in-law, distinguished as ever in her white widow's cap, to order seventy pounds of the cheapest plug chewing-tobacco. On Belle Strong's advice Mrs Thomas Stevenson, Fanny and Valentine were measured by a Chinese tailor for *holakus* or Mother Hubbards, which were cool in the tropics and meant that you could remove your stays. Old Mrs Stevenson ordered some of these garments in black and white lawn and others of muslin. She was delighted with the Chinese tailoring but feared that the *Casco* ladies would be 'queer-looking customers in them!'

On June 26th the *Casco* party went aboard. Friends and reporters swarmed to see them off, but it was not until the 28th that the tug *Pelican* towed the yacht irrevocably out beyond the Golden Gates. The after-cabin was a solid mass of flowers and fruit from well-wishers, the whole dominated by a very large budding magnolia which stood in the centre of the crimson velvet-draped table. Belle Strong and Mrs Virgil Williams waved them good-bye from the wharf, and Mrs Williams found some means of sending Fanny a note on board. It read, simply, '*Ave atque Vale!*' As the *Casco* was being towed towards the open sea, the ferryboats in the Bay saluted her with three blasts, and even the Alamado train, which was passing, did the same. Valentine fell down the hatch and was badly bruised—'I wonder she was not killed' was Fanny's comment, in a note to Belle which she sent back by the tug. Through tear-blurred opera glasses she watched her daughter waving from the wharf. The Stevensons would be out of reach of letters for at least two months. All of the party were feverishly excited by their adventure. 'Isn't it wonderful that we are going to see all these strange, out-of-the-way places?' Mrs Thomas Stevenson wrote to her sister Jane in Edinburgh, a missive also taken back to San Francisco by the tug. 'I cannot yet realize it. I remember so well repeating as a little girl at school:

> Full many are the beauteous isles,
>   Unseen by human eye,
> That sleeping 'mid the ocean's smiles,
>   In sunny silence lie.

I have always longed to see them, and I can hardly believe that all those childish longings are to come true.'

Louis, also, had had his fantasies of the tropics when a child at Colinton Manse:

> I should like to rise and go
> Where the golden apples grow;
> Where below another sky
> Parrot islands anchored lie.

As an ailing youth in Heriot Row he had dreamed of an active life in exotic surroundings. Such dreams seemed now destined to come true. But the *Casco* voyage, at the end of which they had every intention of returning to England via the United States, had the primary purpose less of pandering to Louis's romanticism than of finally restoring him to health. They could not know that they were setting out on a six-year adventure, nor that Louis's incredible new life would now compete with, and later come to overshadow, many of his own books.

11

The South Seas

BEFORE the Stevensons sailed from San Francisco it had been agreed that the *Casco*'s first landfall should be made in the Marquesan Islands, a group lying eight degrees south of the Equator and then under the domination of the French. The Galapagos had been suggested as an alternative, but when Fanny learned that on the way to them you could be becalmed for several weeks or, if you were unlucky, several months, she sensibly insisted on their going to the Marquesas instead. The *Casco* began by making very good time— 206 miles in twenty-four hours, but later they would sometimes make only 35 miles in the same period. They met calms, head-seas and strong easterly currents. Soon they were watching the flying fish skidding above the surface of the sea. Captain Otis, Dr Merritt's cherished but surly American skipper, who had begun by regarding his strangely assorted passengers with open distaste, soon grew to like them very much indeed. In Mrs Thomas Stevenson he found and appreciated a formidable hand at whist. Soon he succumbed to Louis's well-known charm; when Fanny's daughter, Mrs Strong, welcomed the family in Honolulu she was amused to note that Captain Otis, so taciturn in San Francisco, was now giving an unconscious imitation of Louis's mannerisms and turns of speech. As the *Casco* battled on towards the Marquesas, Gibbon's *Decline and Fall* was being read aloud in the cockpit, mainly by Maggie Stevenson since it exhausted Louis to strain his voice in the open air. Soon the women took out their sewing and began making pyjamas and jackets of thin flannel for Louis against the hot weather ahead. Not to be outdone, the Captain busied himself with stitching new canvas covers for the cockpit cushions, his needle strapped sailor-fashion to the palm of his hand.

After thirty days at sea the *Casco* entered the narrow mouth of the lagoon known as Anaho Bay on Nuka-hiva, one of the main Marquesan islands. A pearly, translucent dawn was breaking over the mountain-tops. Even before the *Casco* had dropped anchor, a boat containing a white man and a tattooed native put off from the village on the shore, and approached the ship swiftly. It was soon followed by many more native boats, and in no time the *Casco* was swarming with natives, their brown skin decorated with marvellous arabesque tattoos. They had, not unnaturally, assumed the *Casco* to be a trading vessel, and when they found that the Stevensons had no wish to buy, or barter for, the fruit and the handwoven goods that were being hawked, the natives became hostile and seemed sneering and sarcastic. For the first and last time in the South Seas Louis felt apprehensive. He knew that the natives of the Marquesan islands had until lately been fierce cannibals, and probably, despite French gendarmes, officials and missionaries, continued covertly to be so still. At first the total language barrier unnerved him—for their visitors had a great deal to say but not one word could anyone aboard the *Casco* understand. The way in which the visiting natives squatted in a serried rank on the cabin floor to watch Louis writing up his journal made him feel very uneasy; but during his stay off Anaho Louis found it practicable to make friends with its inhabitants and even to learn some Polynesian words. Many of his new friends insisted on giving as presents to the Stevensons the very objects they had tried in the first place to make them buy. Louis began going on expeditions into the interior of Nuka-hiva, and up the steep mountain tracks, under the guidance of a French missionary, Frère Michel. From him and from the few other Europeans he came across, Louis learned much about the cannibal history of the Marquesas, and the way in which the islands were being gradually depopulated. This initial sight of a South Sea island surpassed his expectations, and he was, as he remained for the rest of his life, spellbound.

I very much doubt if anyone who has not directly experienced it can adequately conceive the enticing effect of a first visit to the islands of the South Seas. It is not a question of 'impact', which in this context is altogether too abrupt and harsh a word. The humid, scented air, the brilliance of the light on land and sea, the brash, virulent colours of the flowers and the flowering trees, the great mountain ranges swathed in their torrential foliage, the limpid, shimmering lagoons, the sights and smells and sounds—none of these combine to assail your senses, as do, say, the mountains and valleys of Switzerland. It is not a question of reacting, but of being soothed and somehow absorbed into this tumultuous, alien world. Quite soon you find that all your values have undergone a soft sea-change. Nothing seems to matter any more, time has no longer any consequence. These Polynesian islands and their people have none of the sadness innate in the islands of the Caribbean. They are merry and haunting and seductive. To yield up your mind to their influence is not only irresistible, it is inevitable as well. Even the current touristic development, so clearly foreseen by Herman Melville more than a century ago, can but superficially impinge upon the true atmosphere of these islands. By diligent reading and by verbal inquiry from travellers, Louis Stevenson had hoped to equip himself for his first voyage in the South Seas. The reality proved to him a revelation, and towered over all that even he had imagined.

'The interest, indeed, has been *incredible*,' Louis wrote to Colvin from an atoll in the Low Archipelago. 'I did not dream there were such places or such races.' To Henry James, Fanny wrote from Nukahiva that she had been so often disappointed that she had lost all faith in travellers' tales of the South Seas. Once there she found that 'the half' had not been told her. In the Marquesas, moreover, Louis's health improved to a startling degree. He would spend four hours wading in the lagoon in search of shells, he would ride a horse for another five, he would wait up till early morning and all the time he was keeping the diary from which he would manufacture travel-letters for Sam McClure's syndicate.

The lack of constraint was infectious. Fanny and Louis and Lloyd went about barefoot, and even Louis's mother gave up wearing stockings, and often shoes as well. 'I wish you could but just get a glimpse of that lady taking a moonlight promenade on the beach in the company of a gentleman dressed in a single handkerchief,' Fanny wrote of her mother-in-law to Henry James. 'It is impossible to believe that these charming people are not fully dressed in their beautiful tattooing.' On one occasion a secondary chief came to call on the *Casco* and got drunk on rum in the after-cabin. When the Stevensons asked him if they could see his tattooing, he (according to Fanny) 'stripped to the buff in a trice'. She found him 'a most beautiful sight', and neither she nor her mother-in-law 'were at all embarrassed' by this exhibition. Gifts of food were being constantly ferried to the *Casco* by the inhabitants of Anaho. The Stevensons were struck by the happiness and contentment of the Marquesans, and Louis's mother, in Edinburgh a pillar of the Missionary Societies, now doubted whether such European activities in Polynesia were either wise or kind. 'Their conduct to each other and to strangers, so far as kindliness and courtesy are concerned, is much more Christlike than that of many professing Christians,' she wrote to her sister Jane.

From the Marquesan islands of Nuka-hiva and Hiva-ao, the *Casco* set sail once more and headed for Tahiti, but stopping at Fakarava atoll on the way. The people of Fakarava were so impressed by the look of the *Casco* that they christened it 'the Silver Ship'—a name which Louis pondered on using for the South Seas book of which he intended his articles for McClure to be the core. He soon found, and presumably they all did, that it was landfall that really made their journey worth while, for conditions on the tiny *Casco* were very restricted, and it was easy to let other people get on one's nerves. On this subject Louis wrote to Colvin in October:

And yet the sea is a horrible place, stupefying to the mind and poisonous to the temper; the sea, the motion, the lack of space, the cruel publicity, the villainous tinned foods, the sailors, the captain, the passengers—but you are amply repaid when you sight an island, and drop anchor in a new world.

The coral atoll of Fakarava, their next port of call, was a sharp contrast to the lush mountainous islands of the Marquesa group. It was of the usual horseshoe shape, and seemed to be only just above the level of the sea; in bad hurricanes, indeed, the sea could wash right over parts of Fakarava with devastating effects. Leaving the *Casco* at anchor in the lagoon, the Stevensons hired a cottage on the beach.

By day Fakarava was exceedingly hot, but they all rose with the sun, bathed in the lagoon, and then ate breakfast cooked on a discarded American cooking-stove which Fanny, with her customary talent for improvisation, had reconditioned, having found it stranded on the beach. The mornings were spent sorting shells gathered the day before. After lunch and a siesta they would cross to the windward side of the atoll to hunt for more shells and to peer at strange highly coloured poisonous tropical fish trapped by the tide in the rock pools.

On Fakarava the evenings turned out to be the best time of all. Once the moon was up it made the shadows of the palm-trees so black and so distinct 'that one involuntarily stepped over them'. When they had dined, and bathed once more in the lagoon, they received their one invariable visitor—the half-Tahitian, half-French acting governor of Fakarava, Monsieur Donat Rimareau.

This intelligent official—seated on the only chair on the veranda, whilst his listeners lay on mattresses at his feet—would entertain his hosts with a recital of the islands' legends, which Louis would cap with narrations of Scottish ones. Monsieur Rimareau was superstitious, and said that he himself had seen many strange things which could not be explained away; in particular he instanced the soul of a dead child which, wrapped in a leaf, had been dropped in at the bereaved parents' door. In his later tale, *The Isle of Voices*, Louis made use of Monsieur Rimareau's gripping stories. 'I know that I never read *The Isle of Voices*', Fanny wrote years later, 'without a mental picture rising before me of the lagoon, and the cocoa palms, and the wonderful moonlight of Fakarava.'

They spent two placid weeks of September 1888 on Fakarava and then set sail south-east for Tahiti. Louis had more pressing things to do than gathering shells or even listening to Monsieur Rimareau's talks. For there was the uncompleted *Master of Ballantrae*, which he felt to be a millstone round his neck. Then he had to think about the syndicated articles for McClure. 'Tuesday, we shall leave for Tai'ti where I shall knock off and do some necessary work ashore,' he wrote to Colvin on September 21st.

[II]

On leaving Fakarava the passengers aboard the *Casco* shared once again regrets that would repeat themselves throughout their next years of cruising the South Seas: regrets that they were leaving places in which they had been very happy, and friendly people whom in the course of nature they were unlikely to see ever again. 'To come to a place so shut into the midst of waters,' wrote Mrs Thomas Stevenson on leaving Fakarava, 'to live in it, grow wonderfully at home in it, and then to leave it so utterly behind, is almost painfully dream-like. I wonder if in my sleep I shall walk in the shade of the cocoa-palms, and hear once more the surf breaking on the ocean beaches.' She, at any rate, still believed in their ultimate return to the British Isles. Whether by now Louis and Fanny in their heart of hearts did so is more questionable. From a little wooden house with grated verandas, set in a mango grove at Papeete, capital of Tahiti, Louis wrote to Colvin an account of a recent verbal exchange with Fanny. 'My chief reason for wishing to go back to England is to see Colvin,' said Louis. 'It is my *only* reason,' Fanny replied.

En route to Papeete from Fakarava, Louis fell ill and was confined to his berth. Arrived in Papeete he caught a species of cold in the head peculiar to Tahiti, where children died from it. A local French doctor, luckily wrong, predicted an imminent haemorrhage. None of the *Casco* party liked Papeete, which they found unattractive and judged to have 'a half and halfness' between western civilization and its own native culture. They inquired about the other side of the island but were fobbed off by being told that, although beautiful, it was inhabited by people as wild as those of Anaho. This decided them, for they had loved the people of Anaho in the Marquesas. They all piled into the *Casco* once more and set sail for Taravao on the southern coast.

This was a dull, empty place, humming with mosquitoes. Captain Otis and Lloyd went off prospecting for somewhere agreeable to live, and came across an aged Chinaman who owned a cart and horses, but refused to hire them out to strangers. On their return to the ship Fanny and Valentine went ashore in their turn, bearded the Chinese, and returned in triumph with his promise of two horses and the cart. This further impressive display of Fanny Stevenson's will-power meant that she could take Louis next day to somewhere he might like. On being asked where she wanted to go, she issued the simple and entirely characteristic direction: 'To the largest village and the most wild.' They thus ended up in Tautira, just along the coast. Tautira, and the friends they made there, seemed to them to constitute an earthly paradise. This was as well, since the fortuitous discovery that the *Casco*'s main masts were riddled with dry-rot meant that they were happily marooned at Tautira for nine weeks.

On Tautira Louis for some reason (perhaps contentment?) ceased to keep his travel journal. He did, however, when he was better, get down to work on *The Master of Ballantrae*, and almost completed this rugged Scottish story in that improbable *venue*. He also wrote large parts of two Polynesian ballads, *The Feast of Famine*, about the Marquesas, and *The Song of Rahero*, based on a legend of the Tivas, the people amongst whom, at Tautira, he was living. Both ballads are of excessive length, and I incline to think that Sidney Colvin, who signally failed to appreciate them, was right.

When Fanny and Valentine had brought Louis by the Chinese cart to Tautira along a track of sixteen miles crossed by twenty-one streams, they were forced to rely on the local gendarme to find them a house. The result was that they were charged an exorbitant rent, but as Louis was by then practically in a coma they had no choice but to agree. Next day there came to Tautira a certain Princess

Moë, the beautiful ex-Queen of Raiatea, whom Pierre Loti had much admired. Hearing of Louis's plight, she hastened over to the rented house with special food cooked by herself. Fanny was convinced that the Princess saved Louis's life. 'He was lying in a deep stupor when she first saw him, suffering from congestion of the lungs and in a burning fever.' Princess Moë declared that the Stevensons were being overcharged for their house, and insisted on them all coming to stay in the house or 'palace' of her relative, the sub-chief Ori a Ori. Both Ori a Ori and Princess Moë proved themselves friends in need. When Louis was better he exchanged names with Ori, thus becoming the sub-chief's brother. Ori, who spoke excellent French, was a handsome and imposing Tahitian, whom Mrs Thomas Stevenson likened to a Roman emperor, while to Fanny he resembled a colonel in the Life Guards.

It was not only Fanny, Louis and Lloyd who were enjoying themselves at Tautira. Mrs Thomas Stevenson was herself made much of by Princess Moë, was feasted by the Protestant community of the place, and herself boldly gave a feast in return. Her co-religionists contributed generously to the feast in her honour, and she listed the items for her sister's benefit: six hens, one dozen eggs, one lobster, one hundred coconuts, two large bunches of green bananas, two baskets of ripe bananas, two bunches of wild bananas for cooking, one basket of sweet potatoes, two bundles of taro, two bunches of bread-fruit and three pineapples. 'Well,' she said to Louis in her prim Edinburgh accent, 'I have always believed that "Godliness was great gain", but I never before had such immediate proof of its holding good even in this world!' She determined to commission a set of church plate for the Protestant church at Tautira, which she had made and despatched from Edinburgh to Tahiti via New Zealand in the summer of 1889.

Meanwhile the *Casco*, which had been taken to Papeete to have its rotted masts strengthened with iron rings and bolts—new masts of the size were utterly unobtainable—failed, day after day, to reappear. The Stevensons' food, and then their money, ran out, and they found themselves in a very awkward situation—or would have done so had Louis's new blood-brother not come to their aid. Ori offered them everything edible which he possessed, and for some weeks they lived pleasantly but monotonously on native food. Finally, despite stormy weather and the Stevensons' pleas, Ori had himself rowed with some retainers by canoe to Papeete, and returned within a week with good news, more money and food. Captain Otis had thoughtfully sent along some champagne, for the

Stevensons and Ori had finished the *Casco* stock celebrating St Andrew's Day.

Although Louis was shut up working away hard at *The Master of Ballantrae*, none of the rest of his party was remotely bored at Tautira. Fanny and her mother-in-law took lessons in hat-plaiting from the local ladies, and Princess Moë herself showed them unusual patterns to plait. The hats could be made of bamboo shavings, Fanny's choice, which were shiny and white, or more simply of tough pandanus fibre, which Mrs Stevenson preferred. Others were confected of sugar-cane leaves, but the best of all were woven from the 'stalks of the arrowroot plant, which was not then in season. Fanny, who was nothing if not versatile and enterprising, did a silhouette of Ori against the wall of his house, using a lamp, drawing the outline and then filling it in. She had intended to take it away as a personal souvenir, but Ori was so gratified that he demanded that she do silhouettes of her family for him in return. Louis, heading the document with his new native name Terliters (which was his brother Ori's surname), printed under the silhouettes: 'Robert Louis Stevenson and party came ashore from the yacht *Casco*, November 1888; and were two months the guests of Ori, to whom, having little else, they gratefully bequeathed their shadows *in memoriam*.'

The long stopover at Tautira not only enabled Louis to work in peace; it also allowed him to catch up once more on his health, which as we have seen had deteriorated on leaving Fakarava. Mrs Thomas Stevenson wrote to her sister that from this point of view 'the long detention has proved a blessing.' Louis's appetite, she said, was splendid, he was a little fatter than he had been even in the Marquesas, he was able to take good long walks and had been swimming almost every day. She had not seen him so well since 1879. 'All this makes us start our journey northward—and in the long-run homeward—in a very thankful frame of mind.'

They sailed from Tahiti for Honolulu on Christmas Day, 1888. Ahead of them lay a very nasty passage indeed.

[III]

On leaving Tahiti the *Casco* ran into such heavy seas that it took a whole month to reach Honolulu. Fanny's daughter Belle, who with her thriftless painter husband Joe Strong and their eight-year-old son Austin was living there in the shadow of King Kalakaua's ostentatious court, began reluctantly to subscribe to the general conviction of the whites in the island capital that the yacht and the whole Stevenson family must have been lost at sea. When, in late January, the *Casco* got fairly into the Trades she sped along; but even so this last lap of the voyage was very wearing, entailing for the passengers a perpetual effort to keep upright on their feet by clutching at the rails or any other fixture that came handy. The spray was so strong that it was impossible to sit out in the cockpit, and one night both Mrs Stevenson senior and Lloyd Osbourne were drenched by water from the cabin skylight as they lay asleep. Fanny was seasick a good deal of the time and swore that once she had landed at Honolulu she would stay ashore and never leave it again. Six months' worth of letters lay waiting for them in Honolulu, a prospect which delighted Louis's mother, while he himself nervously referred to this post-bag as 'Pandora's Box'. Even when they could see the lights of Honolulu they were kept hanging about the Hawaiian group, from lack of wind, for a week. Their last meal on board consisted of salt horse and ship's biscuits, and had they stayed at sea another twenty-four hours they would have starved. At last the wind changed and their drifting came to an end. Instead, caught up by the Trade Winds, they suddenly sped into Honolulu harbour at the rate of thirteen knots, 'flashing past the buoys and men of war,' Lloyd recalled, 'with the pilot in a panic of alarm'. 'Flying round Diamond Head with the speed of an express train,' as Belle described the *Casco*'s overdue but none the less spectacular entry into Honolulu harbour, the yacht almost ran down a small boat carrying Belle and her little son to greet the travellers. The two were hauled on board.

Belle found the *Casco* party looking extremely well, especially Louis, who was as brown as a South Sea islander and 'wildly excited'. All of them seemed to Belle to be obsessed by food and could at first talk of little else. Louis was wearing yellow knitted silk socks upon his slender feet, and Aunt Maggie was dressed in black with touches of white at throat and cuffs. Her white widow's cap was newly starched, but she exchanged it for a hat before they landed. Dinner that night at the old Royal Hawaiian Hotel seemed to the travellers a feast — 'the finest banquet', wrote Louis's mother, 'of which I have ever partaken'. After their island adventures, however, Honolulu seemed to them painfully Americanized and sophisticated : 'But oh dear me, this place is so civilized! And to come back from Tautira to telephones and electric light is at first very bewildering and unpleasant.'

The Stevensons took a rambling old Hawaiian house in a big compound on the beach at Waikiki, just out of town, and here they settled for the next four months. The chief, barn-like room or *lanai* was communal, open, and had verandas. There were many independent, subsidiary rooms. For his writing Louis would withdraw to a solitary hut some distance from the main house. Fanny decorated the walls of the *lanai* with sea-shells, strips of tapa, island weapons and woven mats. They rented a grand piano, and the room was scattered with small tables and easy chairs. Here Louis, who was thirsting for company but at the same time soon grew tired of exclusively white visitors, would receive and entertain, when his work was over. *The Master of Ballantrae* was already running in *Scribner's*, so he pressed on half-heartedly and polished it off at Waikiki. He then turned his attention to *The Wrong Box*, that entertaining story of a tontine and of the disposal of a corpse, drafted by Lloyd Osbourne at Saranac, where Louis had begun to revise it. He was also busy writing his articles for McClure, penning a great many letters home, and involved in producing yet another lengthy South Sea ballad.

Fanny was still unwell from the last buffeting aboard the *Casco*. 'My wife is no great shakes,' Lois wrote to Baxter early in February 1889, when they had been ashore a week, 'she is the one who has suffered most. My mother has had a Huge Old Time. Lloyd is first chop. I so well that I do not know myself—sea bathing, if you please, and what is far more dangerous, entertaining and being entertained by his Majesty here, who is a very fine, intelligent fellow, but O, Charles! what a crop for the drink!' Louis in fact struck up a close friendship with Kalakaua, the last of the kings of Hawaii, after whose death in 1891 the United States Government took over his kingdom. Kalakaua was a highly civilized and inquisitive monarch devoted to champagne and to his Royal Hawaiian Band. He cross-examined Louis about the Marquesas and other places that the *Casco* had visited, for at that time, even in Hawaii, little was known about these remote islands below the line. His entertainments were prolonged and bibulous, and even Aunt Maggie was known to totter from the effects of the royal hospitality.

Meanwhile, the Stevensons still officially planned to return to Europe. Louis wrote to Baxter that he felt it was 'a sort of filial duty' to Colvin to go home, and that he was likewise influenced by the knowledge that Lloyd Osbourne could not be expected to spend his formative years drifting about the South Seas. 'And these two considerations will no doubt bring me back—to go to bed again—in England.' Louis was thinking of his weevil life at Skerryvore.

Louis and Fanny knew that, once they returned to Europe, they would never be in a position to sail the South Seas again; and there was so much that they had not seen. 'We will start next week,' they would say to one another, or 'we will start next month'. And all the time their hearts were following every trading ship that left Honolulu for the islands of the South. The climate even of Honolulu proved too temperate and almost chilly for Louis's health. In the spring they decided to resist the lure no longer, and in early April Louis wrote to Baxter, to whom he had already broached the subject of staying longer in the Pacific, to thank him for condoning their decision: 'For I have decided in that sense.' They were now set on going to Butaritari in the Kingsmills, to be dropped there or at Ponape, and hoped thence to catch a boat going to Manila or to China. The *Morning Star*, a vessel belonging to the Boston Missionary Society, was getting ready for sea, and was actually bound for the Kingsmills. Negotiations with the Boston missionaries seemed full of catches and then, just in the nick of time, the Stevensons heard that a trading schooner, the *Equator*, would shortly anchor off Honolulu on its way south. The owner of the *Equator*, a Mr Wightman of San Francisco, was 'most obliging and liberal'. He let Louis charter the ship on rather unusual terms: Louis could make the *Equator* stop at any port he chose, but he was also not to interfere with the normal itinerary when Captain Reid was trading for copra at some specific island. In the end, Captain Reid, who was twenty-three and wore a Scots bonnet, proved delightful and treated his ship as though it were the Stevensons' private yacht.

The party preparing to embark on the *Equator* was diminished in numbers. Mrs Thomas Stevenson, homesick for Edinburgh New Town, took an American steamer. Valentine Roch had been dismissed and went to San Francisco, where she married, settled down and lived to a ripe old age. Valentine's crime had upset Fanny, but we do not quite know what it was. There is a suggestion that it was to do with dishonesty over money, but it seems more likely that it was connected with some member of the crew of the *Casco* — 'Valentine leaves us here, to mutual glee,' Louis told Baxter, adding rather arcanely that it had been 'the usual tale of the maid on board the yacht'. Young, healthy and attractive, it would have been odd indeed had the Swiss girl not caught the wandering eye of one of the *Casco*'s sailor-boys during that long frustrating voyage of six months. This meant that Louis, Fanny and Lloyd would board the *Equator* by themselves except for Ah Fu, the invaluable Chinese cook from the *Casco* who was working for them at Waikiki. Louis made a new will, and Fanny began preparations for their second voyage of discovery. They recognized that they might even end up in Samoa.

They did not know, and as long as they were island-hopping about the South Seas they did not greatly care.

Louis and Lloyd had made elaborate plans to show magic lantern slides to the natives of 'the Line islands'. Singing, guitar music and the flageolet also bulked large in these projects to beguile. Lloyd was good with the camera but his brother-in-law Joe Strong was far more experienced, and so it was at last agreed that he had better come along on the *Equator*, too. Belle refused, as she would not put Austin into boarding school; she was, in the result, forced to accept tickets for Austin and herself to go to Sydney, where Louis arranged for her to draw money and where she was told to wait 'till called for'. The very idea of leaving her friends in Honolulu outraged Belle Strong and she made a fearful scene to Louis, whom she had in any case secretly never yet forgiven for ousting her father, Sam Osbourne, from her mother's life. When the *Equator* put in and they all went on board, Belle was appalled to find how small a boat she was—only sixty-four tons register. The Captain, Danny Reid, quickly went under to Stevensonian charm. Garlanded with leis, and serenaded by the king and his Royal Hawaiian Band, the Stevensons sailed from what Louis now termed 'vile Honolulu' one night in late June 1889. The family's objectives were even more uncertain, and their fate more risky, than had ever been the case on the *Casco*. Louis wrote to warn Baxter that

> this new cruise of ours is somewhat venturesome, and I think it needful not to be in a hurry to suppose us dead. In these ill-charted seas, it is quite on the cards we might be cast on some unvisited or very rarely visited island; that there we might lie for a long time, even years, unheard of, and yet turn up smiling at the hinder end. So do not let me be 'rowpit'* till you get some certainty we have gone to Davie Jones in a squall or graced the feast of some barbarian in the character of Long Pig.

[IV]

According to Fanny, it was during the first ten days aboard the *Equator*, and after many talks with Captain Reid, that Louis Stevenson made up his mind to spend the remainder of his life in the South Seas. The plan now was that he should buy his own trading schooner on which he and his family could intermittently live, basing

* 'Rowpit'—sold at auction.

themselves, however, on some definite island of their choice. The schooner was to be called the *Northern Light*, was to cost fifteen thousand dollars, and to be paid for out of a new book on which he and Lloyd would collaborate, *The Wrecker*. Captain Reid, who entered into all the details with the greatest enthusiasm, was to be appointed skipper of the *Northern Light*. It seemed a perfect, watertight plan. Fanny probably listened to it without too much comment. The notion of the *Northern Light* shed a radiance upon the future. The ship would make so much money that the family would never have to worry about finance again. Louis's health would get better and better. It was a flawless scheme.

The *Equator* put them ashore at Butaritari in the Kingsmills, where they lingered for six weeks. For a variety of reasons Louis got little writing done there, but he took the occasion to study in detail the methods of South Seas traders, of whom there were several specimens on the atoll. The more he learned of their ways the less he liked them. He found that they did many things—and he and the *Northern Light*'s crew would have to conform—of which he could not morally approve. 'South Sea trading', as Fanny put it, 'could not bear close examination. Without being actually dishonest, it came a little too close to the line to please us. Our fine scheme began to fade away.' By the time they had set off again in the *Equator* the fine scheme was entirely shelved. All that was left was the project for a new South Seas story—*The Wrecker*. In Honolulu Louis had got rid of *The Master of Ballantrae*, which he had described as hanging over him 'like the arm of the gallows'. He was now free to embark upon a new novel.

The plot of *The Wrecker* was dreamed up aboard the *Equator* during moonlit conversations between Louis and his stepson. Their attention had been drawn to the whole question of South Sea wrecks by the appearance in Honolulu, shortly before they themselves left that island, of a handful of shipwrecked mariners from the *Wandering Minstrel*, to whose story some eerie and unfathomable mystery seemed to be attached. Unlike *The Wrong Box*, which Lloyd Osbourne had written himself before giving the manuscript to Louis to polish and re-shape, *The Wrecker* was a work of genuine collaboration from the start, which probably accounts for its manifold faults. There is, on Louis's part, a form of self-indulgence in the construction of *The Wrecker*; it takes seven totally superfluous chapters to reach the story of the purchase of the wreck on Midway Island, and these are padded out with descriptions of the artists' life in Paris and at Barbizon as Louis recalled it from his youth. Edinburgh is then dragged in, as is an imaginary American state,

Muskegon, and memories of San Francisco as he had known that city whilst he was waiting to marry Fanny. Once the wreck is bid for, and the whole mystery set up, *The Wrecker* is very good indeed. The storm, and the tension of investigating a deserted wreck on Midway Island, together with the ultimate explanation and the involuntary, almost innocent massacre of one crew by another form a rattling good suspense story.

Years after Louis's death Lloyd, who always thought finely of himself, published a most implausible claim to have written these, the best parts of *The Wrecker*, himself. In his description of their collaboration Lloyd inadvertently reveals what was clearly wrong with the book from the beginning:

> It was exhilarating to work with Stevenson; he was appreciative, so humorous — brought such gaiety, *camaraderie*, and goodwill to our joint task. We never had a single disagreement as the book ran its course; it was a pastime, not a task ... Am I wrong in thinking that some of that zest is to be found in *The Wrecker*?

Lloyd was indeed wrong, for *The Wrecker*, finally finished in Samoa and sold to *Scribner's* for serialization in 1891–2 for the very welcome sum of 15,000 dollars, not only lacks zest but any vestige of cohesion. It is symptomatic of Louis's good nature that he should once again collaborate with a conceited boy of not yet twenty-one; but he himself must have known perfectly well that a book which is written as a pastime cannot, in the nature of things, add up to a very good book. Writing a book, a story, or even an essay, is a solitary and exacting occupation, as Louis had proved to himself time and time again. The light-hearted attitude towards writing which Lloyd indicates reigned aboard the *Equator* was unpropitious and almost calculated to create a failure.

The fact that, when published, *The Wrecker* sold better than *The Master of Ballantrae* annoyed Louis, and rightly. In his youth he had sometimes shown a tendency to let his life and his mood get in the way of his serious work. He now felt responsible that his bright young stepson was dancing attendance on him when he ought to have been trying to get into Cambridge. Louis therefore, no doubt, reasoned with himself that the next best thing would be to involve this greenhorn in the construction of a new Stevenson novel. As always, Louis was acting from the highest motives, but the result, in *The Wrecker*, shows a dimming of his own talent. In effect, he was prostituting himself to give Fanny's son the illusion of something valuable to do.

Except as a collaborator, young Lloyd Osbourne was a distinct asset on the South Sea journeys. He adapted himself easily, picked up Polynesian phrases, wore semi-native clothing and, his ears pierced, went through the islands in gold ear-rings. His weak eyesight was improving, although he continued to wear gold-rimmed spectacles all his life; it seemed as though the equatorial sun was doing good to his eyes. Louis was, and always remained, devoted to Lloyd who, on his stepfather's sudden death in 1894, collapsed and became so gravely ill himself that it was feared that he would die from grief.

When he married Fanny in 1880 Louis had almost blithely taken on and virtually adopted her two children, although he and Belle were frequently at sixes and sevens. The weak link in the family chain was Joe Strong, Belle's painter husband. From Honolulu Louis complained to Charles Baxter, that the Strong family were 'a sore trial' to him: 'Joe is a loveable fellow,' he wrote, adding however that he was 'one of these truculent fools who do not know the meaning of money'. Having paid all the Strongs' debts in Honolulu, Louis decided that the best solution, when he sailed on the *Equator*, would be to take Joe along as cameraman, and in charge of the magic lantern on shore. But on Apemama 'some miserable misconduct' forced Louis to take the photographic business out of Joe Strong's hands. 'I never felt my affection shaken, even in our rows,' Louis asserted. 'I could far better have parted from his wife.' In the spring of 1890, in Sydney, it really seemed as though Joe Strong was dying (probably from the effects of alcohol). Fanny, who had always opposed Belle's marriage and had never forgiven her furtive elopement with Joe from Monterey, thought that if he did die it would be 'the sooner the better for him and all connected with him ... He is a sweet, engaging, aggravating creature,' she wrote in a postscript to a letter from Louis to Baxter, 'refined, artistic, affectionate, as weak as water, living in vague dreams. One needs to be a millionaire to support him and a philosopher to love him.' By no stretch of the legal imagination could Joe Strong be called his wife's stepfather's responsibility, yet Louis, with his compulsive generosity, himself took on the financial support of both the Strongs and the education of their little son Austin. Lloyd felt so deeply about this saintly attitude towards his sister and her family that he determined to forego Cambridge and thus spare Louis, at any rate, that expense: 'Lloyd was to have gone to Cambridge,' Louis told Baxter about this time. 'Now, seeing me saddled with this mule-load of struggling cormorants, he seems to be about refusing to go. I respect the impulse, yet I feel I shall, and should, oppose the decision.'

Joe Strong did not die in Sydney, but lived on to add his shot of poison to the bitter cup of Louis's last years when all the Osbournes save Lloyd ruined his peace of mind and conceivably precipitated his death from cerebral haemorrhage at Vailima in Samoa. Louis was ever an optimist. In Sydney, in March 1890, he discovered to his surprise that Belle and Joe were living strictly on the allowance he gave them and had not run up a pennyworth of debt. 'I cannot tell you how encouraging this is,' he wrote to Baxter, 'and how it reconciles me with life.' When he, Fanny and Lloyd took ship from Sydney for Samoa that spring he left the Strongs behind, putting them 'under custody of a bank (where the wild teller grows)'.

[V]

To return to the voyage of the *Equator* from Honolulu through the islands of the Line in June 1889: the Stevensons found that aboard the trading vessel they were even more conscious of the sea than on the *Casco*, for the *Equator* rode very low in the water. As they approached the Line they found the South Seas 'desert of ships'. 'No post runs in these islands,' Louis explains in his book entitled *In the South Seas*, 'communication is by accident; where you may have designed to go is one thing, where you shall be able to arrive another.' The Gilberts, through which the *Equator* threaded its way, were inhabited by Micronesians, a people darker, less carefree and altogether less elegant in build than the Polynesians. The Gilbert Islands are a group of atolls, horseshoe-shaped, their lagoons fringed by palms, their scenery miniature and making you more than ever conscious of the giant waste of sea and sky. The two islands on which the Stevensons elected to live, Butaritari and Apemama (the latter only thirty miles from the Line), were rather wider than Fakarava, their first atoll in the days of the *Casco*. These two islands were a quarter of a mile broad, that is to say from beach to beach. Both of them contained strange towns of wood and straw, and trading stations.

Their first step, Butaritari, was controlled by an obese, apprehensive and frequently drunken king, Tebureimoa, and rather surprisingly boasted a roomy, shadow-filled church the size of a cathedral. The Stevensons were installed in the house of Maka, an Hawaiian missionary, who happened to be out of the island when they arrived, but who insisted on their staying on when he reappeared. The situation in which the Stevensons found themselves on Butaritari made writing impossible, for the island was in a state

Woodcut by Joe Strong for the frontispiece of *The Silverado Squatters* (volume 3 in the first collected edition of R.L.S.'s works, 1894–8)

of dangerous ferment. For some reason the islanders had been celebrating the Fourth of July—presumably under the auspices of the representatives of the Wightmans, the San Francisco trading firm from which Louis had chartered the *Equator*. To make this occasion a public holiday the king had raised the taboo on spirits ordinarily in force on the island. The result of this was that the islanders were permanently drunk, and that the two liquor stores, *The Land We In* and the *Sans Soucis*, were doing a delirious trade. So potentially threatening did the situation seem that the Stevensons contemplated going to sleep on the *Equator* out in the lagoon; but Louis thought better of this and simply sent for their pistols from the ship. His *The South Seas* vividly describes Louis's efforts to get the king to reimpose the taboo and to persuade both the bars to close down. He seems to have found the whole crisis invigorating, and did not even flinch when stones thrown from the street came whistling past his head as he and his family sat at supper under an open arbour in the missionary's compound. Their risky Butaritari experiences satisfied those dreams of active life which Louis had always harboured, and in no time he found himself the arbiter in the taboo dispute. In the end the king did reimpose the ban, but none too soon.

From Butaritari the winds sped the *Equator* off her determined course, and carried the travellers to Apamama, the kingdom of the locally notorious Tembinok', who aspired to conquer the whole Gilberts group and was only kept at bay by British men-of-war. Tembinok', who was enormously fat but had a profile which Louis thought resembled Dante's, was an autocrat who had learned enough English to get by, had a bodyguard of armed women, and was always intent on acquiring knowledge. He regarded white men as his books and was, in Fanny's eyes, 'a philosopher, a cynic and a poet'. 'From his little corner,' wrote Fanny, 'he had learned to know the world, both its good side and its bad, and his strong, shrewd mind was insatiable for facts and prone to the right deductions.' He was forever making purchases from trading ships, and had vast collections of broken clocks and sewing-machines, some of the latter used as anchors for his boats out on the lagoon. Tembinok' had decreed that no white people could settle on Apemama without his express permission, which he usually withheld. To Louis's first application to be allowed to stay for three weeks, the king deigned to make no reply. On this and several subsequent occasions he stared at Louis, Fanny and Lloyd fixedly. At last he granted the required permission, and later told Louis that he judged strangers by the eyes and the mouth. The Stevensons had passed muster, and Tembinok' said he was convinced that Louis was a good man because of his eyes.

Captain Reid's idea was to leave his passengers, with Ah Fu to cook for them, on Apemama whilst he did the rounds of the smaller copra islands. He would return to pick them up in three weeks. The king put at their disposal four native houses, made of basket-work and wattle, and standing on stilts a yard high. These houses were moveable, a dozen men running under them to lift them to whatever site was selected. The Stevensons' encampment was near a coconut grove. The king, who had directed the whole moving operations while giddily brandishing a Winchester rifle, walked in a circle round the little settlement, making a taboo line which no one but the servants allotted to the Stevensons was permitted to cross under pain of death. Basking in the favour of Tembinok', whose liking for them grew daily, the Stevenson contingent were happy in their new home, or would have been so had it not been for the flies — 'Never were there so many flies,' Lloyd remembered, 'flies, flies, flies in thousands and millions; and no place to escape them outside your mosquito net.' Fanny resourcefully solved the fly problem by making a gigantic mosquito net — 'a veritable house of mesh' — which they hung in the dining-shed, eating inside this muslin room, and also using it as a study. Louis wrote at one table, while Lloyd crouched in a corner at an improvised desk composed of camera-boxes. They were making a serious start on *The Wrecker*.

Food was a problem, for Apemama seemed to have no fish. There were 'wild chickens' which Ah Fu would shoot and cook, but they were tasteless, or rather they tasted of jellyfish and seagull. They had however a quantity of Californian claret to drink, and on rare occasions there was turtle steak and turtle soup. For exercise they would cross to the seaward side of the island, which was very wild, cool, and devoid of mosquitoes or flies.

Altogether, the Stevensons spent two months in Equator City, as they christened their Apemama encampment. So long a stay was not intentional; Captain Reid had promised to return after three weeks, but six weeks went by and there was still no sign of the *Equator*. Knowing the perils of sailing in these seas, the Stevensons began to fear that the *Equator* had been wrecked. Once again their food ran out, and they were obliged to rely on the king's stores, of which they were made free. One day a strange schooner, the *H. L. Tierman*, appeared in the lagoon at Apemama, and was able to supply them with canned foods from its trade-room. Despairing of the *Equator*,

Louis was greatly tempted to charter the *Tiernan* to take them all to Samoa. The price asked by the *Tiernan*'s skipper turned out to be too high, and, moreover, Louis and Fanny felt that it would be unfair to young Captain Reid, should be finally appear with the *Equator* and find them fled. In this case they were lucky, for the *Tiernan* capsized soon after leaving Apemama, with the loss of sixteen lives. The survivors suffered intense hardship, and all of them save the mate, another man and a demented woman died of starvation and thirst in an open boat trying to reach an inhabited island. Fanny, needless to say, attributed her family's escape to her own second sight, recording that she had begged Louis not to go on the *Tiernan*. The *Equator*, which had been unavoidably delayed, reached Apemama in the end. The night before they sailed away, the king was in tears. 'I think you never see a king cry before,' Tembinok' sobbed.

In the book published two years after his death, under the title *The South Seas*, Louis provides an excellent narrative account of the family's experiences in the Marquesas, and on Fakarava, Butaritari and Apemama atolls. To try to paraphrase his own accounts in this present study would be pointless. Because he did not keep a diary in Tahiti no mention of that happiest of their journeys' halts occurs in the book. A richly rewarding volume, *The South Seas* has been largely forgotten, nor were its component parts considered a success when they were published severally in their author's lifetime. We may remember that Louis had accepted McClure's commission for a series of South Sea letters to be syndicated. After they had published thirty-four of these letters the New York *Sun* told McClure that they wished to cancel the contract since the instalments seemed not to be letters of incident and experience but (in Colvin's words) 'only the advance sheets of a book and a rather dull book at that'. The letters were written up from Louis's diaries during his third voyage in the South Seas aboard the steamship *Janet Nicholl* which, as we shall in due course see, he boarded at Sydney in April 1890. It was not just the editors of the New York *Sun* who expressed themselves disappointed by the South Sea material. An influential critic nearer home was disappointed also: Fanny Stevenson declared that Louis was ruining good material. Her reasons were not clear-cut, and it has even been supposed that Louis's life-style was changing in some way which left his wife at a loss. The trouble had already begun before they left Honolulu in June 1889:

Louis has the most enchanting material that any one ever had in the whole world for his book [Fanny wrote in a confidential letter to Sidney Colvin that May], and I am afraid he is going to spoil it all. He has taken it into his Scotch Stevenson head that a stern duty lies before him, and his book must be a sort of scientific and historical impersonal thing, comparing the different languages (of which he knows nothing) and the different peoples ... the whole thing to be impersonal ... And I believe there is no one living who has got so near to them, or who understands them as he does ... What a thing it is to have 'a man of genius' to deal with. It is like managing an overbred horse. With my own feeble hand I could write a book that the whole world would jump at.

Lloyd, for what that was worth, backed up his mother. What neither of them understood, although Fanny may have had her suspicions, was that Louis was developing. She had now got him away from his English friends and had him entirely to herself in the South Seas, particularly after his mother's return to Scotland. He was, however, no longer the delicate romantic boy she had married in California ten years before. His health was so much improved that at the moment he did not need to depend on her as much as in the past. His literary aims and skills had changed, and he was not prepared to write about his South Seas experiences in the wayward, charming, egocentric manner that had permeated, say, *Travels with a Donkey*. He now intended to be objective, and to rely more on facts than on atmospherics in this new book.

This crescent maturity was, unknown to Fanny, loaded with melancholy regrets for his severance from his distant friends. At the end of a long letter to Baxter in February 1890 he thanked him for his continuing friendship: 'So much has fallen away, death and the worse horror of estrangement have so cut me down and rammed me in, that you and Colvin remain now all in all to me.' He wrote in another letter to Baxter, in August of the same year: 'But I did not ever care for much else than my friends; and some they are dead, etc., and I am at the end of the world from what remains; gone, all gone.' These were moods which he could not share with Fanny. His English friends, so brilliant, so informed and so sophisticated, were now replaced by twenty-year-old Lloyd Osbourne and the raw, squabbling Strongs. A corollary of this mood was that Louis looked closely, almost sternly, at everything and everybody he encountered in the South Seas. Yet all the same he wrote to Colvin in June 1889 in a mood of gusto at the material he was collecting; it would almost seem as if he and Fanny were writing about two different embryonic books. 'By the time I am done with this cruise,' he assured Colvin, 'I shall have the material for a very singular book of travels: names of strange stories and characters, cannibals, pirates, ancient legends, old Polynesian poetry—never was so generous a farrago.' In all he wrote some seventy South Seas articles. The McClure syndicate handled thirty-four, and then went on strike. In 1890 fifteen of them were privately printed as *The South Seas: a Record of Three Cruises*. In 1896, two years after Louis's death, these same fifteen and twenty others were published in the collected Edinburgh Edition of his works, under the title *In the South Seas*. In 1900 the volume was issued separately by Chatto and Windus. This most remarkably interesting and enjoyable book has had scant attention paid to it, yet it is, in the words of one of its few admirers, Miss Janet Adam Smith, a book 'that did not need its author's name to commend it', and is in fact 'the most solid of his general writings, and far from being the least readable'.

With the solitary exception of Henry James, Louis's London friends were already fed up with his panegyrics on the South Seas. Colvin was frankly bored by it all, and other friends were subconsciously irritated by his American successes. It was as though he had escaped them for good. Sam McClure, who went to London in 1890 with letters of introduction to such friends as Colvin, Henley (before the final row), Baxter, Bob Stevenson and so on, records in his autobiography that he had found 'most of Stevenson's set very much annoyed by the attention he had received in America'. Henley had been especially poisonous, partly, McClure thought, from jealousy, but also from anger 'that a nation whom he despised as a rude and uncultivated people should presume to give Stevenson a higher place than he held in England'. Louis's pleasure in the South Seas seemed to add insult to injury.

In June 1891, from sheer discouragement, Louis threw his hand in over the South Sea book. In England sections had been tepidly running in *Black and White* from February of that year until December. By this time the Stevensons were settled in Samoa. They first saw that island when the *Equator* dropped them there in December 1889. Accustomed to the deadly sameness of the 'low islands' or atolls, they had not come across forested mountains since they had left the Marquesas. They could not twig that Samoa was to be their future home, and Louis's sepulchre. Unknowingly, he had reached his journey's end.

12

The Samoan Decision

THE Samoas, or, as Europeans had called them in earlier centuries, the Navigators, form an archipelago of fourteen islands, the largest of which, Savaii, is lava-strewn and was in Stevenson's day only inhabited along the rim of the coast. Upolu, which is separated from Savaii by a channel eight miles wide, contains the capital and port of Apia, for four generations the centre of foreign commerce. Upolu is five hundred and eighty miles square. Forty miles to the east of Upolu is the island of Tutuila, which, now known as American or Eastern Samoa, boasts the great harbour and small township of Pago-Pago. The rainfall at Pago-Pago is greater than at Apia, and it was indeed chosen by Somerset Maugham as the setting for *Rain*. The Samoan islands are in fact a line of extinct volcanoes, although the splendid forests and the veridian undergrowth which shroud the central mountain ranges make this hard to believe. These islands are almost surrounded by coral reefs, which are broken here and there, as at Apia, by fresh-water channels dangerous to navigation; the sound of the surf flung against these reefs is, near the coast, forever in one's ears. It was on Upolu, in an extensive house which he had built for himself three miles above the town of Apia, that Robert Louis Stevenson lived, with brief interludes, from the late autumn of the year 1890 till his sudden death on December 3rd, 1894.

These last four years of Stevenson's life are almost over-documented by the very long and richly detailed letters that he wrote to distant friends, to Sidney Colvin and Charles Baxter in particular. Then there are the various memoirs on his Samoan life and even of his table-talk published by his stepson and his stepdaughter, as well as the copious, slapdash journal kept by Fanny Stevenson with more or less regularity from September 1890 to January 1893. This journal was published in Great Britain for the first time in 1956. Moreover, during the apotheosis which followed Louis Stevenson's unexpected death, several of those who had known him well, or even slightly, in Samoa scampered into print with recollections of unequal value. Shut away at Vailima, as he called his new house from a Samoan word meaning 'five streams', and buoyed up by the adulation of Lloyd Osbourne, Belle Strong and Mrs Thomas Stevenson as well as by the now tempestuous and scary affection of his wife Fanny, Louis gave his natural egoism free rein. In his lengthy missives to Colvin he hardly ever inquired after his recipient's state or after that of his old love Mrs Sitwell.

These letters to Colvin are in fact sections of a journal which happen to be addressed and posted rather than shut up in a drawer. As in the old days of his sickly youth in Heriot Row, when he would pour out his soul to Mrs Sitwell or to Bob Stevenson by the light of a lamp in his attic study, nothing that happened to Louis, no thought that crossed his mind, seemed to him unworthy of record. In his perceptive if rather denigratory book on Stevenson, published in 1924, Frank Swinnerton goes so far as to suggest that, with all his captivating charm, Louis was more loved than loving, accepting his friends' devotion thoughtlessly as his due. In January 1893, Louis wrote to Baxter from Vailima to urge that after his own death his letters should be collated and published by Sidney Colvin to make money for what Louis calls his 'more or less innocent and attractive family'. To this letter he appended a list of correspondents whom Baxter or Colvin should approach, and even suggested a project emanating from Fanny's now megalomaniac brain—that Louis should at once call in all his letters and himself make a suitable selection for publication. This eccentric and introverted proposal Baxter firmly shot down:

> Although no doubt your own selection would be most satis-factory, I don't think the scheme of collecting your letters now practicable. There is a great difficulty in persuading people to make such a search ... Add to this that a selection made by the writer from his own correspondence is naturally to some degree suspect. One feels that here is what the man would wish us to see him, and the picture is not convincing.

Apart from his monthly journal-budgets to Colvin, and his frequent letters to Baxter (many of them concerning business), Louis also wrote occasionally from Samoa to Henry James, E. J. Burlingame, Lady Taylor, George Meredith, Edmund Gosse and certain other friends. To these, Louis was now an accepted authority on the South Seas, for before settling down in Samoa he had, as we have seen, spent the best part of two years touring the Pacific. From April to August 1890 they made one last adventurous journey this time by steamer to the Gilberts, the Marshalls and New Caledonia, but except for disastrous excursions to Sydney, where he invariably fell ill, and an unwise trip to Honolulu in the autumn of 1893, Louis remained in self-imposed exile on Upolu, Samoa. His circumstances caught the imagination of the British reading public. Edmund Gosse summed this interest up when he wrote to Louis that 'since Byron was in Greece, nothing has appealed to the literary man so much as that you should be living in the South Seas'.

At first, for some unexplained reason, the Stevensons did not find Samoa as beautiful as Tahiti. They even had certain reservations about its Polynesian inhabitants, based perhaps on their early experiences of the gossiping, shoddy community of Apia-based whites, half-castes and their native servants which was known, as in every other Pacfic island frequented by white traders, as 'the Beach'. Once up at Vailima they quickly discovered that Samoans are the most civilized, courteous and merry of their scattered race. 'Samoa, Apia at least, is far less beautiful than the Marquesas or Tahiti,' Louis wrote to Baxter in December 1889:

> a more gentle scene, gentler acclivities, a tamer face of nature; and this much aided for the wanderer by the great German plantations with their countless regular avenues of palm ... As I write, the breeze is brisking up; doors are beginning to slam, and shutters; a strong draught sweeps round the balcony; it looks doubtless for tomorrow. Here I shut up.

Louis had chosen to settle on Samoa chiefly because of the excellent postal connections with the rest of the world. The capital of Tahiti was the only other South Sea port which offered services as good, and we may recall that the Stevensons had not much cared for Papeete, with its tawdry compromise between European and Polynesian ways of life. At Apia the monthly ships running from Sydney to San Francisco and back dropped mailbags, and soon began putting into the port for a few hours. A little German steamer, the *Lübeck* of the Norddeutscher Lloyd from Bremen, plied between Apia and Sydney, and a New Zealand boat, the *Richmond*, called at Apia on its circular run from Auckland to Tahiti and back. These were the primary, practical reasons that led Stevenson to select Samoa as a residence, but they were soon supported by the passionate affection which the Samoans and their country evoked in the hearts of Louis and his family. To live in Samoa, they soon discovered, was to love it. After close on a century this statement holds good today.

It is a commonplace, but none the less a true one, to contrast modern air-travel, which really means making a journey as an animated package, with the good old days of travelling by ship. The foreign visitor to Samoa today makes the journey in a small Polynesian Airways machine from Tonga, a Mormon island covered in great stone cairns beneath which the Tongan villagers cosily bury their dead alongside the huts and houses of the living. These, and a tree full of sacred bats, are the chief sights of this island charnelhouse. There is also a beach on which Captain Cook landed before going off to Hawaii to be murdered by the natives of that Pacific group. Your first sight of Upolu from the sky is largely one of grey mist shrouding dark mountains, and then, as the aeroplane dips suddenly and seems to shave the treetops, of wayward coconut palms. In the airport itself, once you have presented your New Zealand visa, you then face an amiable but highly competitive scurry of taxi-drivers, Polynesian and Chinese. The man who secures you — for it is not a question of choosing a taxi but of being chosen and virtually kidnapped — then drives you at a jangling speed along the road to Apia for three-quarters of an hour. You creak through villages dominated by large white or grey Roman Catholic churches. Most of the village houses are hive-shaped with thatched domes, and with walls that roll up by day like blinds, but it is in the inland villages that these charming, convenient thatched houses are to be seen at their most numerous and authentic. The clammy, scented air, to which you have grown accustomed in Fiji and Tonga, makes you wheel down the taxi-window, only to wheel it up again in a sudden squall of rain. You then enter Apia, with its one long street of old wooden houses and a handful of new department stores, facing the bay and the new market. Should you be interested in Robert Louis Stevenson, or have read his Vailima letters, you will think nostalgically of his arrival in the schooner, *Equator*, in the first week of December 1889. You will imagine his sensations on smoothly reaching at last his future South Sea island home. But it was not like that at all.

In the first place Louis Stevenson did not originally intend to stay on Samoa for more than two months. The entry to the bay, a bottleneck opening in the coral reef kept free by fresh water from a river which debouched into it, was then rendered even more perilous of access by the wrecks of four American and two Imperial German naval vessels, sunk in the harbour by a spectacular hurricane some months before. Glad though they might be over this release from cramped quarters on the *Equator*, the Stevensons' first sight of 'the Beach' at Apia was not inspiring, and scarcely even reassuring. At that time the street of shops was, on the whole, squalid and dispiriting, and only the two churches and the German firms, like the German coconut plantations inland, seemed pervaded by any sense of order. Further, there was nobody to meet or welcome them, nobody who expected a famous author and his family, nobody in all probability who had ever heard of the famous author before. The merchants and certainly the scallywags of Apia were not noticeably literate. The town moreover had a dingy reputation and was known to mariners throughout the South Seas as 'the Hell of the Pacific'. Trudging down the main street of Apia the *Equator* party were of course being watched and doubtless they became the subject of a rather listless and sceptical interest. Louis was anyway and by his very nature a strange, implausible figure, emaciated as a skeleton, his thin clothes flapping on his bony frame as he hurried by with his quick nervous step. Fanny was wearing a native straw hat (perhaps of her own plaiting) and was hugging a guitar. Lloyd, in gold earrings and dark blue glasses, clutched his ukulele. Joe Strong presumably looked no more trustworthy than his companions. The Reverend Mr W. E. Clarke, the chief Anglican missionary in Apia, who afterwards became one of Louis's treasured friends and recited the prayers both at his deathbed and at his graveside, formed his own conclusions as he watched the strangers from the *Equator* drift aimlessly up the damp street that arched along the Bay. It was the rainy season, and in no way an ideal time to arrive at Apia. Mr Clarke realized that this was a troupe of downtrodden variety artists, who must have arrived by the San Francisco boat and hoped to turn an honest penny entertaining the citizens of Apia.

How the Stevenson troupe explained themselves in their first days in Apia we do not know. It is awkward to present yourself as a writer of great English and American fame when no one in a tropical island has even heard of you. Apparently Mr Clarke, when he had grasped who Louis was, became friendly and helpful; but the most dependable man of their new acquaintances was an American trader from Michigan, named H. J. Moors. It is not exactly known how Louis and his family got to know Moors so well so soon, and to rely on him so much. The American was nominally a trader, but he was also a great manipulator and intriguer, with an undying hatred of the German firms which were monthly increasing their holdings on

Upola, estates they ran with black imported Melanesian labour, 'boys' who were worked under slave conditions and were subject to their masters' brutality and the lash.

The position of Harry Moors in Samoa has been succinctly epitomised by Mr J. C. Furnas, whose admirable biography of Robert Louis Stevenson, *Voyage to Windward*, was published in 1951. Moors, writes Mr Furnas, 'was no petty swindler of savages on a remote island, but owner of a chain of outlying trading posts and, perforce, banker, factor, import agent, and local politician. No mouse squeaked or plot hatched without his getting some inkling.' Moors seems at once to have asked Louis to stay with him while Fanny and Lloyd took a small house outside the native village of Tanugamanono, which lay above and behind Apia and was on the road which led into the tract of 'bush' which Louis afterwards bought and which became his plantation-estate of Vailima. It was essential for Louis to be down in Apia at that time, as he was collecting first-hand information on the complex internal politics in Samoa, which involved the three powers, Great Britain, Imperial Germany and the United States, and which had in 1888 erupted into an island war.

When Louis was aboard the *Casco* off Honolulu in February 1889, he had already written a letter to *The Times* on the Samoan crisis. The information he was now collecting in English and German in Apia was intended to form a section of the South Seas book into which he hoped to turn his letters for the McClure syndicate in time. So absorbed did he become in Samoan politics, so romantic and so partisan, that he continued sending lengthy screeds to *The Times*, and ended by using all his Samoan material in a separate book, completed in May 1892, and published as *A Footnote to History*, in London in the same year. In these meticulous researches, Harry Moors proved invaluable to Stevenson. Soon Moors was using his newly acquired influence in a manner that, while in no way dishonest, was more questionable.

He persuaded the totally inexperienced and enthusiastic Louis, and through him, Fanny, that the only sensible course was for them to buy what Louis called '314½ acres of beautiful land in the bush behind Apia'. The house once built, a cacao plantation organized, the garden laid out, and cattle kept, this estate would, as Louis saw it through Moors's eyes, 'be something to fall back on for shelter and food'. Informing the cautious Baxter of this rash purchase, Louis added that 'if the island could stumble into political quiet, it is conceivable it might even bring a little income ... I have paid one half of it. The other is due in six months; and if by any accident I should fail in meeting it. H. J. Moors of Apia will drawn on you personally for the amount.'

'I live in Apia for history's sake with Moors, an American trader,' Louis informed Baxter just after Christmas 1889, also telling him that Ah Fu the Chinese cook from the *Casco* was looking after Fanny and Lloyd in the house they had temporarily taken in the bush. Louis was forced by circumstances to rely on Moors, but he did not at first trust him. 'The man himself is a curious being, not of the best character,' he wrote, again to Charles Baxter, 'has been in the labour trade as supercargo; has been partner with Grossmühl, the most infamous trader in these waters … has now settled down at last in Apia, where everyone owes him money'. He wrote that he had not intended to be Moors's guest, as he had not liked the American's looks or 'his round blue eyes, etc.' The repulsion, Louis found, had been mutual, but now—Louis was writing from Sydney in March of 1890—they had grown to like each other. Louis believed that Moors would not cheat him; the American was 'necessarily a feature' in what Louis, in an ominous phrase, called his 'business life', and had 'the marring of many of my affairs'. Moors was married to a Samoan wife, and had a daughter at school in the States.

Louis knew that Charles Baxter would be made uneasy by this innocent faith in H. J. Moors. He tried to defend himself against what he felt would be Baxter's suspicions. 'You may wonder I should become at all intimate with a man of a past so doubtful, but in the South Seas any exclusiveness becomes impossible; they are all in the same boat, or with exceptions so few that they are scarce worth mention … [Moors] is a man of so strong an understanding, and is so well-to-do, that personally I am not in the least alarmed.' However well-to-do he may have been, it was much to Moors's interest to channel all Robert Louis Stevenson's affairs through his own hands, and he certainly led him to believe that money could be made out of what Fanny already referred to as 'our plantation' at Vailima. By this time the seduction of Samoa had gone to Fanny's head; once again it was evident that her pioneering gifts for planting and for improvisation would be urgently required. When they set off for Sydney in February of the new year, 1890, the spell cast over them both by Samoa seems to have been pretty complete.

This spell of Samoa is very potent. Like all such effects, it is hard to analyse. So far as the people themselves are concerned there is undoubtedly a compelling element of the *dolce far niente*. There is also the appeal of the consciously decorative—the manner in which flowers (especially the scarlet bloom of the frangipani) are used as personal ornaments—the garlands of flowers round the neck or on the brow, the Polynesian way in which a single scarlet flower is worn behind a young man's ear, the lithe bodies which Belle Strong correctly described as being of the colour of a light bay horse. The lava-lava, a long skirt falling from men's waists, and foolishly likened by Europeans to a kilt, is a garment of the most carefree yet calculated elegance. Samoa gives an overall impression of brightness, really of brilliance and of clarity—the dazing light of day, the violence of the flower colours or intense sheen of white blossom, the myriad happily chosen tints of the printed trade-cloths from which the lava-lavas or the shirts are made, all these combine to create a permanently shimmering effect. The languorous manner in which most Samoans move, holding themselves, however, very upright, forms yet another aspect of this enchanted island. Yet there is one effect of Samoa upon foreigners to which Louis Stevenson, despite all his long habits of zealous industry, clearly succumbed— it is not a stimulating ambience for the effort of intellectual creation; in Apia there are today current cases of writers whose projected books remain forever unwritten. For Louis, whose livelihood now that he was a landowner and an ambitious house-builder depended more than ever on his pen, this atmosphere imposed a severe strain which, together with those induced in him by Fanny's wavering mental health, her rows with Belle and, later, with her mother-in-law, Joe Strong's insufferable drinking and disloyalty, all may have combined to produce the final crack-up when the weakened arteries of Louis's brain burst their banks and he bled to death.

The trip to Sydney in February 1890 was intended as the first stage of a journey home to get rid of Skerryvore and 17 Heriot Row. Louis had even engaged cabins in the mail-steamer. 'I hope I shall see you in some months from now, when I come home—to break up my establishment—I know no diminutive word for it,' he wrote to Lady Taylor from Apia, just before the ill-fated visit to Sydney. He told her that he now owned an estate behind and above Apia with three streams, two waterfalls, a great cliff, an ancient native fort, several views of the sea and the lowlands and 'a good many head of cattle'—these last, in fact, wandered off and were never traced. He described the whole Vailima estate as at present 'one impassable jungle, which must be cut down and through at considerable expense. Then the house has to be built; and then (as a climax) we may have to stand a siege in it in the next native war.'

Louis did not tell Lady Taylor, indeed he may not have yet known, that the plateau he had bought and christened Vailima was not only the site of an ancient fort but had been a bloody battlefield and was feared by the natives as a region haunted by *aitu* or the ghosts of the slain.* This superstition at least protected the Vailima household from night marauders.

In his first letters home after the purchase of Vailima Louis admitted to a sense of guilt. 'I do feel as if I was a coward and a traitor to desert my friends,' he wrote to Lady Taylor, ' ... [but] here I have some real health, I can walk, I can ride, I can stand some exposure, I am up with the sun, I have a real enjoyment of the world and of myself; it would be hard to go back again to England and to bed; and I think it would be very silly. I am sure it would; and yet I feel shame, and I know I am not writing like myself.' In spite of such pleas, and in the teeth of all the evidence of the South Seas' beneficent effect upon his frail body, Louis's London friends like Gosse and Colvin convinced themselves that he could not write well in the Pacific. In this context Edmund Gosse asserted that it was impossible to write well at more than three miles from Charing Cross.

[II]

When he had been in Honolulu before starting off the voyage on the *Equator*, Louis had gone over to the leper settlement at Molokai, where he had refused to wear gloves when playing with the leper children, had been struck by the sanctity of the dedicated nuns who were there to live and to die, and had heard a great deal, of course, of the famous Father Damien, the Belgian priest who had lately died of leprosy in this insular isolation-ward. In Samoa, Louis heard with horror that a Dr Hyde, a Presbyterian missionary of Honolulu, had denounced Damien in a letter to a fellow missionary, printed in an Australian church magazine. In this letter Dr Hyde denied that Damien was 'a saintly philanthropist', called him 'a coarse, dirty man, headstrong and bigoted' and hinted that the leprosy from which the priest had died was due to 'his vices and careless-ness', particularly in his licentious relations with female lepers. Without explicitly denying Hyde's charges, Louis concocted a

* It is today believed by some Samoans that Louis Stevenson is now himself an *aitu*. He is said to have been recently seen, by a creditable English youth, at night-time hovering and peering in at the two windows of a bedroom at Vailima, now the official residence for entertainment purposes of the Samoan Head of State.

vitriolic 'open letter' to the Presbyterian missionary, which was privately printed in Sydney in March 1890, appeared under Henley's auspices in his paper *Scots Observer* in May, and was then reissued by Chatto and Windus. In this letter Louis most effectively destroys Dr Hyde. He half expected a libel action—'it is *conceivable* an action might be brought, and in that event *probable* that I should be ruined.' He had even consulted a Sydney barrister on the libel angle of his attack on Dr Hyde. The barrister asked him if he had used any epithets or 'coarse expressions', calling Dr Hyde a hell-hound or an atheist? When he heard that Louis had not employed such terms he assured him that there was 'nothing in it'. The Stevensons had known Dr Hyde in Honolulu—'a large, dark, smooth, grave, personable man', and Louis suspected that this made himself and his family think the diatribe more pungent than perhaps it was. In the event, Dr Hyde did not sue and English literature gained a prize example of how to write a diatribe.

In Sydney Louis once again fell gravely ill, and described himself as 'a blooming prisoner' in his bedroom in the Union Club. He and Fanny realized that only another island voyage could save him. In April he telegraphed to Baxter that he was returning for four months amongst the islands and would not be home until September. On the same day he wrote that he had been 'quite knocked over' and was just embarking on a steamer by which Fanny had booked passages. There was a dock strike at Sydney, but the *Janet Nicholl*, because it employed Kanakas as deck-hands, was now the only ship leaving thence for the islands. The ship's owners, a small Scottish trading-firm, refused Fanny's application for passages again and again, wishing to have no truck with a moribund author and his seemingly hysterical wife. By some unknown means Fanny won through again, and she, Louis and Lloyd set off on their new voyage on April 10th. The journey began noisily, when a consignment of fireworks on board caught fire. As they were boarding the vessel another passenger tumbled off the gangway, in a drunken stupor. This young man turned out to be an engaging ne'er-do-well, known throughout the islands as Tin Jack, who became a friend of the Stevensons, visited them at Vailima, was the prototype for the character of Tommy Haddon in the still unfinished novel *The Wrecker* and ended up a suicide.

The Stevensons did not know at just which ports and islands the *Janet Nicholl* would put in, but, during a stop at Auckland, they bought presents for their friends on Apemama and Butaritari in case the ship called there. During this voyage, Fanny kept a diary which was published, in a probably rewritten form, in 1915, the year after her own death. The voyage on the *Janet Nicholl* took them from April to August, and during it they visited thirty-five islands new to them. They met up again with King Tembinok' of Apemama and loaded him with presents from Australia and New Zealand. At sea Louis immediately recovered his health. On the way back in August, he stopped alone at Noumea, in New Caledonia, while Fanny and Lloyd went on to Sydney, where he met them in August; it was arranged that Lloyd should go back to England to wind up affairs at Skerryvore and to arrange for shipment of the Bournemouth furniture. From Noumea, where he found he could order 'decent wine' for Vailima, Louis more or less frankly admitted to Baxter that he would never himself see his English or Scottish friends again, unless they crossed the world to stay with him at Vailima. 'The deuce of the affair is that I do not know when I shall see you and Colvin,' he wrote. 'I guess you will have to come and see me ... We shall be able to give you a decent welcome, and talk of old days.' For some reason Louis was in low spirits in Noumea: 'My dear Charles, it is a very poor affair to (what is called) succeed. My faults, whatever they were, were taken very easily by my friends till I had (what is called) succeeded; then the measure was changed.'

Louis and Fanny stayed on in Sydney until September. By October they were settled in the cottage which, under Moors's supervision, had been erected for them to lodge in during the building of the projected big house at Vailima. They had already inspected the cottage, which was on two floors, when the *Janet Nicholl* had put in at Apia on her way to the Gilberts. 'Black boys', probably runaways from the cruel German plantations, were busily engaged cutting down big trees—though leaving the finest—and burning the stumps and the undergrowth. The little cottage at Vailima looked to Fanny like a German bandstand.

[III]

Once settled in their little house, Louis Stevenson got down to work. He had three projects on hand: the McClure letters, which he described to Colvin as 'grinding along ... the Lord deliver me from the thought of the Letters'; there was *The Wrecker* to finish; and there was the scheme for a very tempting new tale, provisionally called *The Pearl Fishers*, but finally published as *The Ebb Tide*. The pull of *The Pearl Fishers* was strongest, as seems to have been the case with each new story thought up when Louis had got bogged down in his work in hand.

The accommodation in their 'little two-storied wooden box' of a cottage—destined to be the lodge of the large house which was being built some hundreds of yards further away—was extremely limited. On the top floor they had three rooms—a sitting-dining-room fourteen feet by sixteen, a much smaller bedroom, and a tiny pantry and provision room. Below slept 'Ben', then the head ganger, his Samoan wife and child, and three Kanakas. The up-stairs sitting-room had no ceiling, and was open to the iron roof. A dado of cold black paint ran round it to a height of four feet; above that the walls were 'an offensive white', and the whole place had in Fanny's view 'a chilling, death-like aspect'. She soon changed the appearance of this room and the bedroom by unpacking some of her boxes and nailing coloured tapa cloth to the walls, and a flat piece of pink coral fixed above the door that linked sitting-room to bedroom. She invented a makeshift couch covered with a shawl and got a carpenter to put up shelves for some of Louis's books; a pink cloth was spread on the table. 'When we light the lamp ... we feel quite snug and homelike,' wrote Fanny in her journal.

Fanny busied herself also having a pen made for the pigs, which were a distinct problem: 'Fanny ... has been largely occupied in contending publicly with wild swine,' Louis noted. She also had a hen-house built and began on a garden and a kitchen-garden in the wilderness of burned tree-stumps. Gangs of Samoans were at work all day long on the new house; the path from the town was flattened and widened by the traffic of the workmen, and planks and scantlings lined it for upwards of a mile. Two cart-horses were imported from New Zealand.

One October day in 1890 Louis wounded Fanny's feelings very deeply by telling her (we do not know in what tone of voice) that she had 'the soul of a peasant', because she took such pleasure in the mere ownership of the land she was digging; had she had the soul of an artist, he declared, 'the stupidity of possessions' would have had no hold over her. Fanny, who was anyway in odd moods these days, was affronted, but she admitted to her diary that she felt 'not so very far removed from God when the tender leaves put forth and I know that in a manner I am a creator. My heart melts over a bed of young peas, and a blossom on my rose tree is like a poem written by my son.' This was a sentiment, or rather a senti-mentality, which Louis would hardly have appreciated. As Vailima grew in size and grandeur over the years, so did Fanny's sense of proprietorship and her sense of her own consequence, no longer just as the wife of a famous man, but as a remarkable person and a tropical *châtelaine* in her own right. In the same month of October, and, as it happened, in the very week that Louis's comment had bruised Fanny's feelings, two pair of alien and critical eyes inspected the embryo of Vailima. These were the eyes of Henry Adams junior and his friend the American painter John La Farge. Adams was travelling in the South Seas in an attempt to forget the death of his wife. His friend La Farge was engaged in painting what they saw.

During the very earliest days at Vailima, when they were almost as cooped up in their own little house as Fanny's Cochin fowl in theirs, the Stevensons were both engaged in manual labour—Fanny in her future garden, and Louis hacking away in the underbrush along the stream-beds, a struggle he much enjoyed, which seemed to do him physical good rather than harm, and which he celebrated in one of his *Songs of Travel*:

> Thick round me in the teeming mud
> Briar and fern strove to the blood:
> The hooked liana in his gin
> Noosed his reluctant neighbours in:
> There the green murderer throve and spread,
> Upon his smothering victims fed.

Mud-stained and active, Fanny and Louis were accustomed to random calls from Moors or one of the missionaries, or from some other inquisitive Apia acquaintance or business contact. They were not at that moment prepared for a visit from eclectic Bostonian strangers, and as it happened were on that very day struggling to set up a greasy, black cooking stove. The impression the Stevenson couple made on Adams and his companion, who regarded themselves as the first Americans to travel to Samoa for pleasure, not for gain, and who flattered themselves that they understood the Samoan aristocracy, was bizarre:

Our European rival, Robert Louis Stevenson, lives in the hills and forest, where he cannot rival us in social gaiety [Adams wrote to Mrs Lodge in Boston]. We have been to see him and found him, as he declared, very well … I saw a very dirty board cabin, with a still dirtier man and woman in it, in the middle of several hundred burned tree-stumps. Both the man and the woman were lively, and in their respective ways amusing,

but they did not seem passionately eager for constant association with us, and poor Stevenson can't talk and write too. He
naturally prefers writing.

Louis, who later dined to meet Adams and La Farge at the American
consulate, and had to swim his horse across the river and to borrow
dry clothes from his host, wrote to Henry James of his compatriots
that their presence was 'a great privilege'. Fanny was still having
difficulties over provisions at Vailima, and when Adams and La
Farge were asked to breakfast they were surprised to be told to
bring their own food. The Stevenson couple seemed to them as
shabby and unwashed as ever. The Americans

> came round to a sort of liking for Mrs Stevenson, who is more
> human than her husband [wrote Adams]. Stevenson is airu
> [sic]—uncanny. His fragility passes description but his en-
> durance passes his fragility ... Their travels have broken his wife
> up: she is a victim to rheumatism which is becoming paralysis,
> and, I suspect, dyspepsia; she says that their voyages have
> caused it; but Stevenson gloats over discomforts and thinks that
> every traveller should sail for months in small cutters rancid
> with cocoa-nut oil and mouldy with constant rain.

Adams found the Stevensons' 'shanty' disgusting and attributed the
squalor to what he judged, in his sneering, finicky, New England
way, to have been Stevenson's lack of a good education. He found
that his illustrious surname, Adams, meant just nothing to Louis
at all:

> All through him, the education shows. His early associates were
> all second-rate; he seems never to have had the chance to come
> in contact with first-rate people, either men, women or artists.
> He does not know the difference between people ... the Oriental
> delicacy of La Farge seems to be doubled by the Scotch
> eccentricities and barbarisms of Stevenson who is as onesided
> as a crab, and flies off at angles, no matter what rocks stand in
> the way.

Such was the sadly provincial judgment of Henry Adams on the
most popular member of the Savile Club, the chosen friend of
Sidney Colvin, the Henry Taylors, the Percy Shelleys, John Singer
Sargent and Henry James. It is a pity that Adams never returned
to see the hospitable splendours of Vailima when it was completed,
with its fifty-foot long main hall of varnished redwood, its marble

busts, its Rodin and its Piranesis, the great dining-table shining with spotless napery, 'crystal' (as Louis Scottishly called glassware), silver and flowers. When completed Vailima was probably the most spectacular and civilized European house in the Samoas. Henry Adams had many adventages, but the gift of imagination was not amongst them. Nor was he an outstanding judge of comparative values, since he was sure that his companion John La Farge, now only known to a few specialists as a minor nineteenth- and early twentieth-century American painter of genre scenes, would be as well known as Stevenson himself in one hundred years' time. He was writing in 1890.

[IV]

The greatest bother that the Stevensons experienced during their first year at Vailima was the problem of servants. They had tried whites, both in the capacity of overseers, and as cooks. The results were entirely and gnawingly unsatisfactory. Their only adequate retainer was a Savaiian chiefling, Henry Simile, who soon became their right-hand man and to whom Louis began to teach decimals. Later, Fanny Stevenson acquired an invaluable local Samoan tough named Lafaele, who stayed with them until the end. The great change to a non-white, Samoan household occurred during Fanny's absence in Fiji, where she went alone, for her health's sake, in August and September 1891.

As soon as Fanny Stevenson had departed, Lloyd Osbourne and his sister Belle, who had by now arrived in Samoa from Sydney with Joe Strong and their young son Austin, seem to have gone to work on Louis. The expensive German cook was dismissed, the white overseer, who was lazy, but under contract, was bought off, and the white carter, who spoke of all Samoans as niggers, was also discharged. For a time Lloyd and Belle did the cooking, to their own and Louis's satisfaction, but one morning Lloyd discovered 'a young and very handsome Samoan' seated on the ice-chest in the back veranda. His hair was fashionably limed, and he wore a red flower behind his ear. He had come up to claim two Chile dollars which Henry Simele owed him, and was prepared to wait all day until Simele, who was out, returned. By some happy instinct Lloyd realized that this engaging boy must at all costs become their cook. The boy, whose name was Talolo, replied that he did not know how to cook anything. The argument ended with them sending for his chest of possessions and with his being taken on. In no time

Talolo proved a first-rate cook, and he stayed for the four remaining years of Louis Stevenson's life. 'He became', Lloyd wrote, 'in time not only an admirable chef, but the nucleus of the whole native establishment and the loyalest of all our Samoan family. His coming was the turning-point in the history of the house; we had achieved independence of our white masters, and their discontented white faces had disappeared one by one. Honest brown ones took their places, and we gained more than good servants by the change.'

Lloyd, who was learning fluent Samoan, and Louis, with his clannish Scots ideals, soon found that the loose, patriarchal family life of the Samoans, with their habit of adopting others, could be imported into Vailima. Soon the 'Vailima men', who wore a Royal Stuart lava-lava on Sundays and other holidays, formed a closely knit, punctilious élite. Over the years the native Vailima household varied from thirteen to twenty-one young men, picked for their good looks, allegiance, polished manners and physical strength. Louis imposed unquestioning and absolute obedience, and invented an acceptable code of fines for any misbehaviour or thieving of food. The fines went into the coffers of the missionaries, Catholic or Protestant, according to the professed faith of the delinquent. In time the Vailima boys tended to be almost exclusively drawn from the Roman Catholic community, which caused suspicion in some quarters of Apia. Mrs Thomas Stevenson once took it into her head to insist that all the Catholic boys should attend the Protestant family prayers under pain of dismissal, but Fanny naturally refused to issue any such command.

In April 1891, when the big house was almost finished, Louis's mother had come to Vailima from Edinburgh via Sydney, bringing with her a troublesome white Australian boarding-house maid, who did not fit comfortably into the household and soon left. It was raining on Mrs Thomas Stevenson's arrival, and she did not think the house at Vailima sufficiently advanced for her tenancy, so, leaving there a sofa she had brought from Sydney, she returned to what she called 'the colonies' for a few more weeks. She came to Samoa again on May 15th, and expressed herself delighted with the house and its great hall; the large sliding doors, half of glass, which gave on to the huge verandas from which you could gaze down over the harbour; the American stove; and her own chamber, which had thick, soft white Samoan mats upon the floor and painted pale green walls hung with tapa, the flag from the *Casco* and one given the family by King Kalakaua of Honolulu. In May the Strong family arrived. Belle, who had inherited her mother's descriptive gift, was overwhelmed by the beauty of Samoa and its inhabitants.

Belle has written that as soon as she landed on the small Apia jetty and looked at the Samoan crowds she understood why Louis had called the island's natives 'God's best, his sweetest work'. She was used to Honolulu, where the natives crammed themselves into ugly European- or American-style clothes, hats, shoes and stockings. The ravishing freedom with which the Samoans moved, the men in lava-lavas hung from the waist, the girls and women with them caught up just across the breast, enchanted her. The bare arms and shoulders, the pale brown bodies glistening with perfumed coconut oil were like nothing Belle had ever seen before.

She, Joe and Austin were led by Lloyd into the shadows of a great banyan tree on the shore, where the rest of the family, who had come down from Vailima in a cavalcade, were waiting with their horses. Lloyd took little Austin up behind him, Joe Strong was mounted and Belle, her tame white cockatoo on her shoulder, was helped up on to a skittish horse; but the journey proved so romantic that she forgot to feel nervous.

• It was three miles slightly uphill to Vailima. At first the road was excellent, shaded by palms and banana trees as far as the village of Tanungamanono, with its cluster of thatched Samoan huts and its warm, merry greetings from the villagers as the Stevenson contingent wound their way past. The horses and riders then turned into a short road on the right, from which they first perceived the green cone of inaccessible Mount Vaea facing them. The road now led through a forest, entirely shut in overhead by hanging branches, and with virgin jungle on either hand. Another turn brought them their first sight of Vailima and they alighted at the gate in a low stone wall covered with greenery and 'the starry blossoms of jasmine vines'. Before them lay a broad, smooth lawn, from which giant tropical trees rose here and there. The large house was two-storied, with verandas on both floors. It was painted blue, with a red roof, Enormous ironwood trees towered above it. The Strongs were allotted the original cottage in which Louis and Fanny had been pigging it at the time of Henry Adams's visit. This little house had now been shifted bodily, had been improved by verandas and an outdoor staircase, and was known as Pineapple Cottage.

Next day Belle discovered that breakfast at the big house was at six, and that Louis had already been writing even earlier. After this meal her mother, dressed in a blue Mother Hubbard, and attended by Lafaele, a Samoan Hercules, and another local boy, went planting in her garden, while Lloyd and Joe took a band of workmen into the forest to continue cutting out the underbush.. At this time the indolent Mr King was still European overseer, but in that summer he was replaced by a native and, as we have seen, the whole of the Vailima household was developed into a cohesive Samoan family group.

Before they came to Vailima, the Strongs and their child had been living in Sydney, uncertain of their future. During a business visit there by Louis, Belle had had a long and frank talk with him. She had said that her own family were quite capable of taking care of themselves in Sydney and that the *Bulletin* had offered her a steady job as theatrical critic. She said she did not see why she and Joe and their boy should be a financial drag on Louis, who was already spending lavishly on the creation of Vailima. Sitting in the park, and watching the well-known and unusual cow which grazed there and walked its unaided way through heavy traffic each day to be milked, Belle and Louis achieved a moment of truth, and she spoke to him as she had never spoken before. He told her of Lloyd's sacrifice of his chances of going up to Cambridge and that he and she herself were 'all the family' he had got. He said he wanted them round him. Together they cleared up many old mis-understandings, and the upshot of it was that the Strongs agreed to settle at Vailima. Louis, who had never cared much for Belle, now grew fond of her. He did not think her clever, but he thought her good. When, in the summer of 1892, Louis developed a very bad attack of writer's cramp, to which he had always been prone, Belle stepped in and acted as his amanuensis. It was to her that he dictated *St Ives* and *Weir of Hermiston*. Seeing how dark Belle was, even more swarthy than her mother Fanny, the Samoans assumed that she was Louis's daughter by some extra wife.

What did Fanny really think of the introduction of Belle into the household on a basis of increasing intimacy with Louis, with whom her daughter would spend claustral mornings taking his dictation? Belle was extremely pretty, and she was now thirty-two, only a little younger than her mother (whom she resembled) had been when she had first captivated Louis Stevenson in those long-dead days at Grez-sur-Loing. It cannot have been in any way an easy situation. Fanny, now over fifty, was getting heavy and grizzled and was later said by some of Louis's London friends to resemble an old lioness. Belle, who was adored by the household, was now really closer to Louis than was her mother.

In August 1893, Louis wrote to Colvin, 'We have a fly in the ointment here.' Without mentioning names he complains of having 'often bad times' and that he had not borne it as well as he would have hoped: 'It is a hard thing to bear perpetual quarrelling about *nix in creation*.' He described Belle as 'an empty creature and as good hearted as the empty can get to be'. Fanny would attack Belle, who would spend the day in tears, and then Fanny, who had routed her daughter out of Louis's room, would come back to him 'in a dreadful state about person number two, whose condition is entirely of her own making'. Louis said that his head and his heart were 'totally distraught between the pair of them. You must not take such an outburst too seriously,' he warned Colvin, 'but it's hard enough not to be agreeable. As far as regards myself it's rather worse. There are certain catch words which drive me crazy when they recur. Is there a screw loose? Well, I suppose there is.' Earlier on, in the spring of that same year 1893, Fanny seems to have had an attack of insanity, and not for the first time. Apologists for Fanny have suggested that she was suffering from the menopause, but her behaviour in 1893 too closely resembled far earlier mental disturbances in California to render this a convincing explanation.

Well, there is no disguise possible [Louis wrote from Vailima to Colvin on Thursday, April 15th, 1893]. Fanny is not well, and we are miserably anxious. I may as well say now that for nearly 18 months there has been something wrong; I could not write of it; but it was very trying and painful — and mostly fell on me. Now, we are face to face with the question: what next? The doctor has given her a medicine; we think it too strong, yet dare not stop it; and she passes from death-bed scenes to states of stupor. Rosse, Dr in Sydney, warned me to expect trouble so I'm not surprised; and happily Lloyd and Belle and I work together very smoothly and none of us get excited. But it's anxious ... I am stupid and tired and have done little even to my proofs. It is awful good those children are so good to me; or I'd be in a horrid pickle.

He said that when the trouble had started eighteen months before he had

felt so dreadfully alone ... You know about F., there is nothing you can say is *wrong*, only it ain't right, it ain't *she*; at first she annoyed me dreadfully; now of course that one understands, it is more anxious and pitiful. The dr. has been. 'There is no

danger to life' he said twice—'Is there any danger to mind?'
I asked—'That is not excluded' said he. Since then I have had
a scene with which I need not harrow you; and now again she
is quiet and seems without illusions. 'Tis a beastly business.

Louis said that at first her animus had all been directed against
himself: 'She made every talk an argument, then a quarrel; till I
fled her and lived in a kind of isolation in my own room.' Recently
Fanny had wanted to run away, and Louis and Belle had had to
hold her down for about two hours to prevent this. A holiday in
Sydney, when Louis gave up all his time to amusing his wife, had
not proved therapeutic and 'she got bad again'. Since she had
been back she had at least been 'querulously' kind. 'I am broken
on the wheel or I feel like it,' Louis continued in this long letter.
'Belle and Lloyd are both as good as gold. Belle has her faults and
plenty of them; but she has been a blessed friend to me.' Belle was
sleeping in her mother's room and she and Louis took alternate
watches there in daytime.

In a sinister way the wheel had come full circle. In California in
1879 and 1880, as well as later at Davos and Hyères, Louis, though
she had loved him, had been a heavy liability to Fanny. Now it
was she who was to become a burden and even haemorrhages are
more straightforward to deal with than any kind of mental illness.
'Anything is welcome but the one horror of madness!' Louis continued: 'I lie quiet in bed today, and think of the universe with a
good deal of equanimity. I have, at this moment, but one ob-
jection to it: the fracas with which it proceeds. I do not love noise:
I am like my grandfather in that; and so many years in these still
islands has ingrained the sentiment perhaps. Here are no trains,
only men pacing barefoot.'

Altogether, the years 1892 and 1893 were not domestically happy
ones for Louis Stevenson. In July 1892, after a great deal of very
unattractive trouble, Belle's husband, Joe Strong, had been
divorced. Always weak, he seems to have become completely
demoralized by Apia, where he was anyway keeping a Samoan
mistress. He had repeatedly purloined the wine-cellar keys, and had
even been silly enough to steal Louis's whisky and fill the bottles
up with soap-suds. When turned out of the house he had gone down
to the beach at Apia and spread scurrilous libels about his wife
Belle's morals. Louis called him a hound and wrote to Colvin that
such people never die—'death is for the reasonably decent; God
seems to scorn to strike these fellows.'

It is perhaps a sign of Louis's dedication to his work, as well as of his need for money, that he managed to continue with his writing.

[V]

As well as being busied through the year 1892 with his own writing and with Samoan politics Louis had somewhat unwillingly embarked on a huge addition to Vailima, a house which in his letters to Baxter he now began to call Abbotsford. The 'lovely' new house was finished and being painted by December. It was his mother, always rather prone to the stately, who had insisted on this extension. 'To tell you the truth I am most unhappy that I got embarked in the building of this new house,' wrote Louis in October, 'and I know there is going to be the deuce to pay to get to the year's end.' During his occupancy of Vailima he often fussed about money in his letters, apparently unnecessarily. Lloyd Osbourne is on record as stating that Louis was at that time 'making a very large income' and that, while he was spending it all on Vailima, this was in fact a capital investment, and that if he had never written another line he could have 'lived there comfortably and in no lessened state on his income from royalties'. Further, when his mother died he would inherit his father's fortune in which she held only a life-interest. Lloyd admitted that Vailima was 'a fantastic extravagance' but that at least it was well within Louis Stevenson's means. Lloyd and his family should have known, since, as Louis's heirs, they lived very comfortably off his royalties and, later, off their two-thirds of the Thomas Stevenson estate, for the rest of their lives.

Lloyd has emphasized that old photographs, which show a large barn-like building, do not do justice to Vailima. These photographs omit the windswept, quivering vegetation—the dense and symmetrical mango-trees, the glossy bread-fruits, the lemon-trees, orange-trees, chiromoyas, the avocados, the red pods of the cacao, the scented mos'oi trees which bloomed three times a year, the pandanus and the wild creepers, the hedges of double hibiscus in permanent bloom, the pots of jasmine, the tube-roses and the gardenias below the verandas. There was then, as there is today, a sense of space and order about the Vailima estate, and, since it lies six hundred feet above sea-level, the air was fresh and the nights so agreeably chilly that you actually needed a blanket. You were very conscious, from the Vailima verandas, of the vast horizon of the distant sapphire sea. Lloyd says that the house 'dominated the country like a castle' and that it became a superlative standard of comparison in Samoan eyes: 'Like the house of Tusitala.' Abroad a legend of the luxury in which the Stevensons lived spread rapidly. Fanny sensibly puts this in perspective by saying that to a man just off a cruise among the islands an evening spent at Vailima 'would seem like a glimpse into paradise'. A tourist fresh from the Colonies or from San Francisco would take it all for granted, and merely be surprised by the butler's bare feet.

The process of becoming a legend in his lifetime was not confined to European or American admirers of Louis Stevenson's works or of his astounding exile in the South Seas. Within Samoa itself, especially after he had learned the language, Louis was made a hero by the chiefs and by their followers, none of whom, but for a Samoan translation of *The Bottle Imp*, had ever read a word that Tusitala wrote. When the native name Tusitala, loosely translated as 'Teller of Tales', was first applied to Louis is uncertain. Very soon it came into general use. The Samoan household applied private native names to the whole family—Fanny, when she was not 'Tamaitai', which meant 'madame', was called by a word meaning 'Flying Cloud' and another meaning the 'Witch Woman of the Mountain'. Mrs Thomas Stevenson was Tamaitai Matua; Belle was 'Teuila', which meant adorner of the ugly, and was suggested by her habit of suddenly giving ribbons or trinkets to members of the staff; bespectacled Lloyd was 'Loia'; Graham Balfour, Louis's second cousin and future biographer, who came as a stranger to stay with his relatives in the summer of 1892, was 'Palema'.

Except for evenings when the Chief of State entertains, modern Vailima, of which the redwood hall and the other spacious lofty rooms are now all painted white, seems still and empty. It was not so in Stevenson's day. His own nervous temperament, together with Fanny's constant runabout activities, and those of Belle and Lloyd and the flock of servants, kept the household in a state of constant movement or almost of turmoil. Louis would wake early, at five or five-thirty, and ring the study bell for his breakfast; he would then make notes for *St Ives* or *Hermiston*. These notes formed the basis for his dictation to Belle later in the morning or in the afternoon. Louis did not take a siesta, but he still stuck to his ten-minute naps. There were, however, no rigid rules to his working hours—he might spend a morning playing on his flageolet, trying to compose music, or writing the poetry which he never took very seriously. Outside interruptions did not bother him, and he was always ready to come down from the upper veranda to welcome some chief and his retainers who would proceed across the lawns bearing presents and seeking his advice. Bands of boys and girls to dance on the lawn would be equally welcome, or embarrassed knots of alert sailors from some British man of war. A Samoan *melanga* or visiting party would be welcomed by him with a high chief's etiquette, the bowl of chewed kava that was expected was offered by the maids and, like any other Samoan chief, he would receive the visitors with his talking man at his elbow. For these ceremonies Louis would readily break the thread of the narrative he was dictating to Belle, and whole sentences might thus be irretrievably lost. But this constant process of people drifting to and fro was an essential part of Vailima life and nothing was allowed to interfere with it.

All the liveliness and this eager and friendly hospitability must have formed a glorious compensation for the invalid years when Louis could scarcely bear to see anyone, or to move far from his bed. Except for one or two threats of haemorrhage, when he reclined on a bed-rest given him by Sir Percy Shelley, and, clad in a white kimono with a white sash, scribbled notes on a board if he was forbidden by the doctor to speak, Louis's health at Vailima was startlingly good. His hair was now greying and he wrote to a new correspondent, James Barrie, whom he admired but had never met, that he would be a greybeard had he been able to grow one. His appearance nowadays wavered between that of gaunt age and his more perennial look of extreme youth. 'Sometimes he looks like an old man of eighty,' his wife once remarked to the family, 'and then, at a moment's notice, he's a pretty brown boy.' Belle's 'Boswellizing', as Louis called the notes of table-talk she was making in two large manuscript volumes, show that on the whole geniality and merriment played a large part in the family chat. A typical passage recorded by Belle had begun with a talk between her little son, in whose bedroom she was saying goodnight. Austin Strong, who soon became a Roman Catholic, had been much impressed by the funeral services in the Catholic mission in far-off Monterey, where he was sent to school to be with his first cousin Louis Sanchez, Fanny's sister Nelly's son. That evening he told his mother about the pall-bearers at Catholic funerals, but he pronounced the word as 'pall-berry': when Belle came down again, she told the family of this Malapropism:

'What a pretty funeral,' said Louis, 'to be decorated with pall-berries!'

' "That is," said Palema, "if it is in the pall-berry season."

' "In the islands," said Lloyd, "I suppose they would have tinned pall-berries!"

' "Imagine," said Palema, "if you were too early in the season and the pall-berries were green. Unripe pall-berries!"

' "Or too late," said Louis, "fancy if the pall-berries were rotten!" '

As a middle-aged man, Austin Strong, who had grown up to be a famous playwright, author of *Seventh Heaven* and other successes of the New York theatre of the 'twenties, remembered the evenings of his childhood at Vailima, the flying-foxes hanging high up on the house and on the great trees, the pack-horses Donald and Edinburgh coming up from Apia, their iron cages loaded with promising boxes, the diamond-clear mornings, 'the intensity of the life around us—the sounds of the forest awakening—one could almost hear the plants growing.' He remembered the distant boom of the surf and the roar of the nearby waterfall after the rains. In particular he liked to dwell upon the great hall at night, with the lamps lit and the place 'filled with joyous faces and after-dinner arguments'. Louis and Graham Balfour would pace up and down the shining waxed floor of the big room talking, and Austin would watch the lamplight on their faces as they came and went. Old Mrs Thomas Stevenson sat bolt upright and 'queenly', nibbling captain's biscuits and sipping her brandy and soda. Austin's mother would recline in a hammock swung the width of the room. Fanny, or Tamaitai as Austin called her, would be seated on a chair at the head of the table, one foot tucked under her, smoking wispy cigarettes 'while listening with avid interest to everything that was said'. When Fanny spoke everyone stopped talking to listen to what she had to say. Little Austin would take refuge under the table, hoping that he would be forgotten when his bedtime came round. To the child it was a happy family scene, bright and reassuring.

The old photographs, which Lloyd thought made Vailima look so plain and barn-like, are often crowded with members of the family, and such special retainers as Talolo the cook, Louis's devoted personal servant the boy Sosimo, or Fanny's chief gardener, 'old' Lafaela. Others, taken in the great hall, with its wide staircase that sweeps up to the second floor, also show members of the family. There are further pictures of Louis in the act of dictating to Belle in the library, or of Fanny and a Samoan girl seated on either side of the chimney-piece upstairs, which was the only fireplace in the island, and a source of amazed interest to Samoan visitors. These shadows from the past, brown photographs brittle along the edges, serve to evoke what was basically a happy if not an entirely serene household.

Naturally enough the family conversation was not all quips, though Louis still had wild days when he became what his family called 'the Idiot Boy', and what he termed 'the gibbering idiot'. In these puerile, carefree moods he would tangle up his mother's knitting, pull out Fanny and Belle's hairpins, and generally impede whatever his womenfolk were trying to do. The appearance of Sosimo to announce that lunch was ready would alone put an end to these capers, and he would settle down at the table to explain to Graham Balfour why *Will o'the Mill* was not as fine as Graham believed. Palema had said that as a youth he had been so much impressed by this story that he had modelled his character and life upon it. Louis replied that Will's sentiments on life were 'cat's meat'. 'It is the best thing on life that has been written in this age,' Belfour strangely pronounced. Louis replied that it was rather remarkable, then, how little stock he himself took in it. 'If you had stood by your words I would have gone down on my knees to you,' replied Palema. 'But how did you come to write what you don't believe?' 'Well,' Louis rather vaguely answered, 'I was at that age when you begin to look about and wonder if you should live your life—' 'To be or not to be?' 'Exactly,' Louis agreed, 'everything is temperament.' In order to fill her albums with important as well as entertaining matter, Belle would pose serious questions to Louis—why were painters more narrow-minded than writers, for example?

Mail-days were particularly thrilling for the expatriates. Louis would open the mail-bags and throw the letters for each member of the family into his or her heap which could not be touched until he had finished—'Woe betide the person who tries to snatch a letter from the pile!' wrote Belle. Letters to Louis from strangers and autograph-hunters were allotted to Belle to deal with; he always himself answered letters which seemed to him sincere, or those from children or the sick. Most begging letters were ignored. Mail-day deranged Louis for further work, and he and Belle would walk bare-headed and bare-footed in the shade of the forest trees, or sit on a stone by the upper waterfall discussing some Stanley Weyman serial of which they were both enjoying the serialization in *Longman's Magazine*.

When she became his regular amanuensis, Belle was amazed to find that Louis, when he felt like it, could swiftly dictate from his notes from eight o'clock in the morning until four in the afternoon with great earnestness, and that when particularly involved in his characters he would unconsciously act out their parts, bowing to an imaginary Flora when his hero Anne de St Ives was speaking, twirling his moustache, and then imitating the Scots falsetto of Flora's old aunt, and the broad Scots growl of the drover to whom the old lady so uncharacteristically entrusts St Ives on his escape to Swanston Cottage from prison in Edinburgh Castle. Belle evidently mentioned this mimicry to her mother, for Fanny told her that when Louis was writing *The Master of Ballantrae* he had once come into her room to look in the glass 'as he wished to describe a certain haughty, disagreeable expression of his hero's.' He revealed on this occasion that he had actually expected to see the Master's clean-shaven face and powdered head in the mirror, and was 'quite disconcerted that he found only the reflection of himself'. Once Belle asked him why he wrote tales as grim as *The Merry Men* and *Markheim* and not more 'pretty' stories like *Providence and the Guitar*. Belle added that at least he had no mannerisms, whereupon he immediately pointed out one in *The Merry Man*, which she had been reading and which she held in her hand. She maintained that the phrase which he criticized — 'it was a wonderful clear night full of stars' — was in itself a good sentence and presented a picture to the mind. 'It is the mannerisms of the author who can't say "says he" and "says she" that I object to,' Belle declared, 'whose characters hiss, and thunder, and ejaculate and syllable —' 'Oh, my dear,' Louis replied, 'deal gently with me — I once *fluted*.' Belle's efforts at turning Boswell lucidly resuscitate Louis's total and disarming charm.

13

Samoa: The End

IN spite of all the traumas caused by Fanny's health, in spite also of the languid atmosphere of Upolo, Louis Stevenson did manage to get a good deal of work done in the first full year at Vailima, the year 1892. He was also much involved, as we shall presently see, in the whole tangle of Samoan-European politics into which he entered with much zest and great partisanship. In one of the prefaces now to be found in the collected *Tusitala* edition of Louis's work (published ten years after her death) Fanny points out that if Louis had ever had good health he would rather have been a soldier than a writer. Her basis for this categorical statement would seem to be Louis's old invalid yearning for a more active life, his interest in books on military tactics and fortifications and, perhaps, the elaborate war-games with which he had entertained himself and Lloyd in the châlet attic during the two dreary winters at Davos. By the time that Fanny was writing her own views of her husband's character, now available in the *Tusitala* prefaces, there was really no one left alive to gainsay her—or at any rate no one who would have been imprudent enough to contradict the authorized version of her husband's life which she was busy confecting and which Henley, reviewing in 1901 the official Balfour biography, written under Fanny's auspices, alone attacked as presenting a 'Seraph in Chocolate, this barley-sugar effigy of a real man', which was not the 'old, riotous, intrepid, scornful Stevenson at all'.

Whatever her motives—and these were at no time very simple—Fanny suddenly explained Louis's interest in Samoan politics and warfare to her readers by asserting that he had always been a warrior *manqué*. 'One side of my husband's character was almost unknown,' we learn with surprise, 'the profession of letters was a second choice, his ill health, beginning in his childhood, making what he preferred, the career of a soldier, impossible.' As we have seen, Louis Stevenson was a born writer, who slaved away from his youth to achieve the stylistic perfection of his natural gift, and the implication of Fanny's new statement makes nonsense. What she seemed to think she was doing was explaining Louis's restlessness about the Great Powers' activities in Samoa: 'It may be imagined how galling it was to sit writing books on his veranda,' she explains, 'conscious the while of the foolish manœuvres of the opposing parties, and knowing how easy it would be to turn the scale.' Galling or not, Louis fortunately remained writing on his veranda, or rather in his upstairs study, which was really a segment of the top veranda next to the library, cut off and enclosed, with two windows giving him a view of the sea, and another from which he could gaze up at Mount Vaea, a pathless peak he had somewhat heedlessly selected as his place of burial. This choice caused a bout of heavy and hectic pioneering activity for his Samoan friends throughout the night of his death.

It seems to have been their miniature scale that inspired Louis's interest in Samoan politics:

You don't know what news is, nor what politics, nor what the life of man, till you see it on so small a scale and with your own liberty on the board for stake [Louis wrote to Henry James in December 1892]. I would not have missed it for much. And anxious friends beg me to stay at home and study human nature in Brompton drawing-rooms! *Farceurs*! And anyway you know that such is not my talent. I could never be induced to take the faintest interest in Brompton *qua* Brompton or a drawing-room *qua* a drawing-room. I am an Epick writer with a k to it, but without the necessary genius.

He told James that 'in twelve calendar months' he had finished *The Wrecker*, written all of *The Beach of Falesa* (an apparently supernatural story to which he unhappily gave a mundane ending), drafted much of his 'History of Samoa' which was published in August 1892 as *A Footnote to History*, done some work on a book on his grandfather which became part of the unfinished and posthumously published *A Family of Engineers*, and both begun and completed *David Balfour*. This last was a sequel to *Kidnapped*, which, before being retitled *Catriona*, ran as a serial in *Atalanta* (a British magazine for girls) from January to May 1893 and was then produced in book-form by Cassell. He told James that he had also roughed out the first three chapters of a new book, *The Justice Clerk*.

This was left unfinished at Louis's death and appeared post-humously as the tantalizing, snapped-off masterpiece, *Weir of Hermiston*. Louis himself was well aware of what a stride forward *The Justice Clerk* was going to represent: 'Mind you,' he wrote to Baxter in the same month as to Henry James, 'I expect *The Justice Clerk* to be a masterpiece. My Braxfield is already a thing of beauty and a joy forever, and, so far as he has gone, *far* my best character.' With this optimistic estimate of the portrait of Braxfield one would not now venture to disagree.

It was Henry James who had complained, in his article on Robert Louis Stevenson printed in *The Century* in 1888, that the novel *Kipnapped* had stopped 'without ending'. In *David Balfour* (or, as we know it, *Catriona*), Louis made amends, taking up the story where he had relinquished it in Bournemouth six years before, and inventing the rest of Davie's adventures consequent to his having witnessed the Appin murder. The book was written simultaneously with *A Foot-note to History* and went so comparatively smoothly that it was finished in September. Fanny wrote afterwards that 'David Balfour' had 'slipped through this turbulent year so quietly that we were hardly aware of his passage', whereas another Vailima witness, Graham Balfour, presents a different view of the passage through the house of *David Balfour*. 'It was the first of his work which was completed while I was at Vailima,' wrote Graham, 'and I well remember the agitation and stress with which it was brought to a close. It lends no support to the theory that the continuation of a story is doomed to fail.' In *Catriona* Louis attempted two female portraits more ambitious than any he had yet undertaken. He used to say that he thought himself incapable of creating convincing fictional women, until he came to the two Kirsties in his last book, *Weir of Hermiston*.

In Catriona More herself he was not perhaps very successful, for she never gains the reader's sympathy, and very quickly forewent that of her author. Throughout the book it is more and more evident that Lord Prestongrange's witty daughter Barbara Grant is winning Stevenson's allegiance; indeed he is said to have exclaimed, 'But of dear me! I came near to losing my heart to Barbara,' and it does at one moment seem doubtful whether David Balfour will not lose his heart to her as well. One of the mysteries of *Catriona* concerns the motives which guide Lord Prestongrange's behaviour to Davie Balfour—kindly patronizing him at one moment, even throwing his daughter Barbara in the boy's way, and then deceitfully incarcerating him on the Bass Rock to prevent his bearing witness at the

Appin murder trial. A letter from Louis at Vailima to Sidney Colvin explains that David never knew what Lord Prestongrange was up to, and that neither did Stevenson, nor indeed, Prestongrange himself. Louis cited Prestongrange as 'a mask' of a character, in consequence extremely hard to render convincingly.

Miss Evelyn Buchanan Simpson, a memorialist who, we may remember, had developed a contempt for her brother's friend from Heriot Row, repeats in her *The Stevenson Originals* a contemporary comment on Barbara Grant by a critic of *Catriona* in the *Westminster Budget*. It is not without a certain curious interest, especially in the light of Stevenson's remark that he had come near to losing his heart to his own creation, Miss Barbara Grant. 'Stevenson had a sort of coyness and archness which reminds me of nothing so much as Miss Grant in his own *Catriona*,' writes this anonymous witness, who had evidently known Louis in his London days. 'Indeed, I seem to see more of the real Stevenson in that lady than in any male character in his books. He has just that quality of wit, that fine manner and great gentleness under a surface of polished raillery.' If Barbara Grant be indeed an unconscious self-portrait, Louis certainly liked it.

He also liked *Catriona*, by and large. In September 1893 he told George Meredith, to whom he had had a copy of the book despatched, that he was sometimes tempted to think it was about his best work. To Mrs Sitwell, in one of his very rare letters to that old friend nowadays, he wrote: 'I shall never do a better book than *Catriona*, that is my high-water mark.' Frances Sitwell intelligently replied that, good though she thought *Catriona*, she believed that he could do better still—and *Weir of Hermiston*, after all, proves her right. To the American Will Low, his crony of the Parisian Latin Quarter in the 1870s, Louis wrote more revealingly, and evidently from the heart: 'I think *David Balfour** is a nice little book, and very artistic and just the thing to occupy the leisure of a busy man; but for the top flower of a man's life it seems inadequate. Small is the word; it is a small age, and I am of it ... *J'ai honte pour nous*; my ears burn.'

It was Graham Balfour who persuaded Louis to furbish and release *The Ebb Tide*, which was serialized in 1893 and 1894 but not published as a book until the latter year. Originating in another brief bout of collaboration with Lloyd Osbourne, *The Schooner Farallone*, or *The Pearl Fishers* as it was then tentatively called, had been discarded and considered as but the draft for the first chapters

---

* As *Catriona* was called in its American edition.

of a very long projected novel. When Louis showed the manuscript to Balfour, this young man suggested that, properly arranged, the tale could stand on its own feet as a long short story. Louis agreed and, without Lloyd's assistance, but with great anguish to himself, he wrote and rewrote passages of it, and then rewrote them again.

Graham Balfour was a cousin of Louis's on his mother's, the Balfour of Pilgrig, side. He was touring in the South Seas, and naturally came to rest for some months at Vailima. Belle Strong seems to have been much attached to him, and when he subsequently married, she wrote that he must tell his bride, Rhoda, what a blessing 'Palema' had been to them:

> We lived so much in our clan — our family was sufficient to us, and every member of it revolved in a wheel of mutual admiration — and he was our pride and joy — in any political difficulties Louis and Lloyd called him in to consult. He warned us off undesirable friends and we waited for his nod of commendation before we made new ones ... Rhoda should see him crowned with a wreath of white jasmine blossom when he looked 'like an angel from Heaven'.

Graham Balfour certainly achieved a private miracle in compiling an official biography of Robert Louis Stevenson which not only pleased Fanny but is factual, level-headed and discreet while not misleading. Sidney Colvin, who had been originally commissioned for this work, soon lost the confidence of Fanny and Lloyd, who treated him shamefully.

It is now time to glance at that other passion which competed with writing novels in the last three years of Louis Stevenson's life — his absorption in Samoa's political affairs.

[II]

While on the minuscule scale which Stevenson found so attractive, Samoan politics were indeed in an uneasy and ambiguous state during his four years' residence on Upolu. 'We sit and pipe on a volcano, which is being stoked by bland, incompetent amateurs, untaught, I fear unteachable,' he wrote to Baxter in August 1891. But he did not pretend that he was not enjoying it, even to the point of dramatizing the dangers which he said threatened himself. 'This is a strange life,' he told Colvin, 'always on the brink of deportation, men's lives in the scale — and, well, you know my character: if I were to pretend to you that I was not amused, you would justly scorn me.' Needless to say he romanticized the Samoans' rather shapeless troubles: 'Here is, for the first time, a tale of Greeks— Homeric Greeks—mingled with moderns and all true.' His reference was to his own contribution to Samoan affairs—a small book entitled *A Footnote to History*. This was supplemented by eight excessively long letters to *The Times*, in which he sought to draw the attention of the serious British reading public to events in late nineteenth-century Samoa. He himself said that he regarded his substantial pamphlet as mere journalism—'there is not even a good sentence in it'. Here Louis was of course exaggerating, for he had now reached a point in his art in which it was a real teaser for him not to write good sentences. One, taken at random and describing the effect upon the South Sea islands of being awakened 'in the midst of the century of competition', is surely memorable: 'And the island races, comparable to a shopful of crockery launched upon the stream of time, now fall to make their desperate voyage among pots of brass and adamant.'

In Honolulu, under the influence of the 'Royal Crowd' as King Kalakama's circle was called, and aided by Joe Strong, who had been attached in the role of artist to an abortive Hawaiian embassy sent to Apia in 1887, Louis had begun to string together a book about Samoa, which Joe was to illustrate. On reaching Samoa itself and talking to Moors and other witnesses, as well as to participants in the brief war of 1888 and its aftermath, he had laid his manuscript aside as being irrelevant, and began to write an informed treatise from the first-hand evidence he was daily collecting. By November 1891 he had completed one-sixth of *A Footnote*, for he felt that time pressed: 'I do not go in for literature, I address myself to sensible people rather than to the sensitive ... I have no right to dally; if it is to help it must come soon.' 'Will anyone read it?' he wrote rhetorically to Colvin in December 1891: 'I fancy not, people don't read history for reading, but for education and display—and who desires education in the history of Samoa?' Although hardly compulsive reading today, and perhaps not much more so when first published, *A Footnote to History* is a workmanlike piece of reporting and research, and forms a solid item in the rather specialized literature on European and American exploitation of the islands in the South Seas during the later years of the last century. Since Louis Stevenson felt fervidly convinced that he had a duty to do it, *A Footnote* should not be dismissed as a waste of a talented writer's time.

There is no cause for us here to go into the murky detail of Samoa's history before Stevenson's day. It is sufficient to remember that the Samoan islands had always been an independent group, ruled in a complicated tribal fashion by one man selected from among the several high-chiefs, a man whose position depended on his titles, which were not hereditary, and whom it was simplest for the whites, when they came there to trade, to call 'the King'. The Samoans recognized an aristocracy of high chiefs, who were addressed in a particular high-chiefly idiom, which amounted to a court language within the daily language. The Samoans had never been cannibals, a way of life which they regarded with distaste. Although civilized, benevolent, handsome and not too imaginative, they had a ferocious streak which came out in their frequent little civil wars, when the heads not only of warriors slain but of these merely wounded were hacked off and collected in baskets by the winning side. Their daily lives were communal and, despite the role of the aristocracy, they were democratic. Physical perfection was always emphasized in their choice of chiefs, and no one with a noticeable physical defect like a hunched back or an important wen could ever achieve political or social prominence. In the nineteenth century the strategic position of the Samoan islands, and their wealth in copra, attracted the attention of the whites of Europe and the United States, just as their resources of splendid timber are attracting Australian and New Zealand timber-merchants today.

It was in 1839 that the United States of America first evinced an interest in Samoa, especially in the fine harbour of Pago-Pago on the island of Tutuila, forty miles west of Upolu. The Americans were granted commercial and extra-territorial rights on Tutuila in 1873. By this time the islands had also aroused the cupidity of German and British merchants. International friction over these small South Sea territories developed and in 1878 an abortive conference between Germany, Great Britain and the United States to decide the future of Samoa was held in Washington. This conference subsided before anything conclusive could be achieved. Germany was well established on Upolu, with extensive coconut plantations, which the Samoans, not yet understanding the lures of the export trade, thought silly, regarding them as gigantic, well-organized and unused larders from which they could daily help themselves. By Stevenson's time one whole section of Apia, the capital (which in fact consisted of a string of adjoining coastal villages), was a German cantonment, another part was British, and another virtually under the American flag. The Consuls of these three powers were therefore paramount, with the Germans assuming to themselves an ostentatious and loud-mouthed control of the situation.

There were then three native chiefs who could claim the kingship — Tamasese, Laupepa, and an elderly man with seemingly stronger rights than either of these, Mataafa. German, British and American war vessels were now sent to Apia, where they anchored in a throng in the harbour. The Germans deported Laupepa, first to Europe and then to Jaluit. A short war broke out in which the Mataafa men defeated Tamasese's, and took some heads. In a subsequent scurry with German marines on shore, forty of these were killed and some of their heads taken. This was in 1888; meanwhile a hurricane wrecked all but one warship in Apia harbour. In 1889 the Washington conference was reconvened, this time at Berlin. A tripartite rule by the Consuls of the three Powers was established, a Swede was appointed as a compromise to the new post of Chief Justice of Samoa, and a German, von Pilsach, was made President of the Municipal Council. Laupepa was released by the Germans and brought back by them as King of Samoa, with Mataafa as Vice-King, a subsidiary position of which he soon tired.

The Treaty of Berlin was signed in July 1889, but the new Chief Justice, Cedarcantz, did not appear in Samoa until December 1890, or open his court for hearings until the middle of July 1891. The new President Pilsach's first activity was building an expensive jail, which was never used. He also bought up the local newspaper and arrested five Samoan chiefs; in September 1891 it was alleged that the Germans had threatened to dynamite the house in which the five prisoners were shut up. Mataafa made his headquarters along the coast at Malie, a residence which gave him the right to the potent title of Malietoa, a name which the puppet-king, Laupepa, had usurped, calling himself Laupepa Malietoa. Mataafa, who had a majority following among the Samoans, slipped gradually into the role of rebel king, and received delegations and homage at Malie. It was in December 1890, just before the arrival of the Swedish Chief Justice, that Robert Louis Stevenson reached Apia, that same winter that he bought the land at Vailima, and settled down to write *A Footnote to History*.

With his romantic temperament, his idealism and his urge to interpret recent Samoan events in a Jacobite sense, it was entirely predictable that Louis should side with Mataafa, detest the European consuls — with Sewell, the young American consul, he always remained on good terms — and be dazzled by the mirage of Samoan politics. His letters to *The Times* caused the Chief Justice and the

President of the Council to demand his deportation, a threat on which he throve, and which was ultimately dissolved by a contrived and timely letter from the British Foreign Secretary, Lord Rosebery, to Sir John Thurston, High Commissioner of the Western Pacific. Thurston had suddenly prescribed a heavy fine and subsequent imprisonment on any British subject found guilty of trying 'to bring about in Samoa discontent or dissatisfaction, public disturbance, civil war, hatred or contempt towards the King or Government of Samoa or the laws and constitution of the country, and generally to promote public disorder in Samoa.' Rosebery, a fellow-Scot and an admirer of *Treasure Island* among other of Louis Stevenson's books, wrote him a personal letter saying that the Foreign Office were not perturbed by the British Consul's complaints of Stevenson; Thurston was then snubbed by the Colonial Office who told him to take no steps discomforting to Mr Stevenson without first consulting the Secretary of State.

Louis's intense interest in Samoan affairs—affairs which did indeed blow up during his lifetime into a few days' mini-war between the supporters of Lupepa and Mataafa—is quite comprehensible, as is his professed aim to bring about a reconciliation. He made two unsuccessful attempts at such a reconciliation, and in fact he and his family rendered only three visits in all to the rebel King Mataafa in his headquarters at Malie. In August 1892 he managed to exasperate the white officials by arranging that Lady Jersey (wife of the Governor of New South Wales), who was visiting Bazett Haggard, the British Land Commissioner, should visit Mataafa's camp incognita, or rather under the name of Amelia Balfour, a pretended cousin of Louis. The visit went off smoothly, although Mataafa and his followers treated Lady Jersey with all the ceremony due to her as 'Queen of Sydney'. Louis had written her a letter giving her a six-a.m. rendezvous on horseback 'towards the Gasigasi river', and had dated his missive August 14th, 1745. Lady Jersey, with whom Louis struck up what she later called 'a warm friendship', was a specimen of a class which, reared in the professional circles of Edinburgh, he had never yet encountered—the English aristocracy. To judge from Fanny's sharp reaction, he was perhaps somewhat fascinated by this handsome, solitary representative of the great world of Victorian society. 'The Jerseys have been and gone,' Fanny confided to her Journal. 'The dear Haggard has since moved in the clouds. They were a selfish "champagne Charley" set ... Lady Jersey tall and leggy and awkward, with bold black eyes and sensual mouth; very selfish and greedy of admiration,

259

a touch of vulgarity, courageous as a man, and reckless as a woman.'

After the little war of 1893, Mataafa and his more distinguished supporters were banished to the German-held Marshall Islands.* Lesser chiefs, including the Vailima cook Talolo's father, were imprisoned in Apia, in jail quarters which, though not austere, were unsuitable to their rank.

Louis and his family publicly made a state visit to them in the jail by carriage, bringing them kava and tobacco. Later the prisoners gave a feast for the Stevensons inside the jail compound and when, owing to Louis, they were finally released, they came to his house in a deputation to inform him that they had decided to work themselves on a link road to shorten the distance up to Vailima. The grassy 'Road of the Loving Hearts' exists, and is now so labelled, to this day.

[III]

'Yesterday and today we wrote steadily at *Anne*,' Belle noted in her journal for mid-March 1894, 'while war news and rumours flew thick and fast around us.' *Anne* was her name for the novel about Anne de St Ives, a French prisoner in Scotland during the Napoleonic wars, whose escape and subsequent adventures formed a tale already sold through McClure for serialization. *St Ives* is as picaresque as *Kidnapped* and *Catriona*, but below these two in quality. The Vailima woods were full of scouting parties and the beat of war-drums—'but nothing stops the cheerful flow of *Anne*,' wrote Belle. Sometimes she would interrupt Louis's dictation with timorous topical questions—'Louis, have we a pistol or a gun in the house that will shoot?' she asked him one day. 'No,' he replied, 'but we have friends on both sides'—and the dictation continued. Belle found that Louis 'worried terribly over *St Ives*' and that at times it refused to run smoothly. He spent much of 1893 on *St Ives*, which, like *The Master of Ballantrae*, and for much the same reasons, now began to bore him. That sense of exhilaration which Dickens felt when writing a book for serial publication was not a characteristic of Louis or of his writing methods. He liked to suspend work on one book and start on another, alternating backwards and forwards

* In 1899, five years after Louis's death, when Upolu was allotted to the Germans, and Tuitula to the U.S.A., the Germans brought Mataafa back again and set him up as king. Louis's house at Vailima then became the Imperial German Government House, and was again enlarged, almost to the size it is today. The colony was occupied by New Zealand forces in 1914, came under a New Zealand protectorate and attained independence in 1962.

between the two. In July 1893 he told Baxter that *St Ives* would be postponed 'for a good few months, for I have come to one of my regular sticks in it.' In April 1894 he reported the novel as 'well on its way' into the second volume, a month later that it was still plodding along 'not at an alarming rate'. In August he was not yet certain of the length of the book, and by November, the month before his death, *St Ives* was referred to by its unenthusiastic author as 'the blamed thing'. He achieved thirty chapters of *St Ives* before his death; owing to the serial arrangements the book was completed by Quiller-Couch, who added another six chapters to the end of the original manuscript.

A persuasive reason for Louis's interest in *St Ives* turning stale was his passion for a new novel—first called *The Justice Clerk*, but now known as *Weir of Hermiston*. Inspired by an old fascination exerted over Louis by the Edinburgh legends centring on the coarse and illiterate eighteenth-century judge, Robert MacQueen, Lord Braxfield, this book is written with a new maturity and a psychological insight into men and women which Louis had never before displayed in so subtle and sustained a fashion. We have seen that he told Henry James in a letter of December 1892 how, amongst all the other work of that busy year, he had roughed out three chapters of *The Justice Clerk*. In 1894 he returned to his manuscript with breathless vigour. 'Pegging away at Hermiston like one o'clock,' Belle recorded. 'I hardly drew breath, but flew over the paper.' She observed that Louis made very few preliminary notes on Hermiston 'to keep him on the track', that he never faltered for a word and that he dictated to her 'as clearly and steadily as though he were reading from some unseen book'. She found Louis's voice so mellifluous and the story so gripping that she forgot everything else while they were working together. 'Belle, I see it all so clearly!' Louis exclaimed to her one day. 'The story unfolds itself before me to the least detail—there is nothing left in doubt. I never felt so before in anything I ever wrote. It will be my best work; I feel myself so sure of every word!' He told Belle that he was using her as the model for the younger Kirsty (the dark-haired heroine of *Weir*), and that he intended to dedicate the book to her.

In June 1894 work was interrupted by the longed-for arrival of all the furniture from Heriot Row. There were thirty-seven cases of it, some of them fifteen feet square; it was dragged up the Vailima road by German bullock-carts, and must have caused a great sensation. These tangible reminders of his youth in Edinburgh appeared on tropical Samoa at the very time when Louis Stevenson, both in *St Ives* and in *Hermiston*, was writing of his grey native city, the mental vision of which ceased to haunt him and almost to require exorcism.

As Louis's death approached, his imagination became more fertile than ever. Having shown, in his portraits of the two Kirsty Elliots in *Hermiston*, that he could draw women convincingly, he announced to his wife that he wanted to start on yet another new novel, this time to be set in Tahiti, to have mainly female characters and to be called after its heroine, a plantation owner, *Sophia Scarlet*. This novel was never begun, although a fourth project, fully as promising in its three existing chapters as *Hermiston*, was partially drafted. It was entitled *Heathercat*, would have dealt with old Scottish covenanting days (the 'Killing Time'), and was influenced by all that Louis had read in extreme youth and all that his old nurse Cummy had told him of the secret open-air meetings which a Covenanting flock would hold on the solitary grey hillsides and beside the morasses of the North-West. In June 1894 he wrote of his current work to Bob Stevenson, the cousin with whom he was once so intimate, but who never now seemed able to answer his letters:

> My work goes along but slowly. I have got to a crossing place,
> I suppose; the present book, *St Ives*, is nothing; it is in no style in
> particular, a tissue of adventures, the central character not very
> well done ... I like doing it though; and if you ask me why!
> After that I am on *Weir of Hermiston* and *Heathercat*, two Scotch
> stories, which will either be something different or I shall have
> failed.

It had been Louis's long-established habit to read each section of a new book aloud to his family, and await their reactions. On these occasions Lloyd sat with a pencil and paper before him, to make critical comments or suggestions. One evening after dinner, Louis read the company the first chapters of *Weir of Hermiston*. At the end of the reading, Louis noticed that Lloyd Osbourne's paper was blank—he had jotted down no comment on *Weir* at all. Lloyd was, in fact, so dumbfounded by the 'sureness and perfection' of the new book that, as he wrote afterwards, the words seemed to strike against his heart. He could not even speak, and when Louis had finished reading, the stepson silently poured himself a glass of whisky, and, as the party broke up for the night, he merely said, 'Goodnight, Louis,' and crept off to his own cottage in the grounds. In a frantic state of agitation, breathless and trembling, Louis pursued him. 'My God, you shall not go like that!' Louis shouted.

No note? No comment? Not even 'the courtesy of a lie'? He had misunderstood Lloyd's speechlessness, and had thought it reflected, not admiration, but contempt. Lloyd was gradually able to explain to Louis that he was struck dumb by the book—that it was a masterpiece; that Louis had written nothing to compare with it; that 'it promised to be the greatest book in the English language'.

Mollified by his opinion, Louis burst into tears. Lloyd cried, too. They sat side by side on the dark veranda, their arms about each other, 'talking far into the night'. What Louis told his stepson on this occasion we do not know, as Lloyd thought it too sacred to divulge even after thirty years. All we do know is that Louis revealed his 'tortured soul' and 'the falterings of its Calvary'. He spoke of moments when he earnestly longed for death. In this last summer of Louis's life, Lloyd Osbourne often caught him gazing up at the green cone of Mount Vaea, which he had chosen as the site for his tomb. Louis was writing to Mrs Sitwell that the Gods did not love him, because he was meant to die young.

What, at the end of his life, were Robert Louis Stevenson's views of his own achievements? What, as a grateful posterity, do we think that he did achieve?

In October 1894, in one of his monthly letters to Sidney Colvin, Louis Stevenson asked his friend 'to spare *St Ives*' when the holograph reached him: ... 'for the nonce my skill deserts me, such as it is, or was,' he wrote. 'It was a very little dose of inspiration, and a pretty little trick of style, long lost, improved by the most heroic industry ... I am a fictitious article and have long known it. I am read by journalists, by my fellow-novelists, and by boys ... I cannot take myself seriously, as an artist the limitations are so obvious.' At about the same time Louis told Lloyd Osbourne that he knew that he himself was not a man of 'any unusual talent', that he had started off with very moderate abilities and that his success was due to his own 'really remarkable industry'. 'What genius I had,' he explained to Lloyd, 'was for hard work.'

Just eleven months after Louis's death, his old friend Baxter, who was in charge of the newly projected *Edinburgh Edition* of the collected works, wrote to Graham Balfour in doubts as to its ultimate sale. Was there still a demand for R.L.S.? 'With the rush of new writers there is a great problem of Louis's works taking a back place in no distant time,' he suggested, although he could not conceive of Stevenson sinking into the oblivion that clearly awaited the then popular writers of adventure stories. In the eighty years since Robert Louis Stevenson died his reputation has been subject to many a marked ebb and flow. When Lloyd and Fanny released the *Vailima Prayers*, written by Louis for reading aloud to his family and to the Samoan household, texts from these were widely reprinted in Great Britain and the United States, and were framed and hung in children's night-nurseries. This was during the period of the hagiological attitude towards Louis Stevenson's life and works.

The new generation reacted in a way that might have been foreseen; the most lucid of the attacks upon his memory was that of Frank Swinnerton, whose book on Louis was published in 1924. In this readable volume the author not only withholds all admiration, but presents Stevenson's writings as thin, veneered and insincere. Swinnerton also asserts that Louis Stevenson was fundamentally a coldly egotistical character, accepting without returning the love of his friends. Other writers of the postwar period exaggerated the trivial lecheries of Stevenson's Edinburgh youth in an effort to contradict what we may call the Vailima Prayers attitude of his devotees. No writer on him dared to question his industry; it was just any literary gift that was denied him.

Nowadays, in an English-speaking world so far less innocent than that of his contemporaries, certain novels of Robert Louis Stevenson continue to be widely read, and not by boys alone. *Treasure Island* and *Kidnapped* have survived, but not perhaps *Catriona* and certainly not *Prince Otto*. *The Inland Voyage* and *Travels with a Donkey* retain, like a number of his essays, their power to charm. *The Master of Ballantrae*, so admirable for the first two-thirds of the book, then proves a bitter disappointment. *The South Seas* deserves to be read more than it probably is. The stories in the *Island Nights' Entertainments* grip one as sharply as ever. *The Wrecker* contains wonderful passages, particularly the scenes in the Pacific. Grim stories like *Thrawn Janet* and *The Merry Men* are unforgettable, while *The Strange Case of Dr Jekyll and Mr Hyde* is known throughout the civilized world. *The Ebb Tide* is excellent and thrilling. *The Wrong Box* can never fail to amuse. As a poet Louis Stevenson is in a distinctly secondary position, although *A Child's Garden of Verses* has its own form of survival and so do several of his songs. As a letter-writer Stevenson is unsurpassed, and the very deep strain of egotism in his nature renders his correspondence immediately and intimately fascinating. The passage of the years has winnowed his achievements, but what remains is anything but chaff. Whether or no he deeply wished for immortality, such, after now eighty years, has been his lot.

Despite the certainty of his immortality, it is hard precisely to assess Robert Louis Stevenson's gifts. He had style, at which he worked so hard, and which towards the end of his life he analysed as being of two varieties—what he called 'the plastic', described as the piling on of colours to bring a book 'up to key', and another which he saw to be 'the simple placing of words together for harmony'. These words, he asserted, 'should come off the tongue like honey'. 'I began so as a young man,' he explained, 'and I had a pretty talent for it.' He believed that men who began with the 'honey dripping' talent, like Beethoven and Shakespeare, 'often developed in later work a certain brusqueness and ruggedness'. It was perhaps this latter quality that he was seeking when he wrote *Weir of Hermiston* and began *Heathercat*. For, however much one may love Robert Louis Stevenson's works, however good his dialogue and evocative his scenic descriptions and adroit his character-drawing, it remains true that the books and the people in them do not customarily make an indelible impression on your mind. You seem each time to be reading him afresh. Anthony Trollope, who surpassed even Stevenson in industry, has left us characters which are more truly memorable than those of Louis, characters who seem to have a full life of their own far beyond Trollope's pages, whereas too often Stevenson's personages seem to return to the puppet-box whenever you put a book of his down. *Weir* and the sketch of *Heathercat* suggest that their author was at length passing from the phase of puppet-master to that of true creator. It was, alas and alas, at this stage of his development that he prematurely died.

[IV]

Louis's final view of the world outside the island of Upolu, Samoa, was in September 1893 on an expedition to Honolulu, a place he never liked. On this trip, which was intended to be for his health, Louis took the Vailima cook, Tamolo, who was hypnotized by the sight of the tramcars and electric lights of King Kalakaua's capital. Almost inevitably, Louis fell ill in Honolulu, and Fanny was obliged to come up from Samoa to nurse him and to bring him back home. After this bout, and although he now complained of the collapse of his liver and his stomach, Louis seemed and looked, for him, superlatively well. Yet his last letters to old friends sound a note of exhaustion with life. 'Literally no man has more completely lived out life than I have done,' he wrote to Baxter in the autumn of 1894, but he added defiantly, 'And still it's good fun.' In his last letter to Colvin Louis described a naval ball given by the officers and crew of a British warship then on duty at Apia. The Vailima family all stayed the night in town at an hotel. Louis got up at six, and watched from the hotel veranda the 'cold, pink and rust colour' of dawn breaking in the East, and the marshes smoking whitely and the contrast of the golden west. The main street of Apia was empty at that hour, and the setting moon showed 'yellow as an apricot'. At this point Louis's reflections were disturbed by a decrepit drunken acquaintance, covered with boils and smelling 'of the charnel-house'. This alcoholic specimen was only by one month his senior. The very sight of him made Louis reflect upon the horrors of old age. 'O, it is bad to grow old,' he wrote to Colvin in his final missive: 'For it is practically hell. I do not like the consolations of age. I was born a young man; and I have continued so.' Louis Stevenson would doubtless have endured old age with the same carefree courage with which he had survived a near-moribund youth. But he was not put to that test. The sudden death, with his clothes on, for which he used to say he longed, was vouchsafed to him at Vailima less than a month after that Apia ball.

On December 3rd, 1894, Louis seemed to everyone in the house to be very well—as well, indeed, and as resilient as they were now accustomed to seeing him. On the day before, he had lunched with his friend the British Commissioner for Lands, Bazett Haggard, and had left him at six because there was no moon that night. Whenever he returned home after dark Louis was always welcomed by the sight of the lamps of Vailima shining through the trees—for he had ordered that when he was out late every light in the house should provide a luminous welcome for his return. On this particular night, and on the following day, he seems to have had no premonition whatever that his death was so near. He had left Haggard cheerfully, remarking as he did so that he must write his monthly letter to Sidney Colvin, which was overdue. Fanny, on the other hand, who prided herself on second sight, was filled with gloomy apprehensions of some catastrophe to someone close to them. She and Louis agreed that it could not concern either of themselves, and feared it might prove to be that Graham Balfour, then on a cruise down the Islands, was in danger.

All the morning of his last day he was dictating *Weir of Hermiston* to Belle Strong. The very last passage he recited concerns the aftermath of a lovers' misunderstanding between the young Kirsty Elliot and the book's hero, Archie Weir, beside the Weaver's Stone:

Archie ran to her. He took the poor child in his arms, and she nestled to his breast as to a mother's ... Pity, and at the same time a bewildered fear of this explosive engine in his arms, whose works he did not understand, and yet had been tampering with. There arose from before him the curtains of boyhood, and he saw for the first time the ambiguous face of woman as she is. In vain he looked back over the interview; he saw not where he had offended. It seemed unprovoked, a wilful convulsion of brute nature ...

These were the very last words of fiction which Louis Stevenson wrote. Whether Fanny ever understood his references to a beloved woman as an explosive engine, and apt to make a row that seemed a wilful convulsion of brute nature, we shall never know. Most probably and most mercifully, she did not.

At twelve o'clock that morning Louis stopped work and, striding up and down his room in his usual fashion, he talked to Belle of the new book, of further chapters for it, and of experiences in his past life which bore on what he had just been dictating. In the afternoon Belle wrote her own letters, and was amused at the noise and laughter coming from the veranda, where Louis was trying to give her son Austin a French lesson. Some time after five o'clock Belle heard her mother calling for hot water, and, suspecting nothing amiss, walked calmly downstairs. There, in the great hall, she saw Louis slumped back in the big red armchair, unconscious and breathing stertorously, while Fanny and his mother chafed his hands, and Tamolo brought hot water for his feet. Belle rushed to Lloyd's cottage, and met him coming over to the house, happily swinging a wreath he had had made for the Consul-General. Lloyd immediately mounted the swiftest horse in their paddock and galloped down to Apia for the doctor.

The circumstances of Louis's cerebral haemorrhage were sudden and brief. To distract Fanny from her forebodings he had played a card-game, and then he had fetched wine from the cellar and was helping her make a mayonnaise for supper, putting in the oil drop by drop with a steady hand. All at once he put his hands to head and cried out, 'What's that?', or 'What a pain!' (accounts differ), and then, to Fanny, 'Do I look strange?' The next moment he was on his knees on the floor of the veranda. His wife and his boy-valet Sosimo helped him into the great hall, and placed him in a big armchair. He had lost consciousness and never regained it. He died at ten minutes past eight that evening, at the age of forty-four and three weeks.

Down in Apia Lloyd had collected two doctors—the medical officer from the British man-of-war, and an old friend of theirs, a German, Dr Funk. The doctors could do nothing for Louis was past help. The Samoan boys of the household gathered round the brass bedstead which had been brought into the great hall from a guest-room, and on which Louis was now lying. The Catholic boys chanted the prayers for the dying. Gradually the chiefs who had been Louis's friends came in ceremonial groups to bid farewell to the man they had admired, and who had never been sparing of help or advice in their troubles. They brought precious mats, family heir-looms, to lay on the coffin. The question of Louis's burial, which the doctor said must be before noon next day, was now urgent.

Louis had frequently asked Lloyd to have a path cut up to the summit of Mount Vaea, but his stepson, knowing the reason for the request, had superstitiously kept deferring the work. It now had to be done with the utmost speed, and Lloyd appealed to the local chiefs to provide men, whilst he also arranged for sufficient hatchets, machetes and other tools to be brought up from Apia, together with a quantity of white vests and black lava-lava material for the house-hold mourning. Getting the coffin to the top of Mount Vaea was a task that strained even the strongest Samoans, who carried it in relays, starting at one o'clock. Nineteen Europeans and sixty Samoan friends attended the funeral *cortège* as it slithered and scrambled up the steep acclivity to the mountain peak. Alone on the empty verandas of Vailima Louis's wife, his mother and his stepdaughter watched the coffin disappear into the trees.

For each of these three women, standing in their black mourning weeds against the flame-colours of a particularly sunny Samoan noon, Louis's speedy and unheralded exit meant the end, for them, of a rare, indeed of a unique, way of life. Mrs Thomas Stevenson, as she wrote in a letter to Henry James thanking him for his con-dolences, had never quite realized, until Louis died, how dreadfully ill he had often been. Fanny, who had lived for years in the awe-inspiring, frantic knowledge that Louis might die suddenly, was now confronted by the bleak fact that now he had died it was not from a long haemorrhage or from any of the ailments with which, on Louis's behalf, she had so long and so valiantly fought. Belle, though shocked and distraught, had youth on her side.

Mrs Thomas Stevenson returned to Edinburgh after Louis's death, and lived there at the height of his apotheosis. She herself died within three years; her final words before falling back into a coma are reported to have been, 'There is Louis! I must go!' It was she who, from his childhood upwards, until Fanny took over, had preserved her son's life. With his death, the act of living lost all interest for her.

Fanny began by trying to blunder on at Vailima with the help of Belle and Lloyd. She ended by selling the estate. From the stance of protective wife to a world genius she now developed into that of an awkward and touchy widow. After a last interview with Fanny at his house in Rye, Henry James is said to have murmured to himself, 'The old scamp!'

Belle Strong, who had been latterly so close to Louis and to his work, lived on a long time. In 1917 she took her mother's ashes to Apia, to be buried in Louis's mountain-top tomb. Soon after her mother's death she had blithely married Fanny's young beau, Salisbury Field, and, living until 1957, she made herself a watch-dog of Louis's genius, reading the many disagreeable and unkind books published during the years his vogue was on the wane.

These three women — mother, wife and step-daughter — all basked in the gleams of the Robert Louis Stevenson legend. Louis's mother received these gleams gratefully, especially when, for instance, they drew Lord Rosebery to ask himself to tea. To Fanny the gleams could never be bright enough, they never shone as lustrously as she thought that they should, and she spent much of her widowhood trimming the wick, often with disastrous results. Belle, who lived on and made her own happiness and her own life, cherished memories of Louis which were ineffaceable. In 1894 there was no one who had known him personally, or had even only known him through his books, that did not feel a tragic, icy sense of loss. The great exhilarator had vanished, and only his books and the memories of him remained.

Selective Bibliography

This bibliography does not list every published source consulted during the writing of this book, but only those likely to be of interest to the general reader.

Balfour, Graham: *The Life of Robert Louis Stevenson*, 2 vols (Methuen & Co., London, 1901).

Buckley, Jerome Hamilton: *William Ernest Henley* (Princeton University Press, Princeton, New Jersey, 1945).

Boodle, A. A.: *R.L.S. and his Sine Qua Non* (John Murray, London, 1929).

Caldwell, Elsie Noble: *Last Witness for Robert Louis Stevenson* (University of Oklahoma Press, Norman, Oklahoma, 1960).

Charteris, the Hon. Evan: *The Life and Letters of Sir Edmund Gosse* (Heinemann, London, 1931).

Churchward, William B.: *My Consulate in Samoa* (Richard Bentley & Son, London, 1887).

Daiches, David: *Robert Louis Stevenson and His World* (Thames and Hudson, London, 1973).

Elwin, Malcolm: *The Strange Case of Robert Louis Stevenson* (Macdonald, London, 1950).

Ferguson, De Lancey and Marshall Waingrow: *Robert Louis Stevenson's Letters to Charles Baxter* (Oxford University Press, London; Yale University Press, New Haven, Connecticut; 1956).

Field, Isobel: *This Life I've Loved* (Longmans, Green, London, 1936).

Ford, Worthington Chauncey: *Letters of Henry Adams (1858–1891)* (Constable, London, 1930).

Furnas, J. C.: *Voyage to Windward* (Faber and Faber, London, 1952).

Gwynn, Stephen: *Robert Louis Stevenson* (Macmillan, London, 1939).

Japp, Alexander H.: *Robert Louis Stevenson: A Record, an Estimate and a Memorial* (T Werner Laurie, London, 1905).

Kiely, Robert: *Robert Louis Stevenson and the Fiction of Adventure* (Harvard University Press, Cambridge, Massachusetts, 1965)

Lockett, W. G.: *Robert Louis Stevenson at Davos* (Hurst and Blackett, London, n.d.).

Mackay, Margaret: *The Violent Friend* (Doubleday & Co., Garden City, New York, 1968).

Mackenzie, Compton: *Robert Louis Stevenson* (Morgan-Grampian Books, London, 1968).

Masson, Rosalind: *The Life of Robert Louis Stevenson* (W. & R. Chambers, Edinburgh and London, 1923).

—— (ed.): *I Can Remember Robert Louis Stevenson* (W. & R. Chambers, Edinburgh and London, 1922).

McGaw, Sister Martha Mary: *Stevenson in Hawaii* (University of Hawaii Press, Honolulu, 1950).

McLaren, Moray: *Stevenson and Edinburgh* (Chapman & Hall, London, 1950).

Mattheisen, Paul F., and Michael Millgate: *Transatlantic Dialogue: Selected American Correspondence of Edmund Gosse* (University of Texas Press, Austin and London, 1965).

Osbourne, Lloyd: *An Intimate Portrait of R.L.S.* (Scribner's, New York,).

Sanchez, Nellie Van de Grift: *The Life of Mrs Robert Louis Stevenson* (Chatto and Windus, London, 1920).

Simpson, E. Blantyre: *The Robert Louis Stevenson Originals* (T. N. Foulis, Edinburgh and London, 1912).

——: *Robert Louis Stevenson's Edinburgh Days* (Hodder & Stoughton, London, 1898).

Skinner, Robert T. (ed.): *Cummy's Diary* (Chatto and Windus, London, 1926).

Steuart, J. A.: *Robert Louis Stevenson, Man and Writer*, 2 vols (Sampson Low, Marston & Co., London, n.d.).

Smith, Janet Adam: *Henry James and Robert Louis Stevenson: a Record of Friendship and Criticism* (Rupert Hart-Davis, London, 1948).

Stevenson, Fanny and Robert Louis: *Our Samoan Adventure* (Weidenfeld and Nicolson, London, 1956).

Stevenson, Margaret Isabella (Balfour): *From Saranac to the Marquesas and Beyond: being letters written by Margaret Isabella Stevenson, 1887–88, to her sister, Jane Whyte Balfour, with a short introduction by George W. Balfour*, edited and arranged by Marie Clothilde Balfour (Charles Scribner's Sons, New York, 1903).

——: *Letters from Samoa, 1891–93*, edited and arranged by Marie Clothilde Balfour (Charles Scribner's Sons, New York, 1906).

Stevenson, Mrs Robert Louis: *The Cruise of the 'Janet Nichol' Among the South Sea Islands* (Chatto and Windus, London, 1915).

Strong, Isobel, and Lloyd Osbourne: *Memories of Vailima* (Constable, London, 1903).

Swearingen, Roger: *The Early Literary Career of Robert Louis Stevenson, 1850–1881* (Ann Arbor University Microfilms, Michigan, 1971).

Swinnerton, Frank: *R. L. Stevenson: A Critical Study* (London, 1925).

Index

The following books are also available in
Cassell Biographies.

For information about these and other books
write to the publishers at the address on
page 4 of this book.

SIR WALTER SCOTT

**'Buchan brings to his study just that trained
historical imagination which by placing Scott
accurately in his time and place shows us the
real man in the comprehensiveness of his
genius'.**
Times Literary Supplement

John Buchan's novels are so evocative of
Scottish landscape and his tales so much a part
of Border storytelling that he brings special
insight and experience to this biography of Sir
Walter Scott.
He writes with affection about the sickly youth
and the disappointed lover whose writing
brought him fame and prosperity in
Edinburgh and London. The sad decline into
illness, bankruptcy and poverty is told with
sympathy but it is above all Buchan's
description of Scott's novels that are the gems
of this book. They reveal the genius that
produced books enduring enough to give a
name to a railway station, Waverley, and to a
football team 'Heart of Midlothian.'

**'The almost inspired literary criticisms of Sir
Walter Scott show Buchan at his best.'**
Dictionary of National Biography

0-304-31437-4

THE QUEEN OF SCOTS

with a Preface by Gordon Batho

The tragic story and complex personality of
Mary Stuart, the Queen of Scots, has
challenged novelists, poets and historians.
Stefan Zweig's brilliant and dramatic
biography is one of the most penetrating
studies of this proud and passionate woman.
A dramatist himself and steeped in the culture
and history of Europe, he brings special
insights to his account of Mary's childhood at
the French court and her brief marriage to the
sickly Dauphin.

The young widow's return to Scotland, her
marriage to Darnley, the horrifying murder of
Rizzio, Darnley's death and the shameful
marriage to Bothwell, all are recounted with a
mounting tension that reaches a climax – after
the long years of captivity – in the sombre
execution at Fotheringhay in 1587.

'Zweig has succeeded to Strachey's position as
chief European biographer. He is to be
congratulated on having mastered the
intricacies of our history and to have written
about it as to the manner born ...
He has a very subtle knowledge of human
nature and is a careful and sympathetic
observer of the ways of the heart and mind.'
A. L. Rowse in *The Spectator*

0-304-31439-0

KINGS OVER THE WATER
The Saga of the Stuart Pretenders

Of all royal lost causes, none has a stronger
fascination than that of the Stuart Pretenders to
the British throne. For well over a century, four
successive Stuart kings laid claim to the crown.
The first was James II, deposed in 1688 by his
daughter Mary, and her husband, William of
Orange; then came James III (the Old
Pretender) and his son Charles III (Bonnie
Prince Charlie – the Young Pretender); finally,
there was Henry IX (the Cardinal King) who
died in 1807, the last descendant in direct and
legitimate line from James II. This book tells the
story of these four men, and of their families.
Aronson writes about their public and private
lives, their personalities and the extraordinary
hold they exercised over their adherents. This is
a moving book about the twilight of one of the
world's most romantic, colourful and
ill-fated dynasties.

'For a dispassionate account of the claims of
four successive Stuart kings to the British
crown it would be hard to better this.'
Sunday Mail, Glasgow

0-304-32237-7

JOHNSON AND BOSWELL
The story of their lives

with an introduction by
Michael Holroyd

'It would be hard to find a better introduction
to the Johnson-Boswell saga ... he has got all
the best known things in, and many of the
lesser known as well.'
Times Literary Supplement

In writing this lively account of one of the most
famous partnerships in English literature
Hesketh Pearson presents an unusual double
biography, the story of Samuel Johnson and *his*
biographer, James Boswell.
He has drawn upon all the trustworthy
contemporary accounts. Boswell's Journals of
course, but also those of Mrs Thrale, Fanny
Burney, Anna Seward and Frances Reynolds.
Some of these are more intimate and more
revealing than Boswell, and Pearson is able to
present Dr Johnson from many points of view.
In telling Boswell's own story he presents a
skilful interpretation in spite of Boswell's
confused picture of himself.

'Pearson is an expert at the job, readability is
his forte; he couldn't write a dull page if he
tried.'
TLS

0-304-31440-4

DICKENS

His Character, Comedy and Career

Charles Dickens (1812 to 1870) led a life as fascinating as that of any character in his novels and in this book his story is told by a master of English biography.

After a happy childhood in Portsmouth, London and Rochester, the Dickens family fell into poverty and for a while the young Charles experienced the grim side of the London slums that he was later to depict so brilliantly in novels like *Oliver Twist*. But his first successes as a writer came soon, and by 1838 he was famous for the serialised *Pickwick* and for *Nicholas Nickleby*, which sold 50,000 copies of the first number.

For the next thirty years, this human dynamo travelled incessantly in England, America and Europe, wrote and edited and spoke in public, engaged in business and charitable enterprises, was stage producer, actor, friend to the famous and father of a large family. As Pearson says, Dickens's life (and his writing) resembled a catherine wheel, blazing away and throwing off showers of sparks.

The biography shares something of that brilliance.

'Pearson is an expert at the job, readability is his forte; he couldn't write a dull page if he tried.'
Times Literary Supplement
0-304-31553-2

SIR WALTER RALEIGH

'A first-class life of Raleigh ... well-written, accurate, thoughtful, unpretentious.'
BBC Radio

'Raleigh comes through with unusual vividness ...' *Observer*

'Lloyd Williams cuts his witty, perceptive, rather sardonic commentary to a minimum, and concentrates on what are in effect recorded voices from the past ... it is very well done.'
The Sunday Telegraph

'Lloyd Williams has a real sympathy for and insight into his hero without attempting to make him too heroic.'
Christopher Hill, *The Spectator*

Sir Walter Raleigh, poet, scholar, soldier and explorer, was one of the most flamboyant characters in the colourful reign of Elizabeth I. His daring expeditions to the New World, along with his quick wit, handsome face and ostentatious gallantry, made him a favourite with the Queen, but after the accession of James I Raleigh's fortunes changed. He was accused of treason, committed to the Tower of London and executed in 1618.

'A clever, interesting, and rewarding volume.' *The Guardian*

0-304-32241-5

Jan 29, 2007

LADY HESTER STANHOPE

Joan Haslip

'I have no reproaches to make myself but that I went rather too far' so wrote Hester Stanhope in the last weeks of her life. Joan Haslip's biography is a splendid narrative of what that 'rather too far' meant.

The extraordinary story of the arrogant young noblewoman who as Pitt's niece and hostess at 10 Downing Street, queened it over Georgian London with a disregard for convention that shocked society, and ended her days as 'the Sybil of the Lebanon' is here told with sympathy and flair and an eye for vivid detail.

After Pitt's death Lady Hester roamed the Near East, met Byron in Athens, lived with her lover in a villa in Turkey, was shipwrecked off Rhodes, and eventually settled in a ramshackle 'palace' in the Lebanon. Here she lived on for twenty-five years, ill, lonely and in debt, but still intriguing in the violent and complex politics of that country and famed as prophetess and 'Queen of the Arabs.'

0 304 31435 8

VICTORIA AND DISRAELI

'Mr Theo Aronson has given the best
impression of the Queen that I have read.
With much subtlety – and dead-pan humour –
he has used her relationship with Disraeli to
give us an insight into what she was really
like. His book is bright with intelligence and
human wisdom. Very strongly recommended.'
C. P. Snow, *Financial Times*

Theo Aronson, well known for his biographies
of the royal houses of Europe, is ideally
qualified to tell the story of the strange
partnership between the formidable Widow of
Windsor and the flamboyant Jew who once
wrote 'my nature demands that my life should
be perpetual love.'
But were they so ill-matched? Both needed the
intimate support of someone of the opposite
sex and each responded to the romanticism of
the other.
By the mid 1870s the personal and political
association between the imperialist Prime
Minister Disraeli and his Queen Empress was
in full flower. It was a relationship which
brought happiness and fulfilment to them
both.

'A sensitive and stylish account of their
relationship ... skilfully and sympathetically
described. Aronson has produced an
illuminating and entertaining book.'
Observer

0-304-31433-1